The Human
Face of
Global
Mobility

Comparative Urban and Community Research

Series Editor, Michael Peter Smith

The **Human**
Face of
Global
Mobility

**International Highly Skilled Migration in
Europe, North America and the Asia-Pacific**

**Comparative Urban & Community Research
Volume 8**

Edited by

Michael Peter Smith
& Adrian Favell

**Transaction Publishers
New Brunswick (U.S.A.) and London (U.K.)**

Third paperback printing 2009
Copyright © 2006 by Transaction Publishers, New Brunswick, New Jersey.

This book is printed on acid-free paper that meets the American National Standard for Permanence of Paper for Printed Library Materials.

Library of Congress Catalog Number: 2006040414
ISBN: 978-1-4128-0520-9
Printed in the United States of America

Library of Congress Cataloging-in-Publication Data

The human face of global mobility : international highly skilled migration
   in Europe, North America and the Asia-Pacific / Michael Peter Smith and
   Adrian Favell, editors.
         p. cm.—(Comparative urban and community research ; v. 8)
      ISBN 1-4128-0520-1 (alk. paper)
      1. Brain drain.   2. Professional employees.   3.   Skilled labor.
   4. Emigration and immigration.   I. Smith, Michael P.   II. Favell, Adrian.
   III. Series.

HT110.C65 v. 8
[HD8038]
[331.12'791]

Contents

About the Contributors

Authors

Jeanne Batalova, Migration Policy Institute, Washington DC

Ödül Bozkurt, PhD Candidate in Sociology, UCLA

Paula Chakravartty, Assistant Professor of Communication, UMass, Amherst

Dana Zartner Falstrom, PhD Candidate in Political Science, UC Davis

Adrian Favell, Associate Professor of Sociology, UCLA

Miriam Feldblum, Faculty Associate in Humanities and Special Assistant to the President, Caltech

Gary P. Freeman, Professor of Government, University of Texas, Austin

David K. Hill, PhD Candidate in Government, Cornell University

Sandra Lavenex, Assistant Professor of Political Science, University of Bern

B. Lindsay Lowell, Director of Policy Studies, Georgetown University

Jeannette Money, Associate Professor of Political Science, UC Davis

Ettore Recchi, Associate Professor of Sociology, University of Florence

Michael Peter Smith, Professor of Community Studies and Development, UC Davis

Katalin Szelényi, PhD Candidate in Education, UCLA

UCLA International Institute Working Group

Thanks also are due to the several other regular or occasional members of the UCLA working group on global mobility, who contributed papers, ideas and commentaries during our two years of meetings.

Rafael Alarcón, Sociology, El Colegio de la Frontera Norte

William Clark, Geography, UCLA

Jorge Durand, Anthropology, University of Guadalajara

Rubén Hernández-Léon, Sociology, UCLA

David Jacobson, Sociology, Arizona State University

Marian Katz, Sociology, UCLA

Harlan Koff, Political Science, University of Lille

Ivan Light, Sociology, UCLA

Marianne de Laet, Anthropology, Harvey Mudd College

Mingang Lin, Sociology, Suchong University

Steve Loyal, Sociology, University College Dublin

Paul Ong, Urban Planning, UCLA

Philip Martin, Agricultural Economics, UC Davis

Roger Penn, Sociology, University of Lancaster

Renee Reichl, Sociology, UCLA

Sabeen Sandhu, Sociology, UC Irvine

Kristin Surak, Sociology, UCLA

Roger Waldinger, Sociology, UCLA

Takeo Yamamoto, Sociology, Kwansei Gakuin University

Min Zhou, Sociology, UCLA

Xiaolei Wu, Anthropology, UCLA

Thanks also especially to Leah Halvorson, UCLA, for help with logistics throughout. Additional papers and commentaries are available on our wesbite:

http://www.isop.ucla.edu/ccgr/mobility.asp

1

The Human Face of Global Mobility:
A Research Agenda

Adrian Favell, Miriam Feldblum and Michael Peter Smith

Talk of globalization by political economists has familiarized us with the idea that the continued liberalization of world trade, and the movement of goods, capital and services on which it is based, is also leading to a spectacular liberalization of the free movement of persons. Authors such as Saskia Sassen (1996, 2001) link these developments with a consequent decline in the control powers of nation-states over population movement, something seen as the fulfillment of a new "age of migration" (Castles and Miller, 2003). The discussion is, of course, controversial. Despite market forces, the control functions of states do continue to pose obvious obstacles to poorer international migrants. Labor, for other political and cultural reasons, is often not as mobile as other factors of production. Political scientists are also right to remind us that political and institutional factors—the drama of international relations, variation in national policy approaches, attempts to coordinate border control or the policing of movement, and evolving modes of international governance—all pose significant constraints and boundaries on unfettered movement, at all levels of the economy (Zolberg, 1999; Freeman, 1995: Money, 1999; Guiraudon and Joppke, 2001).

In most of these discussions however, labor migration is undifferentiated. Distinctions are rarely drawn between the processes, policies or politics shaping highly skilled or professional migration, as opposed to those behind unskilled migration. To be sure, when the focus turns to the movement of highly educated and talented migrants, many assume there are likely to be fewer barriers of all kinds to these forms of global "free movement" and that the phenomenon

1

is growing in magnitude and significance. To put it in the parlance of global city theorists (Castells 2000; Taylor, 2004), the virtual "space of flows" on which new global networks of capital and trade are based, must also be peopled by mobile persons who, it is assumed, are embodied by the world's growing cadre of international highly skilled migrants (Beaverstock, 2001c). Some authors even speak of the emergence of new "global elites" or a "transnational capitalist class," with unprecedented mobile and cosmopolitan lifestyles, presaging dramatic social change to the national order of things (e.g., Sklair, 2001). These heroes of global free movement—top ranked employees of multinational corporations, international finance, IT companies, scientific research agencies and so on—are, presumably, the human hands, brains and faces behind the impersonal dynamics of global markets and nation-state decline.

brochure This popular image calls for scholarly investigation. The lives and experiences of these frequent-flying, fast-lane, global elites are better known from the editorial and marketing content of glossy magazines or corporate brochures than they are from solid social science research. And behind the image of global elites lie other socially differentiated realities. In fact, the skilled and educated among the globally mobile, also include: students, nurses, mid-level technical and clerical employees, ambitious or adventurous upwardly mobile middle-classes, migrants from a range of intermediate developing states, and many more it would be hard to describe as "elites." In addition, there are those international migrants, of course, who are counted as unskilled migrants in official statistics because of their menial employment destinations after migration but who may have attained high levels of skill and education in their home countries or who have had to move for political reasons. A whole range of types of international migrants, in fact, are not captured by the two stylized images counter-posed at either end of the social spectrum: high-flying corporate elites and desperate, poverty-stricken labor migrants and asylum-seekers. Our volume, thus, seeks to open up a whole new field of research that can begin to fully document the many worlds of international highly skilled, educated or professional migration, as well as integrate the various types of theory and methodology needed to account for these phenomena.

Lacunae in Global and Transnational Studies

Academically speaking, there has been relatively little "human level" research on the diverse, yet prototypical avatars of globalization in the skilled, educated or professional categories. More broadly, there remains a call for more micro-level, phenomenological studies of the everyday reality of "global mobility," despite the avalanche of writings on globalization in all its forms. Looking back, the first generation of global studies was nothing if not sweepingly macro in its scope and argumentation. Rarely did authors consider the "human face" that might be found behind the aggregate data and structural logic that led to the recognition of global cities and global networks in the work of Sassen, Castells, Taylor, and others (see Loughborough University's *Globalization and World Cities* project, for a panorama of this work).[1] The grounded ethnographic work by authors such as Beaverstock (2002, 2005), or Yeoh and Willis (2005) on corporate employees and business networks, is, in fact, exceptional in relation to the general body of work in urban and regional studies on global cities.

A more recent second-generation of global studies has, to some extent, heeded the limitations of the macro-bias with more "agent-centered" studies in anthropology, human geography and sociology on transnational networks, transmigrants and the new "spaces" of the transnational in the global economy and politics (e.g., Pries, 2001; Conradson and Latham, 2005a). The move to "locate" transnationalism has been a positive one, not least in showing how global processes always have locally inflected and mediated expressions (see, e.g., Eade, 1997; Gupta and Ferguson, 1997; Scott, 1997; Guarnizo and Smith, 1998; Smith, 2001; Burawoy et al, 2000). On the other hand, transnationalism in these debates, is, more often than not, presented normatively as a blow against the capitalist, nation-state centered order of things, emphasizing transnational actors' resistance and freedom in its conceptualization of "agency." Building on this, a new wave of social theory focusing on "mobility" has sought to dissolve the category of "society" itself (Urry, 2000), celebrating a variety of new forms of social, gendered or transnational "citizenship" beyond the nation-state supposedly enjoyed by mobile and networked populations (i.e., Glick-Schiller, 2005; Benhabib, 2002). Writing in this vein often tends to be thin on empirical research and to reify the lives and cultures of such groups in order to make theoretical and political points rather than empirical ones. Even more problematically, the cultural and critical theory leanings of much of this work has lead to a complete disconnect from quantitative studies of migration by demographers and economists, as well as institutional studies of the politics of immigration by political scientists and sociologists.

This may be less of a problem within the more specific field of migration research where truly interdisciplinary work using multiple methods is more common. Here it is the contrast between the volume of interest in research topics that is most striking. On highly skilled migration, there have been only one or two attempts to define a broad research agenda (Cornelius et al., 2001; Iredale, 2001) alongside the more policy-targeted work of demographers and economists (Salt, 1992, 1997; Borjas 1989, 1995; Lowell, 1996; Findlay, 1995; Lowell and Findlay, 2001; Peri, 2005). The quite considerable body of empirical work in recent years on transnational communities, meanwhile, has focused on documenting the transnational strategies and resources of more typically lower-end labor and asylum-seeking migrants. Convincing transnational studies are certainly now accumulating, for example of Mexicans (Smith 2005; Bakker and Smith, 2003), Ecuadorans (Kyle, 2000), Moroccans (Salih, 2003; Bousetta, 2000), Turks (Faist, 2000), and Senegalese (Riccio, 2001). Such work is usually driven by an ethnographic interest in ethnicity and inequality and linked to the ways ethnic networks and cultures facilitate the economic and political actions of relatively powerless or underprivileged actors, as well as providing the means for evading the control efforts of states (Portes, 1996a; Levitt, 2001).

The transnational theorists point to these findings as "globalization from below" (Portes, 1996b). But the migrants they portray are also those *more* likely to be subject to control and restriction. A better test case of the supposed liberalization of human mobility in the world economy, then, would be international professional, highly skilled or technical migrants, whose mobility is linked more to choice, professional career and educational opportunities. That is, of those who face the *least* barriers linked to exclusion, domination or economic exploitation. Their experience would reveal not just how far liberalization might go under ideal conditions, but also reveal, in sharp relief, what persisting limitations there might still be to a completely unfettered global economy of mobility. As everyone is aware, such migrants are clearly the most likely candidates to fill the role of genuine transmigrants, privileged as they are by the global economy, recruited by nation-states still keen to slam the doors on many other forms of global migration, and endowed with the kinds of levels of human and social capital most likely to facilitate the real construction of global lives in new national destinations.

The lack of research on these migrants, as well as the empirical weaknesses of many other debates on transnationalism and global mobility, leaves a clear opportunity for a new kind of integrated research agenda on global mobility and the international migration of the highly skilled. The political economy of globalization can too easily become an overly structural and faceless account of the capitalist logics of global investment and labor demand. Yet, without a structural dimension—without an emphasis on the constraining nature of global economic and demographic trends or of efforts to control and/or liberalize migration flows by governments—the imagined "agency" of migrants and movers can become an insubstantial, de-contextualized, reified thing. Both lead to an idealization of social processes that we need to understand from *both* a structural and agent-centered viewpoint. To a large degree, their agency depends on just how distinct this form of highly skilled migration is from other more constrained kinds—in both top-down demographic and policy terms and bottom-up ethnographic ones. There is little or nothing to connect these two sides—partly because they are so separated by the distinct theories and methodologies that different generations of global and migration scholars have used.

Addressing the Methodology Gap

The UCLA International Institute working group on global mobility was brought together with just these issues in mind. We sought to both identify the empirical lacunae in current global and migration studies on highly skilled migrants in the global economy, and to transcend the methodological barriers that leave demographers, economists, political scientists and ethnographers of international migration unable to fully integrate their diverse macro, meso and micro interests—indeed, unable to even *talk* to one another. Methodological divides have ensured that there is rarely an attempt to cross-reference their distinctive contributions: the highly structural quantitative analyses of demographers and political economists; the explanatory process-based approach of comparative policy and institutional analysts; and the ethnographic interviews and life-story approaches of qualitative researchers. The interdisciplinary demands of migration research however, dictate that *all* such dimensions are needed to specify the balance between global structural trends, mediating political forces and the reassertion of agency and context when migrants' voices are listened to. The group established a congenial environment in which a genuinely inter-methodological dialogue between these three types of research became possible. Focus came from both the topic and its locations; looking at highly skilled migration in the U.S., particularly from the Asia-Pacific, and at the new openness to highly skilled internal migration and selective immigration in the integrating European Union.

The organization of this book reflects our combined efforts to respect the strengths of each respective methodology. Qualitative work is rarely in an authoritative position by itself to generalize its case study or small sample findings; a quantitative backdrop is always necessary. Explanatory efforts to isolate causal factors determining political processes still always benefit from interpretative work about the meanings and contexts of specific actors. Yet macro-level analyses equally, should always be carried through meso-level institutional mediation to micro-level insights into an appreciation of the very real consequences of these structures on the lives of actual individuals and groups. Having first established something quantitatively or structurally, the most useful role of qualitative work is, thus, usually to show how these trends express themselves in the real life experiences of agents, both individual and collective, as mediated by context, contingency and the unpredictability of life stories and circumstances. Our book, therefore, sets out various analyses of demographic and political evidence before moving into a substantial selection of specific ethnographic and interviews-based case studies. Along the way several key themes can be highlighted. These take the form of challenging assumptions often made in global and migration studies about highly skilled migrants and migration; and of rethinking three of the major regional contexts in which such migration is taking place. This will enable us to identify the various components of an ambitious research agenda that is reflected in both the finished chapters we present here as well as the contributory research of other members of our group that can be accessed via our website.[2]

Challenging Assumptions

Despite its visibility as a conceptual reference point in migration studies there has, as we have argued, been a lack of research on international skilled and professional migration; both from the experiential point of view of migrants and in terms of more structural analysis of demographics and politics. What we find instead in much of the global and transnational literatures is an explicit, or implicit, discussion about highly skilled migration, often lodged in studies of other kinds of migration or global phenomena, and in which a series of "assumptions" about this kind of migration can be found. These assumptions may be true or false but all need to be interrogated in the light of concrete empirical studies. Working through *five* such assumptions then, in fact, leads to the emergence of a new, more specified and more differentiated research agenda on "elite," "professional," "highly skilled" or "highly educated" international migration—in all its forms.

A Polarized World of "Elites" and "Proles"?

prole = proletarian

The first assumption concerns the question of who and what constitutes highly skilled migration. Authors routinely refer to higher-end migrants as "elites," usually as a stylized contrast to the disadvantaged, lower-class, typically ethnically distinct, putatively "proletariat" migration that is the concern—for other political reasons—of most researchers in the field. The dichotomy of highly skilled versus unskilled migration glosses over the stratifications within and across categories as well as significant mediating factors such as the gendered nature of some highly skilled movements like nursing (Hardill, 2000; Kofman, 2000). Further, the dichotomy obscures the hard realities of the many highly skilled, educated migrants who cross borders as unskilled migrants leaving their unconvertible human capital, as it were, behind at the border. Finally, the terminology—if dependent on education, profession and migrant status—can leave out key populations: particularly international students who, perhaps more than nearly all other groups, are the quintessential avatars of globalization. This will determine data sources as much as the theoretical arguments that are made from them. Jeanne Batalova and B. Lindsay Lowell in fact offer a clear analysis of the hard methodological choices faced by researchers on this question, as part of their contribution.

quintessence 精髓 真髓 典型

The explosion of literature on migration is linked—quite rightly—to concerns with global inequalities, development and the exclusionary workings of ethnicity and race. But with these kinds of concerns uppermost for most researchers, the field has not been well equipped to study or understand other forms of apparently "less disadvantaged" migration except through a dismissive ("elites") lens. The globalization literature cemented this two-sided view of international migration with the social polarization theme promoted by leading studies of the global city (Sassen, 2001; Friedmann and Goetz-Wolff, 1982; Friedmann, 1986). The image of high-rise corporate downtowns populated by a sharp-suited global elite service industry workforce, but serviced by an army of lower-class immigrant cleaners, shop owners, domestic home help and sex workers, is a powerful one that rings true in many contexts. A graphic example is Kloosterman, van der Leun and Rath's study (1998) of the two sides of the tracks that bifurcate the *Bijlmer* suburb of Amsterdam. But it belies many other forms of migration and work in a mobile global context that would be better seen as "middling" in class terms (for a useful discussion of "middling transnationalism", see Conradson and Latham, 2005a). All forms of migration require thorough empirical investigation, and one of the effects of globalization has, in fact, been a downward "massification," through the middle-classes, of international migration opportunities linked to careers and education, such that it is by no means only those who might be thought of as "elites" who are able to move. Moving beyond the image of free-moving elites brings to the fore questions of mobility and incorporation for these other highly skilled migrants. As Batalova (2005) shows in research linked to her paper in this volume, the evidence suggests highly skilled foreign-origin workers in the U.S. are, in fact, systematically underpaid—that is, discriminated against—in relation to the qualification levels of domestic workers.

Using contrasting methodologies, both Ettore *Recchi and Adrian Favell* in this volume build on the observation that the real action in international migration is, in future, likely to be in the broad middle of society. Highly developed societies typically have fat, bell-shaped, class structures that mean the massification of hitherto "elite" professional career opportunities internationally—particularly within an integrating Europe—become the acid test of whether transnational mobility beyond the nation-state is, in fact, a sociologically significant reality. It may turn out so-called "elites," who have opted to move internationally under present conditions of globalization, are often not at all from elite backgrounds but provincial, career-frustrated "spiralists," who have gambled with dramatic spatial mobility in their education and careers abroad to improve social mobility opportunities that are otherwise blocked at home. Now, as in the past, "real" elites tend to have routine access to international travel and experience through family connections and schooling—as well as a far better chance of success in their chosen career at home—without needing to propel themselves individually on an international stage. They are not necessarily the ones most using new educational opportunities such as the EU's *Erasmus* and *Socrates* schemes. As Katalin Szelényi suggests in her research, presented here in different graduate student nationalities in the U.S., the less-developed the country internationally, the more elites of this country choose to move internationally in their educations and careers. Favell argues it is no surprise the North Africans and Latin Americans one meets in finance or the media in London are from relatively elite backgrounds—one *has* to be an elite in these countries to have the chance to move. This is not the case with nationals from the more highly developed countries, where mobility opportunities are more broadly shared and where people who move internationally have made much more marginal, risky, career decisions compared to those in nationalized careers from welfare-states with stable pay-offs at home. They may have been free to move out in order to move up but this always has costs; it is not for the risk-averse or psychologically conservative and will not be chosen if they already have easier, elite-based access to success in their own societies. As more countries move into the ranks of the highly developed, we are likely to observe more migrants of modest, middle-class backgrounds amongst the highly skilled, as the economies of their home countries afford more broadly distributed opportunities for migration.

A Demand-Driven Migration?

Demographers and economists have often battled to assert the demand-driven nature of much migration to show it is much less of a threat than politicians suggest (Fischer and Straubhaar, 1996; Piore, 1989). Yet, clearly, it is much harder to defuse the relevance of such sending conditions regarding lower-end, poverty-and conflict-related migration. As a corollary, one might assume higher-end migration much more perfectly fulfills market demand. Consequences follow from this assumption: that skilled migration is always "selected" by the receiving country; that it is governed by efficient not sub-optimal politics; and that such skilled workers are not replacing or suppressing the job opportunities of natives. If this view were true it would reflect migration at its pareto-efficient best, operating in a George Borjas-type neo-classical world (Borjas, 1989).

The papers in this volume empirically challenge this neo-classical worldview in several respects. First and foremost, they show in the case of skilled, no less than unskilled global migration, the macroeconomic logic of market forces is mediated by institutional barriers and channeling mechanisms. State policies regarding entry and exit, the granting or withholding of visas and work permits, and the establishment of numerical quotas on certain categories of migrants, set the permissions and constraints under which various regimes of immigration are established by receiving nation-states. A good example is the complicated politics behind the number of skilled workers allowed H-1B visas, the principal legal channel of temporary labor migration in the U.S. While the politics of low-skilled migration may be more visible and contentious, both highly skilled and unskilled migration are shaped by distinctive policy processes and political structures. The papers by Gary Freeman and David Hill and by Jeannette Money and Dana Zartner Falstrom, in particular, offer useful analytical frameworks to differentiate between distinct forms of migration, and the often contradictory state policies and the politics linked to them.

It is within the context of such mediating state policies and political processes that other institutional-level factors challenge simplistic notions of global demand-driven migration. Sandra Lavenex offers a striking overview of how global governance structures, such as the World Trade Organization's (WTO) negotiations on General Agreement on Trade in Services (GATS), have reshaped international migration of this kind. The contributors to this volume also specify numerous corporate and professional steering mechanisms that structure the opportunities and constraints experienced by skilled professionals who wish to advance their life chances by transnational migration. These include, but are not limited to: intra-corporate transfer policies, the existing division of labor within transnational corporations, professional information networks and social connections, and corporate and professional training regimes. All of these institu-

tional-level policies and practices shape the contours of skilled global migration, often in ways quite different from pareto-optimal assumptions about market efficiency. Finally, our studies reveal neo-
classical assumptions about the efficient operation of markets ignore the normative and ideological constraints that may affect the
dynamics of skilled migrants' global mobility. For example, the norms
of multinational corporate cultures, as well as the prevailing national
cultures of sending and receiving societies, may affect processes of
global mobility in different ways. Such conceptions can help create
subtle forms of social exclusion or set internalized limits on the vision and imagination of potentially mobile subjects.

So is there an efficient global competition for skills in which countries with "points based" quotas come out on top (Freeman, 1999;
Salt and McLaughlan, 2002)? This is a familiar refrain from "immi- *putative*
gration reformers" seeking to make the case for more high-end immigration, usually at the expense of the putatively less desirable. The
argument is made that U.S. immigration policy must place greater emphasis on attracting skilled migrants, if the nation in a global-era is to
efficiently compete for the skilled with such countries as Canada and
Australia whose skill-based approaches are the models. No one would
claim the Byzantine U.S. system was a model. It has created a pleni-
tude of peculiar migration channels sustained by vested client interests, and a veritable alphabet soup of visa categories. But it might be
argued U.S. immigration policy reflects more an efficient *political*
process than an efficient economic competition for skills, as Money
and Zartner Falstrom argue. Politics here clearly matters.

Brains Keep on Draining?

In decades past, high skilled migration raised the specter of "brain
drain" from developing countries with the resulting enormous attendant literature and policy debate. Since then, highly skilled and educated mobility has become far more complex and diversified, with
the "brain drain" assumption challenged on numerous fronts. From
"brain drain" to "brain gain" and "brain circulation" in a competitive global economy, the migration literature and popular press now
underscore the new patterns in which engineers and services can be
more easily found, and more cheaply located, in regions previously
identified as "brain drain" origin regions, especially in China and
India. This, in fact, is the very root of the "outsourcing" phenomenon now so prevalent in the global economy.

Again, a simple equation lies behind the supposed distinctiveness of higher-end migration: that the highest skilled are freer to move; that they are more able to carry away with them the benefits of their own human capital; and, hence, that they automatically represent a "brain loss" for their countries of origin. The brain drain/gain/circulation question has, in fact, become the biggest single area of research on skilled migrants, as reviewed in depth by Szelenyi, and Batalova and Lowell in this volume. This is because of its sharp policy implications in developing countries in terms of economic development and political stability. Such fears of the developmental costs of "brain drain" assume a zero-sum game in which sending countries lose as the developed world creams off the best and the brightest. But is it always the best and the brightest who move?

As global movement becomes easier, in fact, this need not be the case. In a more global world the best and the brightest might, in fact, be potentially hyper-mobile entrepreneurs who are now able to stay at home with the new emergence of technical industries in developing countries or, when they do move, use transnational networks and contribute to the economic development of their countries and regions of origin. In fact, these new patterns are already evident. Whereas in the past thirty years large numbers of Asian students came to the United States for graduate study, today many more, including top students, are staying in Asia for their higher education. More Asian scientists, schooled in the United States, are returning home. In particular, the Chinese and Indian governments are investing heavily in university systems and hi-tech and science infrastructure in their respective countries; as are American companies by opening up engineering facilities and laboratories in these countries. In her chapter in this volume, Paula Chakravartty contrasts the everyday experiences of Indian entrepreneurs from Bangalore, who are very successfully developing that region as a high-tech global metropolis, with the often unhappy, mid-level educated Indian migrants to the U.S. who now come to the U.S. on H-1B visas because they were not "good enough" to break into the elite schools and best high-tech operations in India.

A second problem with the zero-sum assumption underlying the "brain gain/drain" debate is that this formulation ignores or, at best, understates the frequent back and forth movement of migrants, ideas, knowledge, information and skill sets, that is now a routine part of contemporary transnationalism. These back and forth movements are part of a pattern of trans-local interconnectivity that many skilled migrants, like their unskilled counterparts, maintain to their regions and localities of origin (Cheng and Yang, 1998). In fact, their relative affluence and privileged status may, in fact, encourage them to be more transnational in outlook and allegiance, contrary to individualist expectations. As the respective chapters by Szelényi, Chakravartty, and Bozkurt demonstrate, the evolving ties of international students in the U.S., high-tech workers from India in Silicon Valley, and workers in a multinational corporations in Finland and Sweden, lead to continuing kinds of global circulation and incorporation. The implications of this complex interconnectivity clearly weaken the brain drain hypothesis. For example, Zhou and Tseng (2001) have shown in the case of Chinese high-tech and accounting business in Los Angeles, these types of network-based translocal connections implicate the economic growth of L.A. with the activities of overseas investment networks from Taiwan and Hong Kong, thereby contributing to the economic benefit of both sending and receiving locations rather than draining the sending locales. This kind of scenario may be becoming the norm rather than the exception.

"Controlled" Immigration Versus "Frictionless" Mobility?

International migration studies have benefited considerably from geographers and critical theorists reminding them geographical mobility in all its forms is something they should consider part of the subject, even when it is not officially classified as typical state-to-state "immigration." One of the benefits of this has been the recognition that those forms of spatial mobility—moving from place *a* to place *b*—which get classified as *im*-migration, are so classified for *political* reasons. They signal the historical state monopoly on freedom of movement that was one of the key emergent "pastoral" features of the modern territorially-defined nation-state and its growing bureaucratic powers to "penetrate" society and, thus, shape society in its own image (Torpey, 2000). Without sovereign political regulation of movement—in the shape of citizenship and naturalization laws, welfare rights for members, and the control and classification of border crossing and re-settlement—migration would just be people moving around (Zolberg 1999; Joppke, 1998). Typically, among those moving across the borders of territorial "container" states, there are the "immigrants" (e.g., refugees and the economically desperate), who are moved by forces beyond their control; and then there are others, most generally thought of as "international travelers" (e.g., tourists, business people, expatriates, exchange students, retirees) who move by choice alone. The first form—the story goes—elicit categorization and strict state control of numbers; the second melt through borders, untouched by the state, their uncapped numbers reflecting only market demand, commercial interests and the dictates of economic and human capital accumulation. In a globalizing world, these are the masters of collapsing time/space coordinates, to echo the much discussed thesis of Zygmunt Bauman on mobility as the new index of global stratification (Bauman, 1998). The clarity of the stark official lines between the two are such that even many questioning scholars do not put into doubt the construction of such routine bureaucratic legal classifications.

Trends in global mobility support these distinctions in some senses but go quite against then in others. On the affirmative side, as Lavenex (this volume) points out, even after two successive decades of control rhetoric and all kinds of efforts at international police cooperation, there is evidence of new forms of mobility slipping through the immigration category. There is, she argues, a reinforced disassociation of regulated or unwanted migration, as officially viewed, from other forms of international mobility that can be allowed, even encouraged and institutionalized, under various international business and trade agreements such as the GATS. In some ways, these latter forms of migration are becoming more like trade in goods and capital, transformed into a temporary mobility that is less visible on the state's radar. Tourist migration and the business migration of temporary "non-immigrant" workers or "posted" service personnel are cases in point, illustrating the multiple new ways temporary mobility is possible. In cases that are more politically visible, such as the outsourcing of skilled services, national attempts to enact "clawback" measures at the national level have been blocked by WTO regulations. These are part and parcel of the process of supra-national private governance that authors such as Sassen (1996) and Strange (1996) have feted as states "losing control." These new developments do not mean that the state has ceased to be a player in the politics of skilled labor migration but rather that it is no longer a clearly controlling player.

Look closer however, at the apparently clear disassociation and the two kinds of mobility are approaching each other. Migration is not what it used to be given the ever-increasing diversity of channels and opportunities. Many of those moving into and through these mobility channels are not rich white folk from Europe and America but Indian software engineers, Central and South Americans able to get six-month tourist visas to the global North or Koreans and Chinese using U.S. immigration loopholes to get their children educated in the U.S. and on a fast track to U.S. citizenship. These movements are using visa categories available to anyone who can get enough money together and who happens to come from a U.S.- or Europe-approved country; all can only be thought of very ambiguously as "immigration," although "temporary" in these cases, as Lavenex points out, can mean anywhere between three months and five years. However, this time dimension can often lead to a kind of immigrant experience. The experience of an international traveler is often assumed to be that of a "sojourner" and no more; a "frictionless" mobility characterized by an absence of any kind of meaningful encounter or incorporation in the host society. But, in fact, highly skilled migration brings with it both different mechanisms for entry and distinctive challenges and opportunities for incorporation. It is not a frictionless mobility but rather a differently tracked mobility with its own costs and constraints.

While the unchallenged transnational sojournment of the highly skilled and educated might once have been seen as evidence of the state losing control, this is no longer so as migration bleeds into mobility. There is a *re*-regulation of these new forms, such that immigration is arguably becoming a *less* important focus of control than the new global mobility. In the aftermath of 9/11, it is increasingly these *other* forms of movement/mobility that are the big state security concerns. There has been a growing perception the "alien threat" might come more from the ranks of students, tourists and business travelers—hitherto a massive blind spot in border scrutiny—rather than official immigrant categories. After all, "true" immigrants have been subject to much more stringent screening than others coming through on a waiver basis or study visa, and they have also, of course, expressed a desire to become (for example) American rather than simply exploiting mobility opportunities as free floating global movers. The new control technologies of the American state have been targeted at these now suspect movers, turning to bio-metric monitoring and multiple new layers of bureaucratic paperwork, as the fulfilling of an almost Foucauldian effort in bio-power to cleanse a globalizing world from "terrorists." Katalin Szelényi documents some of the difficulties international students have encountered in this new environment.

The cooperative attitudes of other major world players indicate states might seek to outdo each other technologically in their enthusiasm for these new forms of bureaucratic "governmentality." The compliant stance of the European Union—the U.S.'s supposed nemesis in international relations—is hard to square with the continent's extraordinary transnational commitment to freedom of movement as a legal right for European citizens. In fact, the U.S. is exploiting some of the EU's experience of new modes of control as this has shifted inwards to the welfare state and policing of access to the interior society rather than the border (Brochmann, 1999; Guiraudon and Lahav, 2000; Feldblum, 2000). Although formal "immigration control" still ends the moment the agent stamps your passport and lets you by, current developments suggest states are becoming more concerned with heretofore unregulated elites and the affluent in other ways. The U.S. state is clamping down on tax loopholes for the hypermobile and looking to enforce more citizenship responsibilities. A side effect of the new security environment appears to be an increase in governments' technological capacity and motivation to monitor all transnational activities, whether it be the financial transactions of religious charities with alleged "terrorist" connections, or squeezing expatriates and permanent residents on long-term, hidden tax obligations to the U.S. state. At the other end of the scale, 9/11 has licensed new powers for states seeking to escape the binding constraints of international law; arrogating human rights in cases when "terrorists" can be tried outside of the law for reasons of "national security." The specter of "stateless persons" being held indefinitely in legal quarantine outside of international law is an Arendtian reminder of how vulnerable all so-called "post-national" populations still are to the claims of the sovereign state.

Human Capital: All You Need to Succeed?

The all purpose lubricant of the (allegedly) frictionless world of elite global mobility is human capital, in which the "human" part is measured in terms of internationally recognized qualifications and quantifiable talent and is every bit as universal and inalienable as human rights. Economic capital might indeed matter less in a truly neo-classical market for migration, in which talent and enterprise would drive the migration calculus and where internationally recognized education or experience (rather than the right family background) would be the one way ticket to global elite status (Borjas, 1989). Again, the economists' theory here does not match empirical realities. It turns out that faster social and spatial mobility, based on the "universal" metric of skill and talent, does not, in fact, remove the challenge of incorporation. Culture and particularistic know-how still impose all the difficulties of integration on these kinds of migrants. Moreover, even if mobility itself has become a form of privileged capital, not all other forms of capital are as mobile as elite status is supposed to guarantee.

Social networks (i.e., who you know and how this can help you) might be the secret of success globally as much as nationally or in your home town, but the real power of the global mobility myth stems from its individualist faith; the idea that the human capital of education can take you where you want to go regardless of social structure or social reproduction. The globally talented are supposed to be able to make it anywhere, even without local connections or embedded networks. One assumption of this kind would be that the human capital-rich face fewer problems of discrimination, exploitation and/or exclusion from receiving societies than do other foreigners.

On many straightforward issues regarding attitudes to migrants, this is still likely to be true. However, the very idea of a world uncritically open to the globally mobile is premised on the idea, promoted by some theorists of mobility (i.e., Urry, 2000), that societies (for the highly mobile at least) no longer exist—and therefore that non-spatially located forms of capital have essentially interchangeable values in different locations. Were this the case, the obstacles encountered and submitted to by other migrants less rich in capital (the less talented)—forces of integration, such as national norms, sanctions for difference, or hierarchies of insider/outsider status manifested as privilege and exclusion— should simply not apply here. Those with human capital mobility are thought to be able to exist "outside" of society and yet be effortlessly able to integrate when they choose to in their host destination. Integration, for them, would somehow escape the coercion of a sociological process and become more of an *à la carte* set of individualistic choices, in which one can always out-trump the imposition of any particular norm or constraint by an appeal to post-national rights or one's mobility right of exit/entry.

Evidence on this question needs to be qualitative. We must look at the experiences of some of the most mobile, talented, human capital-rich migrants on the planet and see just how they get along in their chosen host societies. The chapters by Chavravartty, Szelényi, Bozkurt and Favell in part three of the book offer rich material to this end. High earnings, comfortable unquestioned status and accelerated professional success through mobility are not uncommon. These migrants are indeed choosing their own paths and garnering rewards from corporate or educational systems that reward universal rather than local standards. However, the picture muddies a great deal over time. It is rare to find that selective integration really works. We find instead their power to choose only means they are choosing to stay *out* of local societies they may be very functional parts of the cities they live in, but they have no voice politically or socially. Their ability to change or impact the places to which they have migrated is limited. This might seem a negligible drawback for the globally mobile until we remember that over time "everyday" issues of housing, taxation, health, child-care, schooling and retirement, all require some engagement and negotiation with local social structures that inevitably favor insiders. Failure to master the local rules of the game, in fact, may lead to a subtle exclusion from the benefits of long-term residence. Freed of the less pressurized, coercive adaptation imposed on less capital-rich immigrants, they may remain constrained to live the expensive life of the permanent expatriate, exploited by the city around them and forced, instead, into a less than easily sustainable transnational lifestyle that debars them from any meaningful "settlement."

For the highly mobile, the work environment is at least meant to function as well as a place where human capital is recognized and convertible. Here too, however, mobility has costs as well as benefits. Skilled migrants, because of foreign status, can face "glass ceilings" in professional advancement not commensurate with education, experience or professional attainment, as Chakravartty points out. Because of the precariousness of the H-1B type immigration status, it can be argued skilled migrants to the U.S. have frequently been exploited by employers, having become the equivalent of "high-tech *braceros*" (Smith, 1998). Batalova and Lowell find there has been a persistent downward transnational mobility of skilled workers in the U.S. and elsewhere—data that would be even more dramatic if it included the highly educated migrants from developing countries who move into unskilled labor with no recognition of their experience or education. Flexibility and mobility can also equal vulnerability when there is a turn down (as Bozkurt points out) or as age creeps up and family responsibilities begin to weigh (Favell, this volume). This can become a form of transnational "fragility" of lifestyle, if the host state decides to start pressurizing the non-integrated to clarify their residency status or commit themselves to cultural and linguistic rights of passage—as has been the case for expatriates in the Netherlands, for example, in recent years. Whatever else they are experiencing, their privileged formal position also does not prevent exploitation of precariousness in other ways. Skilled migrants from developing countries can still be easily racialized or ethnicized negatively, as Chakravartty shows. Expatriates can also still be stigmatized culturally for non-conformity to local ways. The "post-national" mover in the U.S., for example, can also be viewed as "un-American" if they too openly affirm a lack of interest in long-term immigration and citizenship in the country.

In his incendiary manifesto on offshore living for the globally mobile, libertarian Ian Angell recommends living like a "new barbarian" as a way to escape the burdens and responsibilities of nation-state membership in a fast globalizing world (Angell, 2000). Like master thief Robert de Niro in the classic Michael Mann movie, tax- and citizenship-evading barbarians have got to be able to take everything they own or care about and run the moment they feel the *Heat* around the corner. But states are always catching up and globalizing their reach too. U.S. citizens abroad, for example, always have to file a tax return or they may lose their citizenship. This can turn into a nasty catch-22 for dual citizens or permanent residents when they then find they cannot voluntarily "lose" their citizenship or residence status unless they can demonstrate they are not giving it up for financial reasons. In short, the offshore world in which it is easy to be a transnational barbarian may not really exist. Life outside of such everyday structures as we have is an impossible life to imagine. The permanently mobile and moving need to remember, live like a barbarian and you might just die like one.

Rethinking Regional Contexts

The second part of our research agenda has been to look again at the major world regional contexts in which highly skilled migration is happening. This involves thinking through and differentiating the specific contextual research questions that might be asked in different global locations and in relation to different forms of mobility such as: international students, workers in multi-national corporations and high-tech professionals. Across the board, as Batalova and Lowell point out, one issue that immediately arises is the dearth of instruments to calculate and break down the magnitude of highly skilled migration *wherever* it is occurring. One immediate research agenda, therefore, concerns the question of what are the best analytical frameworks for ascertaining both the scale and specificity of such mobility. Research in future is likely to have to think creatively about combining official national and international sources with other kinds of investigative procedures.

Europe

In terms of free movement of persons, the European Union is the global leader, as it were, of regional mobility possibilities, far outstripping those to be found within the regional groupings of NAFTA (the North American Free Trade Association) or ASEAN (the Association of South East Asian Nations, which sometimes meets as ASEAN "plus three," i.e., the big three of Japan, South Korea, and China). Only in Europe has a genuine freedom of movement of persons been legally institutionalized alongside the freedom of movement of goods and capital (services remain a problematic area). The legal creation of these provisions—which dates back to the 1950s and Italy's insistence on a legal framework for the migration of its workers to the north of Europe—has, over time, had an enormous effect on the decline of state monopoly on free movement in Europe. The anti-discriminatory provisions about the employment of foreign Europeans have proven quite dramatic in European jurisprudence as they have been extended over time to non-economically active persons such as spouses, students and retirees. The EU has now enlarged dramatically with the accession of ten new, mostly Central and East European, members in May 2004. Although all these countries face a transition period before attaining full freedom of movement, the *de facto* free movement of East European workers, tourists and visitors in the West is long established through existing bi-lateral agreements and the open call for labor in the construction, homemaking and agricultural industries in many countries. The logic is economic, the willingness to see the freedom of movement of labor alongside trade and services as an efficient factor of production that does not admit other political or cultural forms of restriction for national reasons. To block this in an integrated regional economy is now seen straightforwardly as an example of discrimination, hence unfair competition, in this frame.

Ironically, the dramatic institutional encouragement of free movement in Europe has not been accompanied by a dramatic rise in the small number of European nationals actually moving and resettling within Europe. Recchi sees evidence of a growth in mobility and it is certainly true that new forms of cross-border movement, linked to tourism, retirement, shopping and so on, have become more significant. But in another sense there has been a decline in intra-EU mobility since the early 1970s, as working class south-to-north migration has dried up. It remains to be seen whether this is going to be replaced by a new kind of middle-class professional "spiralist" movement that accompanies the emergence of a more European-minded younger generation.

Several interesting research questions are suggested by the chapters dealing with European migration trends in this volume. For one, why is it that Europeans no longer move much, particularly in the light of their dramatic mobility in previous eras? The point where the ultra-mobile economic theory of economic integration hits the apparent cultural fact of local and regional identities, and their relative *immobility*, is a fertile place for understanding some of specificities of European society. Is there a distinctive form of regionalized capitalism embedded in contemporary European social and institutional forms? Or, put another way, how is the unfettered neo-liberal notion of mobility tempered by welfarist, community-based or other forms of closure when mobility threatens social reproduction, identity over time or stable long-term returns? An equally keen indicator of the specificities of European society is the encounter of non-Europeans with receiving host countries struggling with the long-term consequences of immigration. Much work has been done on the immigrant experience in post-war Europe but much less has been done on the putatively more privileged, skilled, educated or "elite" migrants that have been a growing part of these flows. For example, where do the new migrants fit alongside older post-colonial immigrants in France or Britain? How are highly skilled Asians or Africans getting along in unlikely new destinations such as Sweden or Finland? What are the reasons for the apparent failure of the so-called German "green card" scheme to recruit highly skilled technical workers from India and elsewhere in recent years?

North America

In a North American context, it is Canada that is often seen as the model for highly skilled migration policies. On this question, at least, Canada is typically seen as a globally open immigrant nation efficiently offering all potential newcomers access to the country through a rational talent and human capital-based evaluation of immigrant applications. In the U.S., family- and ethnicity-based immigration has long trumped skills-based criteria, something often blamed for the declining quality of "selection" in the U.S. In recent work by Reitz (1998) the economic rationality of the Canadian model has been challenged but the model itself still seems to appeal strongly to reformers pushing for new high end immigration channels in countries such as the U.S., Britain and Germany.

As shown in the chapters by Freeman and Hill, and Money and Falstrom, the U.S. system of multiple visa categories and the often distorting business interests behind these, point to a far from rational economic construction of policy. They indicate the difficulties of reform, even in the absence of strongly organized public opposition, and the degree to which path-dependence seems to determine overall outcomes in the policy process. Curiously, all the authors here suggest that highly skilled migration policy in the U.S. is a wholly self-contained national affair. National politics, rather than global economic pressures, drive the twists and turns of U.S. immigration policies, with key roles being played by high tech employers, professional associations, pro and anti-immigrant organizations, and even associations of immigration lawyers. There appears to be little space in their accounts for the kind of global legal/institutional influences signaled by Lavenex's study of WTO reforms or by the importance of global multinationals as in the stories told by Bozkurt and Favell. Further work on highly skilled migration in the U.S. might look to see how far U.S. policy is also subject to the same kind of global economic pressures forcing other nations to give way on control over some forms of economic mobility.

The questionable self-containment of the U.S. is likely to be challenged in other ways as the consequences of new empirical trends begin to be felt. How, for example, will the more mobile "brain circulation" and global competition—evidenced by students staying in or returning to their countries of origin, especially India and China—reshape the landscape of highly skilled migration in the U.S.? Will the benefits of open door policies on students and highly skilled migrants continue to accrue to the U.S., or are these influential factors in national GDP also mobile across borders? What new types of translocal geographical, business and social connections are likely to be forged between sending and receiving regions of skilled and business migration along the lines of those now established between Taipei and Los Angeles? Are these likely to be significant enough to constitute future new global city regions? Alternatively, might hostility towards highly skilled migrants grow as they increasingly become identified as "un-American" in their footloose attitude to residence in America? What, in fact, are going to be the medium- and long-term effects of the U.S.'s new bureaucratic controls on international students which led to such a dramatic dropoff in new arrivals in the years immediately after 9/11? On the other hand, it is clear the chapters here on the U.S. by Freeman and Hill, and Money and Falstrom, pioneer the study of the politics of the highly skilled with explanatory frameworks that need testing in other contexts. The politics of visa categories in the U.S. are a remarkable site of competition between business and societal interests as well as the different scales of local and national interest. The strongly regionalized differences pointed to by Money and Falstrom, and by Batalova and Lowell, suggest, too, that more qualitative studies of migrants in and between particular regions and industries—as suggested by Chakravartty's research project on Boston, New Jersey and the Silicon Valley—could be usefully developed.

Asia-Pacific

No work has done more to cement the image of Asian migrants across the Asia-Pacific as the paradigmatic transnational global movers than Aihwa Ong's widely read work on *Flexible Citizenship* (1999), about Chinese transmigrants in the region. Remarkable new ethnographic work of this kind will surely still be done on the manifold forms of migrant "agency" displayed by Chinese, Korean, or Japanese migrants, and others using loopholes in national immigration regimes in the U.S. and Canada to create new kinds of networks and practices across the region. Scholars are beginning to conceive of fascinating new projects looking at the social organization of "astronaut" families jetting between Asia, Australia and North America and the strategic planning of pregnancies and schooling that these families use to gain U.S. citizenship and access to the U.S. educational systemfor their children. The relatively invisible migration of long-term, overstaying visitors from Japan and Korea, and the dramatic role they play in their remarkable "offshore" cultures in cities such as Los Angeles, is also a highly suggestive transnational topic.

Increasingly, Mexicans and Central Americans deserve to be seen in a similar light, as participants in a Pacific Rim regional space, centered on the very porous economic opportunities moving in and out of the U.S. New research has been done on the increasing social differentiation within Mexican migration, for example, that looks at the movement of highly skilled Mexicans within migration systems between particular U.S. and Mexican cities in a post-industrial context (Hernández-Léon, 2004). Mexicans themselves count among some of the new "high tech *braceros*" using various visa channels to work in the US economy (Alarcón, 1999).

Research on migration in the Asia-Pacific or Pacific Rim needs, above all, to differentiate between sending countries in terms of their political relationship with the U.S.; the dominant defining factor in migrant flows between countries (Waldinger and Fitzgerald, 2004). The post-war emergence of South Korea, for example, owes everything to the privileged economic position given to the fast developing nation because of its geo-political significance in Cold War politics and the very easy forms of mobility established as a side effect of ever-increasing business flows between these unequal partners. Similar things can be said about U.S.-Japanese, U.S.-Filipino or U.S.-Indian relations and China has emerged as the biggest transnational question of all in the last decade. Sending countries have, however, found there are ways to subvert the dominated position they find themselves in by opening their arms to former expatriates and children of expatriates and seeking to pull back reserves of economic and human capital through the open business and education channels with the U.S. (see Chakravartty's overview of recent research on Indian migration in this volume). Given the economic success enjoyed by India in pro-actively managing its migration relations with the U.S., it is unlikely that other notable sending countries will remain passive in their attitudes to the crucial national resource represented by their most mobile native populations. As a result of these various migration patterns, the changing character of inter-ethnic relations within transnational cities like Los Angeles and New York and the effects of these relations on future trends in global mobility along the Pacific Rim, remain important research questions.

Conclusion

The Human Face of Global Mobility aims to put the empirical study of highly skilled, professional or educated migrants back on to research agendas in migration and global studies, which are more attuned to thinking about immigrants and immigration at the lower end of the labor market and then usually in terms of minority race, ethnicity or culture. Instead, we seek to open up opportunities for researchers seeking to resist the clichéd opposition of "elite" and "ethnic" migrants in a polarized global economy.

Our chapters offer different views on whether highly skilled migration is fundamentally different from unskilled migration as well as how the idea of "global mobility" differs from more conventional notions of "international migration." The chapters in this volume certainly document how highly skilled movements are looked upon more favorably in the context of liberalizing international trade regimes and argues for their growing importance in national and international policy. We point to the distinctive dimensions of national policies on highly skilled migration, showing how it is as important to differentiate among different instances and types of highly skilled migration as it is to recognize differences between highly skilled and unskilled migration. Evidence we bring forward here certainly suggests the economic impact of the highly skilled migration movement has moved beyond mere "brain drain" in many contexts and is now encouraging "brain circulation" that feeds new forms of global competition. We also offer good qualitative evidence for thinking that, although mobility *across* and integration *into* receiving societies may differ quite considerably in its patterns to the experiences of less skilled migrants, these privileges far from remove the challenges and difficulties involved in global mobility and international relocation. All of these themes, explored here through detailed quantitative, institutional and ethnographic work, add up to an open invitation to further research. Mobility is clearly a feature of the globalizing contemporary world and mobility breaks open and extends many of our conventional ideas about international migration. What is needed now is a whole new range of empirical studies that can begin to fill out the research agenda sketched here.

Notes

1. Their excellent website can be found at: http://www.lboro.ac.uk/gawc
2. See our UCLA website: http://www.isop.ucla.edu/ccgr/mobility.asp

Part One

Global and Regional Contexts

2

The Competition State and Multilateral Liberalization of Highly Skilled Migration

Sandra Lavenex

In the light of increasingly politicized publics and the recurrent restrictions of national asylum and immigration laws, the entry and stay of foreign nationals is usually regarded as one of the last bastions of state sovereignty. This view is backed by the relative weakness of multilateralism in states' attempts to regulate migration flows. In contrast to the flow of goods and finance, where states have established strong international regimes to co-ordinate their (highly liberal) policies, no similar development has taken place with regard to the international mobility of persons. With the exception of the codification of a weak international refugee regime after World War II, states have shown little effort to co-operate at the global level (Hollifield, 1992b; Sassen, 2000). In so far as coordination takes place, this is limited to the aspect of immigration control either in form of supranational integration projects such as the European Union (EU), or in loose, largely informal intergovernmental consultations with a low degree of institutionalization and enforcement.

This chapter argues that this view depicts only part of the reality of immigration politics which has to do with states' desire to maintain control over politically and socially contested forms of immigration. A look at states' approach towards desired forms of economic migration shows a very different picture and confirms the emergence and consolidation of supranational regulatory structures at both the regional and global level which, rather than enhancing immigration control, aim at the liberalization of labor mobility. Whereas the free movement regime inside the EU may be seen as an exception in the international context, the extension of parts of this regime to non-EU member states, and the inclusion of free movement provisions in a number of other regional trade agreements, points to a broader trend which has found its preliminary peak with the liberalization of certain aspects of labor mobility in the General Agreement on Trade in Services (GATS) concluded within the World Trade Organization (WTO).

Linking the phenomenon of migration with the literature on globalization and its transformative impact on the nation state, this chapter scrutinizes the dynamics and constraints behind the emergent structures of global governance of labor mobility. Whereas many aspects of these developments herald a growing dissociation between different categories of migration policies—that is, humanitarian, irregular, low-skilled and highly skilled—they may also trigger a greater awareness of the mutual gains of co-operation between sending and receiving countries as reflected in recent discussions on the viability of an international migration regime. The chapter starts with a discussion of labor mobility in the context of globalization and highlights the dynamics which push for a stronger liberalization of particular labor flows in the global economy. The second section approaches the question of a growing pressure for liberalization and deregulation in the context of contemporary debates in the political science literature and argues for a stronger differentiation of the theoretical approaches applied to different aspects of international migrations. The question of how states respond to these developments is addressed in sections three and four. Section three analyzes the handling of labor mobility in different regional trade agreements. The emerging global regulatory structures in the WTO (GATS) are scrutinized in section four. Section five addresses additional manifestations of post-national forms of regulation in the field of highly skilled migration and discusses in particular the role of multinational corporations and professional associations in the internationalization of labor markets. The broader implications of these processes for both the regulation of migration and the role of the nation state are addressed in the last section. Here the relationship between the liberalization of highly skilled labor mobility and other forms of migration is again addressed as well as the prospects for more inclusive forms of cooperation in these matters (see also Lavenex, 2004).

Globalization and Labor Mobility

Globalization may be conceived of "as a process (or set of processes) which embodies a transformation in the spatial organization of social relations and transactions—assessed in terms of their extensity, intensity, velocity and impact—generating transcontinental or interregional flows and networks of activity, interaction and the exercise of power" (Held et al., 2000: 15). In economic terms, globalization describes the progressive global integration of formerly national or regional markets and the transformation of the state from the nationally bound welfare state of the second industrial revolution to a neoliberal "competition state" (Cerny, 1994). Globalization cuts across the traditional division of labor between the two pillars of the postwar grand design—the Keynesian welfare state at the national level and the system of free trade at the international level— and promotes the commodification of all factors of production including human labor.

The restructuring of the global economy and the emergence of the "competition state" impact in several ways on international migration and generally enhances both the demand and supply for foreign labor at all levels of skills. Whereas the potential exploitation of manual labor through the relocation of labor-intensive production processes from the industrial countries to low-wage economies in Africa and Asia has been observed from the 1970s onwards (Fröbel, Heinrichts, and Kreye, 1977), another phenomenon is the transnationalization of the flows of skilled migrants. In contrast to unskilled workers, whose movements have been the focus of Western regulatory endeavors since the closing down of active recruitment policies, skilled labor has experienced a substantial degree of deregulation and liberalization which shares many more characteristics with the general patterns of neoliberal globalization than is often assumed. Three aspects of the global economy are particularly pertinent to the liberalization of skilled migration: the growth of the third sector in developed countries and the rising importance of trade in services in contrast to trade in goods; the transnationalization of production and the spread of multinational enterprises; and technological change.

Although labor is an integral factor to all modes of production, the rise of the service sector has specific implications for labor migration as the delivery of services, in contrast to goods, is often not separable from the physical presence of the person providing the service (Sapir, 1999: 52). This is particularly pertinent for international trade in services as, in absence of electronic alternatives, the cross-border transactions will usually involve the movement of the service supplier. The potential implications of this become clear when one looks at the importance of the service sector in Europe that, according to the European Commission, is "a harbinger of a fundamental restructuring of the world economy" (European Commission, 1995). It accounts for almost 70 percent of EU GDP and roughly 60 percent of foreign direct investments (FDI) of the major trading nations (Ghosh, 1997:1). The expansion of trade in services began in the early 1980s and has, by far, exceeded growth patterns for trade in goods. In addition to its expanding contribution to economic growth, the service sector bears the biggest potential for job creation: 18 million new jobs have been created in services in Europe over the past fifteen years, compared with a reduction of some 13 million jobs in industry and agriculture (European Commission, 1996).

The transnationalization of production is another major force behind the integration of previously nationally bounded labor markets. Portfolio and foreign direct investment (FDI) often imply migration, as the cross-border establishment of new enterprises, usually involves the movement of the entrepreneur or, in the case of the MNCs, managers and other key personnel (Sassen, 1998). Thus, tight immigration laws and bureaucratic admission procedures are increasingly identified as potential barriers to the inflow of foreign capital. The spread of multinational corporations has two implications for Western immigration policies: it increases the risk of an outward movement of jobs from affluent societies to countries with a surplus of labor or where the foreign intake of labor is easier; and leads to the establishment of internal labor markets which are largely independent from the domestic labor markets where the firms operate. The possibility to recruit within internal labor markets limits the opportunities for the creation of new jobs for the domestic labor force and, in case of labor shortages, gives MNCs an advantage over small and medium enterprises (SME) in the competition for qualified workers.

Technological change, as well as change in the modes of production, have created additional drivers for the liberalization of labor movements. In transnational production networks, shortening product cycles and "just in time" production implies a greater mobility of the labor force and a growing need for the temporary assignment of expert personnel to support short-term projects abroad. Apart from raising the level of skills required, technological change provides the broader infrastructure with both transportation and communication.

Nowhere is the relationship between jobs, investment, technological change and dynamic economic growth clearer than in the information and communication technology (ICT) sector that is central to economic restructuring and international competitiveness. Even after the 'crisis' of telecoms and computer and electronic industries during 2001 and 2002, when many mainly less-qualified employees in the ICT sector lost their jobs, the "gap" between supply and demand in ICT workers was estimated to have reached 1.6 million jobs in 2003 (European Commission, 2002). Yet, apart from ICT, shortages also persisted in other sectors such as health and education. Notwithstanding the current economic downturn, studies conducted by the OECD and others found the most intense labor shortages OECD-member countries will have to face in the next 20 years or so are in the skilled and highly skilled job market (OECD, 2002). Of course, this is also influenced by the negative demographic trends in northern countries (United Nations, 2001).

Challenges to the Nation State: Migration and the "Competition State"

The globalization debate is split between the globalists on the one hand, who observe a decline of the state in the face of denationalized economies (Ohmae, 1990, 1995; Strange, 1996) and the skeptics, on the other, who refute the unprecedentedness of current levels of interdependence and underline the continuity of states' interventionist powers (Boyer and Drache, 1996; Hirst and Thompson, 1996). The same divide is at the core of contemporary accounts of the impact of migration on the nation state. From a globalist perspective, the expansion of migrant flows beyond states' control is seen as a function of economic globalization (Sassen, 1996). According to Sassen, globalization results in "the relocation of various components of state authority to supranational organizations" and "the de-facto privatization of public sector activities" to firms and multinational enterprises, thereby undermining state sovereignty (Sassen, 1999: 177). A similar unintended expansion of immigration flows has also been sited by students of domestic politics. From this perspective, however, the growing "gap" (Cornelius, Martin, and Hollifield, 1994) between the desire to limit the intake and actual flows is not a consequence of external pressure, but a homemade problem. Refuting the globalists' thesis of a weakening of the state, these authors stress the role of domestic structures in liberal democracies as explanations "why states accept unwanted immigration" (Joppke, 1998). These domestic constraints on restrictionist policies include, in particular, pluralism and the freedom of interest groups to organize themselves and lobby for immigration (Freeman, 1995) and legal systems with the judiciary playing an important role in the expansion of immigrant rights (Guiraudon, 1998).

While these two poles highlight important constraints on the ability of states to control undesired immigration, I argue that they divert our view of the deeper transformative impact of globalization including the way states approach the phenomenon of international migration. By framing the question in terms of how far states are able to avert undesired migration flows, this debate fails to account for states' approach to desired forms of migration. Hence, we need to differentiate more strongly between the different flows of migrants and their relationship with globalization and the role of the state. The question then, is less how far global migration flows weaken or strengthen the nation state, but rather how, and in which direction, the processes associated with globalization transform both the goals and the means of the state with regard to international migration.

This framing of the research question concurs with an alternative view in the broader international relations (IR) literature on the nature of globalization proposed by the "transformationals" (the term is taken from Held et al., 2000): scholars who, without problematizing the end-state of these processes, conceive of globalization as a historically unprecedented transformation in which states and societies across the world face the challenge of adapting to the gradual dissolution of the distinction between international and domestic as well as external and internal affairs.

Drawing on this literature, the transformative impact of globalization on the role and the shape of the state points to four major trends (Giddens, 1990; Rosenau, 1997; Ruggie, 1993; Zürn, 1998; Prakash and Hart, 1999). First, nation states no longer operate autonomously in the realm of foreign policy or international relations but are increasingly enmeshed in complex multilevel systems in which resources and responsibilities are shared with actors at the international and subnational level. Second, the traditional distinction between domestic and foreign policy as "not part of the same universe" (Lowi, 1964a: 689) is no longer clear cut. Third, globalization transforms core aspects of statehood, namely sovereignty (both with regard to its internal and external legitimacy), resources and the formulation and realization of the goals of government which are increasingly defined at the international level with the nation-states taking the task of implementation (Zürn, 1998: 329ff). Finally, a fourth trend refers to power shifts between states, the economy and what is commonly referred to as civil society. This concerns, in particular, the belief in the superiority of market-based over state-managed solutions and the growing authority of private actors in domains formerly reserved to the state (Héritier, 2002; Knill and Lehmkuhl, 2002).

As a result of these processes, today widespread opinion maintains that "the main task or function of the contemporary state is the promotion of economic activities, whether at home or abroad, which make firms and sectors located within the territory of the state competitive in international markets" (Cerny, 1999: 199). This transformation of the state, which has inspired the concept of the "competition state," should be at the very heart of contemporary approaches to skilled migration. Skilled migration, often referred to as labor mobility in this context, has become an important element in the external economic policy of the competition state. These developments find support in the economic theory of migration that, in contrast to the wider debate about the economic advantages and disadvantages of liberalizing labor flows—where no clear consensus exists among economists—clearly affirms the gains from skilled immigration. The reason is in this view skilled immigrants make a positive contribution to the stock of human capital in the receiving economy and, by bringing in new skills and innovation, enhance the level or rate of growth and may also promote higher incomes. According to a recent OECD publication, the immigration of highly skilled workers is seen: "i) to respond to cyclical labor market shortages; ii) to increase the stock of human capital; and iii) to encourage the circulation of the knowledge embodied in highly skilled workers and promote innovation" (OECD, 2002: 9). The intake of skilled immigrants is particularly profitable for a receiving economy since it receives persons with skills and professional experience without having to contribute to their training and education (Borjas, 2000). For sending countries, the economic gains from the emigration of skilled workers are less clear cut. The economic advantages from emigration concern, first and foremost, remittances that, for many developing countries, by far exceed the level of official development aid (United Nations, 2003). Other advantages are the reduction of unemployment and, in the advent of return migration, also the acquirement of additional skills and technological transfer. The danger in the emigration of especially skilled workers is the phenomenon of "brain drain" and losses in the return on investment in education and training. Notwithstanding these disadvantages, a growing number of developing countries actively promote the export of migrant workers. Special government-sponsored programs to promote emigration have been set in place in Bangladesh, China, Egypt, India, Indonesia, Pakistan, the Philippines, South Korea, Sri Lanka and Vietnam (Massey, 1999). The next sections of this chapter thus scrutinize new developments toward the liberalization of skilled migration in regional and global trade agreements that highlight the growing similarities between the regulatory structures in this policy field and the "classic" themes of international political economy, trade and finance. The role of these initiatives in the general context of migration politics is discussed in the conclusion.

Neo-liberal Arrangements in Regional Trade Agreements

The economic integration project with the most prominent neoliberal regime for labor migration is the European Union with its internal free movement regime. However, most regional free trade agreements include provisions on the liberalization of certain types of labor movements. These provisions range from the full free movement of labor and service providers, to a limited liberalization of the temporary movement of intra-corporate transferees and business visitors. Notwithstanding these differences, all agreements provide more favorable treatment for skilled workers. The following review is based on the texts of formal treaties and does not look at their implementation. This section reviews the pertinent provisions in regional trade agreements and shows at least with regard to skilled migrants, states' approaches have reached a considerable degree of openness (OECD, 2002; Nielson, 2002). These regional developments are paralleled by the introduction of more flexible arrangements in domestic regulations that are geared to facilitate the intake of skilled immigrants. These activities cover a wider range of measures and are not limited to the specific aspect of entry requirement alone. Rather, government policies to attract foreign expertise, include the introduction of specific immigration schemes for highly skilled personnel such as: the German "green card" or the H-1B visas in the U.S.; the simplification and acceleration of existing work permit systems; mutual recognition of professional qualifications; the provision of tax incentives; the internationalization of higher education; and, more generally, measures to promote the country as attractive working and living environment (McLaughlan and Salt 2002; OECD, 2002).

The Extended EU Free Movement Regime

Among the regional free trade agreements, the EU clearly has the most liberal free movement regime. The free movement of workers was included from the onset as one of the four freedoms of the single market (together with the free movement of goods, capital and services, Art. 18 EC). The Treaty of Rome included three types of economic activity in the free movement provisions: work (Article 39 EC, old Art. 48); self-employment (Article 43 EC, old Art. 52); and service (Article 49 EC, old Art. 59). The realization of these provisions was based on the abolition of discrimination on the ground of nationality between workers of member states as regards their employment, remuneration and other conditions of work and employment. Limitations to these rights were held narrow and are circumscribed by states' serious concerns of public policy, security and health. All occupations were opened up to workers from other member states with the exception of occupations in the public sector. The full free movement of workers was introduced in 1968 with Regulation 1612/68. Following the decision in the 1987 Single European Act to fully realize the single market by 1992, the free movement norm was extended from the group of workers to the economically inactive and today covers all EU citizens as well as their foreign relatives.

Whereas one can interpret this free movement regime as a politically motivated aspect of the European integration project, its extension to certain non-EU member states confirms the strong economic logic behind this approach. Full freedom of movement has thus been introduced through the Treaty on the European Economic Area (EEA) of 1992 with the remaining members of the European Free Trade

Association (EFTA), for example, Norway and Iceland, and with Switzerland by the bilateral treaty of 1999. In addition, partial free movement rights were included in the Europe Agreements concluded with the (then) candidate countries for EU membership, and two Balkan countries (Croatia and Macedonia). Limited to the category of service providers, the agreements allow for the temporary entry of natural persons providing a service or who are employed by a service provider as key personnel, as well as nationals of the contracting parties who seek temporary entry for the purpose of negotiating for the sale of services. Although the agreements don't provide general freedom of movement for workers, rights of establishment are extended without discrimination. Nationals of the contracting parties have the right to enter any member state for the purpose of setting up and operating a business on a self-employed basis. The same right applies to companies that establish a branch in the EU. These may send key personnel to a member state on a long-term basis for the activities linked to the establishment and operation of the firm (Guild, 2001).

Less inclusive provisions relating to the mobility of service providers are also included in the EU-Mexico Free Trade Agreement and the Euro-Med Association Agreements concluded with Morocco and Tunisia. These agreements address labor mobility through trade in services and add certain entitlements to the mutual commitments undertaken under the GATS (see below). In the EU-Mexico Agreement, this is, in particular, regulations with regard to "work, labor conditions and establishment of natural persons" (Art. 27) and measures relating to "key personnel" (Art. 16 and 17). The wording of the Euro-Med Agreements exceeds the more narrow category of service providers and foresees a regular dialogue to find ways to achieve progress in the field of movement of workers (Art. 69(2)). In their present shape, these agreements however resemble more the kind of co-operation agreements modeled on the basis of the GATS than the expansive free movement provisions of the EU.

The North American Free Trade Agreement (NAFTA)

NAFTA includes important provisions with regard to the mobility of skilled workers. Chapter 16 of the agreement, which deals with the temporary entry for business persons, facilitates the movement of four categories of persons: "business visitors," that is, persons engaged in international business activities for the purpose of conducting activities related to research and design, growth and manufacture and production, marketing, sales, distribution, after-sales service and other general services; "traders and investors," defined as persons who conduct substantial trade in goods and services between two of the contracting parties, or who commit a substantial amount of capital to that country, provided such persons are employed or operate in a supervisory or executive capacity or one that involves essential skills; "intra-company transferees," that is, persons employed by a company in a managerial or executive capacity or one that involves specialized knowledge and who are transferred within that company to another country; and other categories of "professionals," with a university degree or other specific skills who seek to engage in business activities at a professional level. The highest degree of liberalization applies to business visitors who are exempt from both labor certification and work permit requirements, provided they do not enter the labor market and do not receive remuneration for services provided in a member country. The other three categories are exempt from labor certification or labor market tests but still require a work permit.

In addition, the U.S. permits a quota of 5,500 Mexican professionals to enter the country under the provisions of Chapter 16. Canada, in contrast, applies no quotas on Mexican professionals under NAFTA. Finally, the agreement also provides for a special "Trade NAFTA" (TN) visa for citizens of Canada or Mexico visiting the U.S. whose profession falls under the Chapter 16 list and who qualify under the agreement. This visa lasts for one year and is renewable. However, the regulations concerning Mexican nationals are more strict than those for Canadians. While Canadians can receive TN status at the port of entry without needing a visa or prior approval, Mexicans must apply for a visa at the U.S. Embassy in Mexico on the basis of a labor condition application filed by the employer.

While NAFTA thus applies a rather cautious approach to labor mobility, a Working Group on Temporary Entry has been established with the task to expand the scope of Chapter 16. Proposals currently under discussion include extending the waiving of labor certification requirements for accompanying spouses and the establishment of an additional category to cover business people who do not fall under the existing categories but whose movement is essential to the liberalization benefits granted under the agreement.

Other Agreements

Like the EU, the Australia-New Zealand Closer Economic Relations (ANZCERTA) and Trans-Tasman Travel Arrangement provide for full liberalization of labor flows between Australia and New Zealand. The ANZCERTA Treaty provides for full market access and full national treatment for all service suppliers without distinction (Art. 4 and 5 Services Protocol). Although this treaty does not provide for general labor mobility, it is supplemented by the Trans-Tasman Travel Arrangement, which allows the citizens of the contracting parties to live and work freely in the other country for an indefinite period. However, this arrangement is not legally binding.

Another agreement with far-reaching provisions is the Common Market for Eastern and Southern Africa (COMESA). This treaty provides for the establishment of a common market within which goods, services, capital and labor shall move freely within 20 African member states. Like the EU, COMESA also aims in the longer term at the establishment of a monetary union. Full free movement of persons and right of establishment shall be realized by 2025.

In addition, there are a number of regional agreements using free movement provisions similar to the GATS model. Protocol II of the Caribbean Community (CARICOM) provides for the free movement of university graduates, other professionals and skilled persons in selected occupations. In addition, freedom of travel and the exercise of a profession are granted (i.e., elimination of passport requirements, elimination of work permit requirements). CARICOM also guarantees national treatment but not the Most Favoured Nation (MFN) principle. These provisions were adopted after the coming into force of the GATS (see section four). The 15 CARICOM member states are Antigua and Barbuda, the Bahamas, Barbados, Belize, Dominica, Grenada, Guyana, Haiti, Jamaica, Montserrat, St. Kitts and Nevis, Santa Lucia, St. Vincent and the Grenadines, Surinam and Trinidad and Tobago. Provisions on the movement of natural persons, in particular business people, investors, short-term business visitors and intra-corporate transferees are also included in Chapter 9 of the Japan-Singapore Free Trade Agreement. The ASEAN Free Trade Area (AFTA) also covers the mobility of natural persons in its provisions on trade in services. The ten ASEAN/AFTA member states are Brunei Darussalam, Cambodia, Indonesia, Laos., Malaysia, Myanmar, Philippines, Singapore, Thailand and Vietnam. The 1995 ASEAN Framework Agreement on Services committed members to negotiations aimed at achieving commitments beyond those in their existing GATS schedules. The promotion of the freer flow of skilled labor and professionals was also included in the Framework Agreement on the ASEAN Investment Area of 1998 together with the free movement of capital and technology. Another agreement that draws directly on the GATS model is the Southern Common Market Agreement (MERCOSUR). Mercosur member countries include Argentina; Brazil; Paraguay and Uruguay. Chile and Bolivia are associated members. The wording of the GATS is practically replicated in this agreement.

Relevant provisions are also found in the twenty-one-nation Asia Pacific Economic Co-operation Forum (APEC), in particular its action plan adopted in Osaka in November 1995. APEC members include Australia, Brunei, Canada, Chile, China, Hong Kong, Indonesia, Japan, Korea, Malaysia, Mexico, New Zealand, Papua New Guinea, Peru, Philippines, Russia, Singapore, Taipei, Thailand, the U.S. and Vietnam. Among other things, this plan aims at is the promotion of the mobility of business people engaged in trade and investment in the region. APEC does not grant any right of entry but has established a scheme to facilitate the entry of business visitors under the APEC Business Travel Card Scheme. The Card has a validity of three years and permits multiple short-term business visits for a period of two or three months on each arrival. Finally, the seven member countries of the South Asian Association for Regional Co-operation (SAARC) include Bangladesh, Bhutan, India, Maldives, Nepal, Pakistan and Sri Lanka, although this association does not cover trade in services. However, a Visa Exemption Scheme was adopted in 1992 that waives visa requirements for twenty-one categories of persons and simplifies visa procedures and requirements for business people to promote trade and tourism in the region.

A tentative summary of the relevant approaches in the different regional trade agreements is provided in Table 2.1 below.

In sum, the liberalization of the movement of certain groups of skilled workers and/or service providers is a common phenomenon in all regional economic integration agreements. The diffusion of these free movement norms has taken different paths. Whereas the EU provisions and NAFTA preceded the conclusion of the multilateral GATS Treaty, several regional initiatives in South America and Asia have taken the GATS as a model for the liberalization of their own regional service markets. This model is presented below.

Table 2.1
Overview of Labor Mobility Provisions in Regional Trade Agreements

Agreements providing full mobility of labor	Agreements providing market access exceeding the GATS	Agreements using the GATS model	Agreements providing no market access but facilitated entry
EU	NAFTA	MERCOSUR	APEC
EEA	CARICOM		SAARC
EFTA	Europe Agreements		
COMESA	Japan-Singapore FTA		
ANZCERTA	EU-Mexico FTA		
	Euro-Med Agreements		
	AFTA		

Source: Nielson, 2002.

Liberalization in the GATS Framework

The WTO's GATS (General Agreement on Trade in Services) covers the cross-border movement of all production factors in service trade, including the cross-border movement of natural persons who enter another country for the purpose of service supply. Concluded in 1994, the general aim of this treaty is to abolish barriers to trade in services, including domestic regulatory practices that prevent the efficient cross-border movement of service providers. According to the Annex on Movement of Natural Persons attached to the treaty, "Members may negotiate specific commitments applying to the movement of all categories of natural persons supplying services." In accordance with the different modes of service trade distinguished in the treaty, measures relating to the movement of natural persons are referred to as "mode 4" liberalization in the GATS framework. Movement of natural persons is contained as one out of four modes of delivery of services in the GATS negotiations. These modes are as follows (Art. 1(2) GATS): "cross border supply" which denotes the possibility for non-resident service suppliers to supply services cross-border into the Member's territory; "consumption abroad" which means the freedom of the Member's residents to purchase services in the territory of another Member; "commercial presence" indicating the opportunities for foreign service suppliers to estab-lish, operate or expand a commercial presence as legal persons in the Member's territory, such as a branch, agency or wholly-owned subsidiary; and finally "presence of natural persons" which opens the possibilities offered for the entry and temporary stay in the member's territory of foreign individuals in order to supply a service. This treaty includes both service suppliers who are employed by a foreign or national firm and independent workers, irrespective of skills and hierarchical position. Although tackling only temporary movement, the term "temporary" has been left deliberately open in the treaty. In practice, temporary entry may reach from a couple of weeks up to five years (WTO, 1998:1).

Temporary Mobility vs. Immigration

The general limits of labor mobility under the GATS are fixed in the Annex on Movement of Natural Persons. Its first paragraph clearly states the members' commitments under this mode relate only to the temporary admission of foreign nationals or foreign permanent residents as "service providers" in their territory. Accordingly, the GATS does not "apply to measures affecting natural persons seeking access to the employment market of a Member, nor shall it apply to measures regarding citizenship, residence or employment on a permanent basis..." Furthermore, the fourth paragraph contains a safeguard according to which the agreement does not "prevent a member from applying measures to regulate the entry of natural persons into, or their temporary stay in, its territory, including those measures necessary to protection the integrity of, and to ensure the orderly movement of natural persons across, its borders, provided such measures are not applied in such a manner as to nullify or impair the benefits accruing to any member under the terms of a specific commitment". Notwithstanding these clear limitations, the GATS does have an important impact on national immigration systems in so far as it seeks to abolish domestic regulations which hinder the international mobility of service providers. Barriers to the provision of services by natural persons may be categorized in three groups:

1. general immigration legislation including visa requirements;
2. labor market regulation governing the issuance of work permits etc.;
3. and regulations defining foreigners' ability to work in individual areas.

Member states' official consensus says that limitations falling under the first category are beyond the formal scope of the GATS. The Annex on the Movement of Natural Persons expressly exempts measures regarding citizenship and residence, as well as the rules governing permanent employment from the disciplines of the agreement. Accordingly, the commitments made under the schedules do not go beyond existing regulations regarding, for example, the issue of visas for temporary stay. Moreover, the operation of visa requirements only for natural persons of certain members, but not for others, is not *per se* regarded as contrary to the agreement. Still, even if the formal scope of the treaty is thus limited, the processes engendered by it do have implications for national immigration policies in so far as global competition over labor (in particular skilled labor) is increasingly recognized as a scarce resource. National immigration and labor market regulations may also be affected by Article IV.4 in GATS which is designed to allow members to simultaneously maintain domestic regulatory policies regarding qualification requirements and procedures, technical standards and licensing requirements, while ensuring any trade distorting effects of those policies are minimized as much as possible. In particular, this article stipulates domestic regulations shall be "a) based on objective and transparent criteria; b) not more burdensome than necessary to ensure the quality of the service; and c) in case of licensing procedures, not in themselves a restriction on the supply of the service."

Measures falling under the two other groups of barriers to "mode 4" supply do formally fall under the scope of the treaty and may be captured either under the general horizontal commitments or in specific sectoral commitments falling under Articles XVI (market access), XVII (national treatment) and XVIII (other additional commitments). These may include numerical quota for access to the national labor market; licensing and qualification requirements; residency requirements and non-eligibility under subsidy schemes; discrimination with regard to mandatory social insurance systems (e.g., denial of pension entitlements); or restrictions affecting the mobility of family members, etc (WTO, 1998: 11ff.).

Scope of Commitments

The exact scope of the GATS provisions must be sought in the members' commitments laid down in the schedules. The vast majority of entries cover only key personnel and highly skilled professionals. The EC's horizontal commitments under the current schedules provide for the temporary presence, as intra-corporate transferee, of natural persons working in a senior position or who possess uncommon knowledge essential to the establishment's service, research equipment, techniques or management. In addition, the agreement covers representatives of service suppliers who are seeking temporary entry for the purpose of negotiating for the sale of services and persons working in a senior position who are responsible for the setting up, in a member state, of a commercial presence of a service provider. In general, commitments adopted by industrialized countries under "mode 4" are strongly linked to their commitments regarding commercial presence and the right to establish a company ("mode 3").

The entries in schedules constitute binding commitments for the country to allow the supply of the service in question under the specified terms and conditions and not to introduce any new measure that could restrict its access to the market. The importance of such terms and conditions is enforced by the stipulation the commitments cannot be withdrawn or modified until the agreement has been in force for three years and such changes should be subject to agreed arrangements with the affected countries on compensatory adjustment (Ghosh, 1997: 94). In addition, the WTO's dispute settlement process offers a means of authoritative enforcement in case of infringement of agreed commitments. Yet only governments have access to this dispute settlement procedure. The only possibility for a company or an individual person who feels he or she is not given fair treatment in a foreign market according to GATS rule is to request his or her home government to seek redress with the other government in question. In case no agreement can be reached, the process goes before the WTO's Dispute Settlement Body that may decide retaliation against the offending member.

The current schedules regarding mobility of persons are the result of an additional year of negotiations taking place after conclusion of the Uruguay Round in 1994, on the initiative of developing countries which called for more liberalization in this respect (Koehler, 1999: 192ff.). As a consequence, six GATS members presented modified schedules in 1995, including the European Union, Australia, Canada, India, Norway and Switzerland.

The review of the schedules shows a more restrictive approach to commitments under "mode 4" than on other modes and a preference for qualified labor. According an OECD analysis, 240 out of 328 entries relate to executives, managers and specialists. More than half of these, 135, concern intra-corporate transferees. Yet, 17 percent of all horizontal entries cover low skilled personnel (e.g., "business sellers") and ten countries have allowed some forms of restricted entry to "other level" personnel (OECD, 2002: 31). When compared to other modes of service trade, this review confirms the caution of member states to take up binding commitments with regard to foreign service providers. Although this caution is more pronounced with regard to "mode 4" than in other modes, it corresponds to a more general feature of the GATS.

According to a note by the WTO Secretariat, the treaty permits the signatories to circumvent their commitments in several ways (WTO, 1995). The agreement allows a considerable flexibility in applying the general principles of liberalization. It is a sectoral agreement in the sense it only applies to specific sectors in service trade which are specifically listed in the national schedules (Mukherjee, 1999:89). Unlike other agreements in the GATT Uruguay Round, which adopt a "negative list" (naming exceptions to the rules) approach, the GATS provisions for market access and national treatment follow a "positive list" approach, in the sense only those service industries that are specifically listed in national schedules come under GATS disciplines. Furthermore, the national schedules may impose limitations and conditions on the—in principle—unrestricted provisions on market access and national treatment for specific modes of supply. Thus within a sector listed in the national schedule, a member country may include restrictions on movement of persons as service providers while liberalizing other modes of supply. This means the extent of movement of persons is largely determined by the commitments concerning sector coverage and the nature and extent of limitations imposed on market access and national treatment (Ghosh, 1997: 107). Together with the lack of specific definitions in central terminology (such as "temporary" stay, "specialist" etc.) this approach increases the scope for discretionary administrative practices in the implementation process and, from an economic perspective, reduces transparency of barriers to trade (Ghosh, 1997: 92; Mukherjee, 1999: 89ff.; Lee, 1999: 48ff.).

Notwithstanding the caution of industrial countries in their current commitments, it is generally expected that the ongoing "GATS 2000" negotiations will bring some extensions in this respect (OECD, Trade Directorate 2002: 8). A first indication in the direction of further openings are the negotiating proposals tabled in the current round of negotiations. The main proposals include:

- expansion of existing market access, either through the development of sectoral commitments or by expanding access of particular groups or categories of personnel (such as e.g., contractual service providers or independent professionals);
- improvement of the level of access by removing obstacles to the utilization of existing commitments through increased transparency and information or the stream-lining of administrative procedures, such as e.g., a specific GATS-visa, eventually to be self-administered by companies once certified by the immigration authorities;
- other domestic regulations (Art. VI.4 GATS), such as the limitation of economic needs tests and recognition of qualifications.

To sum up, the GATS is the first multilateral treaty to include binding multilateral rules on migration. Although the treaty allows for a great degree of flexibility, and does not, in practice, exceed existing national commitments of the participating countries, it does have direct implications for national immigration systems and labor market regulations, especially since once adopted, these commitments cannot be unilaterally reversed. In addition, the WTO's dispute settlement system provides for a supranational enforcement mechanism to ensure compliance. In the longer run, the importance of these developments lies maybe less in the current commitments than in the dynamics set free by the process of institutionalization of multilateral rules.

As shown in the case of the GATT and other multilateral negotiations, in the context of "framework" conventions such as the International Climate Convention or the Convention on Biodiversity, iterative negotiations tend to lead to both normal expansion and institutional consolidation over time. Yet, apart from these endogenous institutional dynamics, at least two exogenous developments are likely to push "mode 4" liberalization further. The first are market forces and the pressure of the service industries for further openings. In Europe and North America, service industries have joined forces in two influential interests groups (the European Service Forum, EFS and the US Coalition of Service Industries, CIS) which have engaged in an active lobbying of the EU Commission and the US government in the services negotiations (ESF, 2000; ESF, 2001; ESN, 1999 and CSI, 2000). The second important factors is the pressure exerted from an influential group of developing countries in the GATS negotiations which, under the lead of India, expect important gains from the export of parts of their skilled and less-skilled workforce (WTO 2000). Given the interest of the industrial countries in the opening up of service markets in the South, linking concessions with regard to "mode 4" with the grant of market access through other modes of delivery, is likely to give the developing countries some leverage in the current negotiations. This might also be expected from the general goals declared in the opening of the Doha round of trade talks and of the industrial countries' assertion to put greater emphasis on the interests of the developing countries.

For the receiving countries, the content of future commitments will ultimately depend on how the interests inherent in the trade agenda will be weighed against national concerns with immigration and labor market control. It is precisely in this logic that advocates of greater liberalization now call for an intensified "dialogue and co-operation between all relevant agencies, both at the national and international level" (OECD, 2002: 6). By this it is meant immigration, labor and trade ministries, as well as social partners and other relevant actors. The consequence would be moving the issues discussed in the GATS "from a migration to a trade framework" (ibid.).

The Emergence of Private Authority

In addition to liberalization in the framework of regional and multilateral trade agreements, the mobility of skilled professionals is also an area where the first instances of private transnational regulatory authority have developed. This holds first and foremost for the movement of intra-corporate transferees, managers and other key personnel within the internal labor market of MNCs. With the significant liberalization of these movements, authority over (temporary) entry and stay in a third country has been nearly fully delegated to the firm as a transnational actor. This approach has also been codified in the GATS framework in which private enterprises are the determiners of labor migration. It is the firms who select, recruit and move workers within their transnational internal labor market, according to their own market needs (see Salt and Findlay, 1989).

This delegation of authority to MNCs may on the one hand respond to their need for rapid and flexible admission procedures. In countries with a longer tradition of immigration systems based on the selection and evaluation of skills such as Canada, the U.S. or Australia and New Zealand, this trend may also be the result of a conscious decision for market-based solutions in the light of the difficulties faced with existing administrative procedures (on this last point see Freeman, 1999). A salient example of the increasing influence of private actors in this field is the new pilot scheme launched in the U.K. in 2000 to enable multinational corporations to self-certify work permits for their intra-company transferees. The GATS-visa, that has been proposed by a number of countries in the current round of negotiations, points exactly this direction.

A second area where this liberalization of high skilled migration yields a certain delegation of public authority is in changes occurring in the operation of professions and systems of education, including the formal procedures for recognizing skills across national systems. According to Robyn Iredale (Iredale, 2001), highly skilled migration leads to an "internationalization of the professions" understood as a "convergence towards international standards and procedures away from nationally defined standards and national forms of regulation" (ibid: 10). In so far as these processes involve delegation of regulatory authority to private actors such as occupational groups, one could also speak of a transnationalization of the professions. These processes are most developed within regional blocks, where transnational recognition and accreditation have been promoted to different degrees. With its free movement regime, the EU is most developed in this respect and has introduced measures to achieve general mutual recognition and harmonized training. NAFTA has least mutual recognition, while the Trans-Tasman MRA provides for mutual reciprocity arrangements in some occupations and a sharing of resources in others. Interestingly, this works not on the basis of directives such as in the EU but through self-regulation by occupational groups (Iredale, 2001: 11).

The progressive liberalization in professional services through the GATS is a second important development where professional associations have gained increasing influence. This is most salient in the accountancy profession, where mutual recognition agreements have been negotiated by professional bodies that set minimum educational requirements for international trade in accountancy services (ibid: 11). A similar development which is not linked to multilateral trade talks can be seen in the field of actuarial science, where the international professional body has concluded a "Society of Actuaries Mutual Recognition Agreement" setting minimum standards for the admission of international actuarial services (ibid: 12). These trends are also visible outside the accountancy or actuarial science professions. Examples of professions organized at the European level are nurses, lawyers and engineers, while international federations exist for pharmacists and engineers. Even if these organizations do not possess regulatory authority as such, they have become powerful advisory bodies that, by monitoring professional standards and making recommendations to regulatory bodies, now play an essential role in the global regulation of the professions (Evetts, 1999).

Conclusion: Migration and the Mobility of the Highly Skilled

This chapter has shown that the international regulatory structures addressing the mobility of skilled professionals increasingly resemble the neoliberal structures regulating the global flow of goods and finance. Spurred by the restructuring of the global economy and the rise of global trade in services, the mobility of skilled professionals is increasingly recognized as an important factor generating growth, innovation and employment. In stark contrast to the broader phenomenon of international migration, where states have sought to maintain control and independence, the approach developed towards the highly skilled manifests both an orientation towards liberalization and multilateralism. In addition to the commitments undertaken under regional trade agreements and the GATS, the regulation of transnational flows of skilled labor also bears some important signs of increasing private authority, as reflected in the influence of multinational firms over intra-corporate transfers or in the role of professional associations in the regulation of the professions.

It should be noted, however, the formal treaties discussed in this chapter are not equally implemented across the different regions and countries. Generally speaking, the GATS, as well as several of the regional free trade agreements, do not force members to deregulate; nor does GATS directly regulate members' policies through harmonization. Instead, WTO members remain free to shape their domestic policies and laws, provided they respect their international obligations under GATS. In most cases, "mode 4" commitments are hence "accommodated" within existing regulatory frameworks and countries have hitherto mainly committed to the status quo. Rather than legal incompatibility, implementation of the GATS provisions suffers from the absence of common definitions and categories regarding the persons and professions falling under the commitments and a lack of transparency concerning the administrative procedures for admission under the GATS. As noted above, these problems of implementation are a focus of the current round of negotiations in the WTO.

The questions that can now be posed are whether these developments should be discussed under the heading of international migration at all and how they relate to other forms of migration. Three obvious differences from the conventional understanding of international migration include the fact most liberalization initiatives cover only temporary movements for specific purposes (i.e. service trade), are often confined to one sector and do not normally include access to the labor market for the purpose of employment. Yet these distinctions are less clear cut than the texts of the trade agreements analyzed above might suggest. First, as mentioned above, temporary entry in the framework of the GATS may extend from short-term movements below three months to a maximum of five years. This situation may be contrasted with other definitions of migration, such as the standard definitions for categories of persons crossing borders used by the UN. These use the criterion "duration of stay" to distinguish between migrant and non-migrant for stays below three months (e.g., tourists, short-term business travelers, frontier workers, etc.). Second, the term "migrant" is itself further sub-divided into long-term migrants (a person who moves to another country for a period of at least twelve months) and short term migrants (between three and twelve months of stay). Thus, intra-corporate transferees moving abroad for more than twelve months under the GATS could fall under the UN definition of long-term migrants. Notwithstanding these categorizations, the guest worker experience has shown that temporary movement can often turn into permanent residence and involve professional mobility. This is especially the case since the evolution of social rights associated with "postnational membership" (Soysal, 1994; Jacobson, 1996). Finally, the question whether under temporary entry service providers actually "enter" national labor markets or not is not completely clear cut. From the wording of the GATS treaty, several observers have concluded that GATS commitments can be read to suggest that foreigners employed by host country companies are also included under "mode 4" (WTO, 1998; Young, 1999).

Thus, although the liberalization of skilled mobility has so-far been promoted by trade representatives rather than immigration officials and—partly because of that—has often escaped the attention of migration scholars, the contents of issues already negotiated and those which are currently on the negotiation table show that the liberalization of movement of skilled professionals is very much an aspect of immigration policy. The fact that these phenomena are addressed in terms of "mobility" or, even more abstractly, "mode 4," instead of international migration, is an instance of the growing differentiation of migration—and perhaps also the dissociation of immigration politics under the influence of globalization.

We need to pay attention to these different types and forms of movement if we want to account for the ways international migration challenges the nation state in an era of globalization. With its inclusion in regional trade agreements and the GATS, mobility of the highly skilled has taken an important step out of the state-centered framework of national immigration policies, toward the market-led, multilateral framework of international trade. In the long-term, however, what looks today as a dissociation may also have broader implications for the way states deal with the broader phenomenon of international migration. On the one hand, it is doubtful whether an international organization focused on liberalization such as the WTO will prove the right place to deal with the issues of positive integration and re-regulation resulting from increasing labor mobility. On the other hand, the very exercise of formulating the interests of both sending and receiving countries in multilateral trade talks may also pave the way for more inclusive debates on the possibilities for multilateral cooperation in the field of migration.

3

From Migrants to Movers: Citizenship and Mobility in the European Union

Ettore Recchi

Once They were Migrants: Europeans on the Move in the Industrial Age (and Beyond)

The Ellis Island Immigration Museum in New York informs visitors that the descendents of the 12 million people landed on the island from 1892 to 1954 "account for almost 40 percent of the country's population."[1] No place conveys the image of America's immigrant heritage so vividly. To a European eye, the museum equally appears as a monument to the enduring and widespread outflow of people from Europe—the principle origin of Ellis Island's past guests. With few exceptions (most noticeably France), no European nation has been exempted, at different historical times, from sending a significant part of its younger population out of its borders. Between 1851 and 1890 three-quarters of them went to the U.S. and in later decades other destinations grew to about half the total (Bade, 2000: 137). However, America remained the epitome of the land of migration (Hoerder, 1996: 220-221). In Italy, for example, the "American uncle" stood out as the popular image of the successful relative abroad, regardless of the place where the migrant had actually settled.

In total, from 1824 until 1924, 52 million people were shipped from European ports to North and South America, Australia, and New Zealand. About three-quarters of them are likely to have stayed forever out of their home country (Moch, 1996: 124).[2] The United States took in 60 to 70 percent of European migrants, while Canada, Argentina, and Brazil received 7 to 15 percent each (Nugent, 1996: 79). The apex of transatlantic flows was reached between 1911 and 1915 and again in the early 1920s when about one and a half-million Europeans crossed the ocean yearly (Bade, 2000: 143). To these one must add movements to colonies (what in Britain was called "empire settlement" to be achieved through the "export of the poor") as well as to other European countries. In particular, the latter movements were almost as large as the migrations out of the continent; for instance, 44 percent of all Italian emigrants from 1871 to 1914 left for another European country (Bade, 2000: 162). Numbers are controversial, and perhaps underestimate total movers. As transport technology improved and costs of travel declined, the proportion of "rotation" or "seasonal" migrants among long-distance travelers also increased.

The 1929 recession and the rise of fascist and nazi regimes halted these population flows, which nonetheless reemerged soon after World War II. In the 1950s, Europe lost 2.7 millions residents, who mainly followed the transatlantic migration tracks beaten by European migrants about one generation earlier (Bade, 2000: 301–302). In the 1960s, however, movement to the Americas dropped. Intra–continental migrations replaced them (figure 3.1). In an age of reconstruction and economic expansion, central–northern European industrial areas attracted migrant workers within and between countries, particularly from the Mediterranean countries. A model was established, in which the migrants were absorbed by sectors such as construction, heavy industry and low-grade service occupations, poorly paid jobs now shunned by the local work force, because of rising standards of education, and hence, social mobility aspirations (King, 1993: 23).

The bulk of intra–European migrants left rural and mountainous areas of southern Italy, western Spain, northern Portugal, and northern Greece. Italians moved first, already in the 1950s, encouraged by their membership in the newly established European Community, and then the Spanish. Spanish international migration soared in 1960, as a consequence of the economic shock caused by Franco's *Plan de estabilización y liberalización* of 1959 (Ródenas Calatayud, 1994: 63 ff.). Moreover, in 1960 a labor recruitment agreement was signed with Germany, following similar agreements with Italy, channeling Spanish migrants to the strongest market for "guest" work in Europe. From the 1960s on, the ranks of moving Portuguese and Greeks also swelled. The Portuguese presence in France, in particular, skyrocketed in the 1960s from 50,000 at the beginning of the decade to more than 800,000 ten years later (Moch, 1992: 185).

Many of them settled in miserable *favelas* in the outskirts of Paris, eventually to be incorporated into French society (and more decent dwellings). Generally speaking, in the 1946 to 1970 period, Italy was the most common origin and West Germany the most common destination of all these flows. On the one hand, 1,520,000 Italians settled in another European country—more than 80 percent of them in Germany and Switzerland (Pugliese, 2002: 21–22). In fact, this was a net migration figure: four-and-a-half-million people left Italy but around 3 million returned. Taking the four south European Mediterranean origin countries together, at its highest level in the early 1970s, there were about 1.5 million such "guests" in Western Germany (Rogers, 1985: 5–9).

Figure 3.1
Switching to Europe. Proportion of emigration flows from Southern European countries to other European countries in the 1950s and 1960s

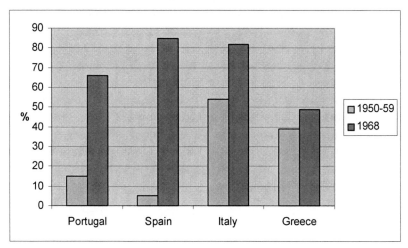

Source: Livi Bacci (1972: 114)

In retrospect, any social history of Europe would be highly deficient were it to overlook international migration. The option to expatriate was regarded by many generations of Europeans as an extremely plausible and socially respectable life choice. As senders, receivers, or both, almost all regions of Europe have been somewhat familiar with migration experiences: "Migration was a long–standing part of the family, land–holding and inheritance systems of the continent" (Moch, 1996: 7). At least until some thirty years ago,

Europeans were movers. Narratives of migration soaked national identities and folkways. Although migrants packed their carton luggage to escape poverty, their travels had a much deeper impact. In particular after World War II, they left for jobs, and found city life, technology, trade unions, open-minded customs, class consciousness, leisure, equality between men and women, and, frequently, a partner and a new family. Acting as bridges between remote villages of the south and industrial cities of the north, migrants sustained the rise of a more homogenous culture and lifestyle at both the national and the European level. In brief, they smoothed cultural and economic differences, serving as key vectors of modernization.

The oil shock of 1973 was the occasion—more than the direct cause—to put a halt to mass migration within Europe. Signs of growing xenophobia, linked to the awareness of an incumbent economic crisis, had driven Britain (in 1962 and 1968), Switzerland (in 1970) and Sweden (in 1972) to already tighten their immigration policies. While repatriation schemes failed and family reunification never stopped, in the early 1970s the age of mass European migration came to an its end. Thereafter, the size of movements between European countries declined; destinations diversified; motivations and settlement projects became more individualized.

In the last three decades of the twentieth century, as the number of people leaving European countries dropped, Western Europe reached positive net immigration. At the eve of enlargement in 2004, even the bulk of new EU member states (exceptions being the Baltic countries and Poland, albeit with small negative figures) had larger population inflows than outflows (Holzmann and Münz, 2004: 84). The rest of this chapter illustrates how the European integration process has interacted with migration dynamics in Western Europe, easing population flows and possibly reshaping their nature and scope.

European Integration and the Evolution of Free Movement Policies

Given the backdrop of existing migration flows, free movement across member countries was, from its inception, one of the chief goals of the European integration project. Indeed, it was first introduced by the pioneer supranational organization of shared economic interests, the European Coal and Steel Community (formed in 1951), to ease specialized workforce recruitment across national borders. Among the six founding states of the Community (Germany, France,

Belgium, the Netherlands, Luxembourg, and Italy) Italy was particularly keen to support this goal, as a way to lower domestic unemployment and underemployment, while also improving living conditions of nationals who had already migrated abroad (cf. Willis, 1971: 150; Ascoli, 1979: 29–36; Dumoulin, 1989; Romero, 1991: 29–34; Maas, 2004).

Whereas the ECSC Treaty limited it to "workers who are nationals of member states and have recognized qualifications in a coalmining or steel-making occupation" (article 69), the right of free movement was generalized in the founding Treaty of the European Economic Community signed in Rome in 1957. Basically, article 48 of this Treaty affirmed the right to accept offers of employment made in another member state, to move freely within the Community, as well as to reside and remain in another member state after having been employed. In its original version, however, the treaty conditioned the right to move upon the creation of job commitments, as it explicitly referred to "workers" rather than "citizens." At this stage, community law openly treated migrants as production factors rather than persons *tout court*, which remained in line with the functionalist conception of European integration as an essentially economic enterprise. While bilateral agreements between national governments had been established soon after World War II, and extended later to more peripheral countries—Germany and Portugal signed one in 1964 and Germany and Yugoslavia in 1968 (Salt, 1976)—the EEC Treaty built a more solid legal framework around the intra-European mass migration system of its age, taking into account that free movement met the interests of both would–be foreign workers in Italy and potential employers in Germany, Benelux, and France.

However, the enactment of the "free movement doctrine" proceeded at a slow and discontinuous pace. For more than a decade, in spite of the Rome Treaty, citizens of EEC member states, who intended to work in a different member state, continued to be subject to national immigration laws just like Third World nationals. They had to apply for work and residence permits, which could be discretionarily denied. According to article 49 of the Treaty, free movement was a fully intergovernmental policy left to decisions taken in the Council of Ministers. Central and Northern European EEC member states resisted the interference of supranational regulations on their sovereign power to control aliens. More specifically, in these countries, free movement was often argued to give a competitive advantage to Italians over other Southern European migrants, possibly making them less controllable and stable workers. It is true free circulation norms allowed these migrants from EEC Member states (basically Italians) to circumvent the official 'guest worker' employment channels by which 84 percent of Spanish and 86 percent of Portuguese, but only 8 percent of Italian workers, were hired in Germany in 1969 (Romero, 2001: 413). However, even before the full enactment of free movement rights, the popularity of commuting between Italy and other EEC countries had been very high in the post–World War II period (Corti, 2003: 93).

The real implementation of free movement was postponed until 1968, when Council Regulation 1612/68 and Council Directive 68/360 abolished movement and residence restrictions of member state workers and their families in the entire EEC territory. Regulation 1612/68 forbade all nationality–based discrimination between workers of member states in work conditions, salary, and unemployment benefits. Furthermore, it established the foreign workers' right to the same social and tax benefits as national workers, including access to training in vocational schools and housing benefits (when existing). Family members of foreign workers (including TCN spouses) were entitled to reside with them and allowed access to any kind of employment in the host country. In accordance with Regulation 1612/68, Directive 68/360 reduced the bureaucratic formalities of moving within the EU considerably, recognizing the workers' and their families' rights to enter a different member state by simply showing an identity card or valid passport, without being forced to obtain a visa. Community migrants were also entitled to a "residence permit," with a validity of at least five years and an automatic renewal, by presenting an employment certificate. In addition, permanence in the host country was guaranteed thereafter, as the residence permit could not be withdrawn in case of involuntarily unemployment and its lack could not justify expulsion.

The 1968 provisions ended the transitional regime set by article 49 of the Treaty and created the conditions for a full exercise of the free movement right. They represented a turning point on this matter. In the following decades until the present, vast secondary legislation has dealt with admission, residence and equal treatment of foreign residents from other member states. Community law and the European Court of Justice have increasingly spread the matter and scope of the right to free movement originally contained in the Treaty.

In particular, since the 1970s the ECJ has played a fundamental role in widening the scope of free movement by shifting its focus progressively from the free movement of *workers* to the free movement of *persons*. Due to the contribution of European citizens submitting their cases, the Court was able to give a broader interpretation of article 39 (ex 48) of the Treaty and of the Regulation 1612/68, emphasizing the social and individual dimension of free movement. According to the ECJ, the right to equal treatment implies a fully–fledged integration, not only in the job market, but in the whole society, including social, cultural, and educational aspects of workers' and their families' lives (O'Keeffe, 1998: 20–25). It was the decisive contribution of ECJ jurisprudence that, in the 1970s, led to the extension of free movement laws to include self–employed workers and, in the 1980s, to persons who take up a paid apprenticeship, who enter university in a member state different from their own after having taken up a job activity, and seasonal workers (Baldoni, 2003: 8–9). Other issues moved more slowly. The controversial position of posted workers—that is, workers who are temporarily sent to another member state to perform services there and who return to their country of origin after completion of their work—was clarified only twenty years later with the Council Directive 96/71.

As a logical consequence of the Single European Act of 1986—which aimed at creating an "area without internal frontiers in which the free movement of goods, persons, services and capital is ensured"—a significant step forward was made in 1990, when the freedom of movement and residence was explicitly extended to non-economically active personal categories (as well as their families) including students, pensioners, and the unemployed (Directives 90/364, 90/365, 90/366, the latter replaced by Directive 93/96). Still, such arrangements are subject to two conditions from which workers are exempted: students, pensioners, and the unemployed must have sickness insurance, and hold sufficient resources to avoid becoming a burden on the national health systems and social assistance of the host member state.[3]

Symbolically, however, the most spectacular step in the process took place with the Treaty on the European Union, signed in Maastricht in 1992 and entered into force on the November 1, 1993. The Maastricht Treaty introduces citizenship of the European Union to "reinforce the protection of the rights and interests of the nationals of its member states." Concretely, EU citizenship consists of a set of rights allowing people to: a) vote and stand as candidates in elections of the European Parliament and in municipal elections in the member state in which individuals reside, regardless of their nationality; b) submit petitions to the European Parliament and appeal to the EU ombudsman; c) be protected by the consular authorities of another member state in third countries that lack diplomatic representation of one's state; and d) to move and reside freely on the territory of any of the EU member states.

The first three rights in fact have a small scope compared to the last. For the ordinary EU citizen, access to diplomatic protection in third countries is an extremely unusual event; petitions to the EP or the ombudsman look like quite remote options; and the EP vote has limited political relevance, suffering from higher abstention rates than all other elections in Europe (this is admittedly less the case for local elections). Indeed, the exercise of voting rights for the EP and local governments, regardless of the country of residence, is a second–order right requiring the exercise of the right to free residence abroad first. Thus, the rights to free movement and settlement in the entire EU territory essentially form the cornerstone of EU citizenship. Furthermore, this is exactly what Europeans perceive the EU is for. When questioned about the 'meaning of the European Union', young EU citizens—39 percent of respondents in 2001, 35 percent in 1997—point predominantly to "the ability to go wherever I want" (Eurobarometer, 2001: 16; see Recchi and Nebe, 2003).

In conclusion, the free movement of persons across national borders—evoked as a long–term aim in the early years of the European integration process—has turned into a real possibility in the EU by the end of the twentieth century. The two major legal steps in this process were the abolition of restrictions on movement and residence for workers of member states and their families in 1968, and the introduction of EU citizenship in 1992. Another practical advancement was the adoption of the Schengen system, which took place progressively in the 1990s, to eliminate passport controls between EU national borders. No less important, albeit less visible, was the action of the European Court of Justice. The ECJ promoted free movement significantly and progressively through its judgments, in particular by extending and reinforcing the rights of workers in host countries and combating discriminations based on nationality. Especially at times when community legislation on the matter lingered, the Court stood as a bulwark against all attempts to maintain privileges rooted in preexisting or reemerging nationality–based pieces of legislation. Even semantically, all these changes have turned intra–community "migrant workers," as they were called in the ECSC Treaty of 1951, to "movers," as they are now usually referred to in EU documents.

Taking European Citizenship Seriously:
Intra–EU Movements after the Maastricht Treaty

European Community rules on free circulation began to be effective in the late 1960s—ironically just as the interest to migrate from Southern to Northern Europe was declining. Economic growth in fast developing sending countries discouraged migration. Free movement laws certainly removed the prior constraints to settling abroad, but in the midst of a substantial weakening of both demand and supply of alien workforce (figure 3.2). Foreign workers from the European Community of nine shrank from 1.8 to 1.2 million in the 1973 to 1985 time period (Molle and Van Mourik, 1988: 326). Outflows from Italy, in spite of Community legislation, did not cease to drop from 1961 onwards. Greeks could not exploit free movement opportunities until 1988; seven years after their country joined the European Community, while Spaniards and Portuguese had to wait until 1992, when the moratorium period for the extension of free movement rights to Spanish and Portuguese citizens ended. Even in these cases, the generalization of the rights to move, settle, and work abroad in Western Europe did not revive the traditional sources of European migration. In economists' language, "the stock of foreign residents from the Southern EU members had already reached its equilibrium level when the free movement was introduced" (Boeri and Brücker, 2001: 12).

Is this still a faithful picture? Although the introduction of EU citizenship did not prompt a renewed tide of intra–European migration, it probably changed its profile and character. In particular, in absence of border controls, visa, and sanctions for non–registration in state offices, Europeans are entitled to move back and forth between home and host countries at their own will and pace. Thus, free movement is likely to have fostered short–term, commuting, and rotation mobility at the expenses of permanent settlement abroad. These are definitely more "invisible" movements which further complicate the already difficult task of assembling migration data that differ from one EU member state to another because of discrepancies in the sources and methods of statistics collection (Poulain, 1996 and 1999).

Figure 3.2

Rise and fall of post–World War II European migration. Intra–continental yearly flows from Spain, Italy and Portugal, 1960–1985 (thousands)

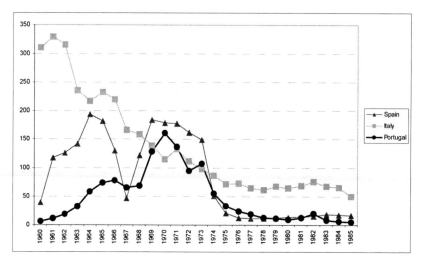

Sources: Golini and Amato (2001: 50); Pugliese (2002: 56); Istat (various years); Ródenas Calatayud (1994: 261 and 267); Baganha (2002: 19)

In looking at the data, it makes sense to concentrate on stocks of migrants, as comparative data on migration flows in the EU are much less complete. On the entire migrant population (i.e., workers and non–workers), sufficient time series are available only for Belgium, Denmark, France, Germany, the Netherlands, Portugal, and Sweden (Recchi et al., 2003). During the 1990s, the inflow of EU citizens in all of these countries tended to either rise slightly or remain constant. Eurostat indicates that "over the second half of the 1990s, an average of only just over one in 1,000 of those resident in the EU moved from one member state to another each year" (Thorogood and Winqvist, 2003: 2). Among workers only, EU citizens made up 19 percent of the entire immigration flows into EU member states in the 1995 to 2000 period (Bailly et al., 2004: 39). Significantly, 10 percent of them did not move away from their own country—that is they were "global movers" with other migration experiences in their background (ibidem). This was most often the case for EU citizens settling in peripheral member states, both in southern and northern Europe (i.e., Portugal, Spain, Greece and Denmark). The bulk of them were probably expatriates of multinational companies.

Table 3.1
Stocks of foreign and non–national EU citizens in EU–15 countries, 1990–2000
(thousands)

	1990	1991	1992	1993	1994	1995	1996	1997	1998	1999	2000
B	904,5	922,5	909,3	920,6	922,3	909,8	911,9	903,2	892,0	897,1	861,7
	555,6	559,3	541,6	548,5	552,3	554,5	559,6	562,0	562,5	563,6	–
DK	160,6	169,5	180,1	189,0	196,7	222,7	237,7	249,6	256,3	259,4	258,6
	38,4	39,2	40,5	42,4	44,6	46,5	48,9	51,2	53,2	53,8	54,3
D	5342,5	5882,3	6495,8	6878,1	6990,5	7173,9	7314,0	7365,8	7319,5	7343,6	7296,8
	1644,8	1698,8	–	1750,2	1779,9	1811,7	1839,9	1850,0	1854,3	1858,7	1872,7
EL	229,1	253,3	262,3	149,1	152,8	155,5	161,1	165,7	–	–	–
	59,1	61,6	64,7	42,9	43,7	44,4	45,0	44,1	–	–	–
E	278,7	360,7	393,1	430,4	461,4	499,8	539,0	609,8	719,6	801,3	895,7
	255,8	289,8	181,8	200,5	219,8	235,6	251,9	260,6	295,3	312,2	375,5
F	3596,6	–	–	–	–	–	–	–	–	3263,1	–
	1311,9	–	–	–	–	–	–	–	–	1195,5	–
IRL	80,0	87,7	94,9	89,9	91,1	96,1	118,0	114,4	111,0	117,8	126,5
	–	–	73,0	67,0	70,7	73,4	86,8	81,3	85,3	85,0	92,2
I	781,1	863,0	925,2	987,4	922,7	991,4	1095,6	1240,7	1250,2	1252,0	1338,2
	163,9	160,7	160,8	120,3	124,9	128,5	133,5	–	–	148,5	153,8
L	113,1	117,8	122,7	127,6	132,5	138,1	142,8	147,7	152,9	159,4	164,7
	–	–	–	–	–	–	127,8	131,4	–	–	–
NL	692,4	732,9	757,4	779,8	757,1	725,4	679,9	678,1	662,4	651,5	667,8
	174,0	181,9	188,7	193,9	193,1	191,1	188,3	190,2	192,2	195,9	201,6
A	456,1	532,7	623,0	689,6	713,5	723,5	728,2	732,7	737,3	748,2	757,9
	–	79,4	–	–	–	–	–	–	–	–	219,8
P	107,8	114,0	123,6	131,6	157,1	168,3	172,9	175,3	177,8	190,9	208,2
	29,9	–	–	32,7	36,2	–	41,5	43,7	48,2	52,4	56,8
FIN	26,3	37,6	46,3	55,6	62,0	68,6	73,8	80,6	85,1	87,7	91,1
	11,4	11,9	12,2	12,5	12,9	13,7	14,1	14,9	15,7	16,3	16,7
S	483,7	493,8	499,1	507,5	537,4	531,8	526,6	522,0	499,9	487,2	477,3
	195,7	190,5	186,3	182,6	180,3	179	178,2	176,8	177	177,4	180,1
UK	1723,0	1750,0	1985,0	2001,0	2032,0	1948,0	1934,0	2066,0	2207,0	2208,0	2342,0
	781,0	818,0	–	812,0	–	818,0	805,0	877,7	859,1	856,2	–
Total foreigners	14975,5			15551,4			16249,7				18915,3
Total non–national EU citizens	5501,7			4832,6			5735,8				6014,3

Source: SOPEMI (2002); Eurostat New Cronos database (2001)
Note: Totals are calculated on the basis of the closest available year for missing data

With these caveats in mind, there are few doubts that migration has nevertheless been on the rise again in the European Union in the 1990s. This is true for both TCNs and EU citizens. However, while the proportion of TCNs in the EU has increased by 33 percent over the decade, the proportion of EU citizens living in another EU country has grown by a less spectacular 10 percent. More precisely, the foreign population has risen from 14.9 million in 1990 to 18.9 million in 2000 and the number of EU–foreign residents has gone from 5.5 million to 6 million (table 3.1). The basis being one of citizenship and not birth, these figures exclude holders of dual citizenship (forbidden in some EU countries) and naturalized migrants. Nevertheless, as has been aptly noted, "citizens of EU countries usually have little to gain from adopting the citizenship of another member state. This is why the number of such acquisitions is limited" (Eurostat, 2004: 2). In the whole EU (Ireland excluded) in 2000, only 22,800 EU citizens acquired the citizenship of another member state. This corresponds to 4.1 percent of all naturalizations and 0.3 percent of all intra–EU migrants (ibidem: 4–5). Naturalization did give some advantage before the introduction of EU citizenship, so that the proportion of pre–Maastricht intra–EU migrants who naturalized—particularly among the older generations of labor migrants—is likely to be significant. For instance, Maas (2004: 16–17) shows that naturalizations of EU foreigners in France in 1986 were twice and a half more numerous than in 1996.

Figure 3.3
Growth in the Stocks of TCNs and Non-National EU–Citizens in EU Member States, 1990–2000 (1990=100)

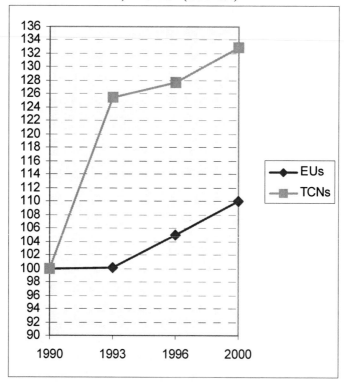

Sources: SOPEMI (2002), Eurostat New Cronos database (2001).

The highest growth rate of TCNs took place at the beginning of the decade, when in fact, the number of EU–foreigners stagnated. After 1993, however, the curves of increase of the two categories of migrants assumed a similar slope (figure 3.3). By the turn of the century, intra–EU movers represented 31 percent of the total population of non–nationals legally residing in other EU member states. This proportion varies greatly from one country to another. Only in Luxembourg, Belgium, and Ireland are intra–EU migrants a majority among non–national residents. In spite of restrictive migration policies for TCNs (cf. Geddes, 2003), in all other EU member states the bulk of foreign residents come from outside the European Union. Labor immigration and family reunification of TCNs make for a larger share of the immigrant population in those countries where the stocks of immigrants are higher: Germany (74 percent of foreign residents are not EU citizens), France (63 percent), the United Kingdom (61 percent) and Italy (almost 90 percent). Yet, in the 1990s, the number of EU immigrants has grown all over Europe—the exceptions being Greece, France, Sweden, and Italy. This increase has been spectacular in Austria (their number has almost tripled) and Portugal (their number has almost doubled). In Finland, Spain, and Denmark there are about 50 percent more EU immigrants in 2000 than there were in 1990, while in Ireland, the Netherlands, and the United Kingdom the increase has been smaller. Generally speaking, the rising trend is quite regular, save for Greece which experienced some growth in the 1990 to 1992 biennium, then followed by a downturn in 1993 and some reprise afterwards.

The national communities that settled abroad during the post–World War II period of industrial recovery and mass migration along the south–north axis of the continent, still largely determine the total amount of European migrants in EU member states (table 3.2). In the host countries of traditional immigration, the most recent free movers have not altered the pre–existing picture. France still has the second largest Portuguese–speaking and Spanish–speaking populations in the EU (64.3 percent of Portuguese and 37 percent of Spanish immigrants in the EU live there), and Germany is second-home for the Greeks (82.5 percent of those who live outside Greece in Europe) and the Italians abroad (51.5 percent). In absolute figures, Italians in Germany form the single largest community of EU non–nationals in a EU member state (619,000 persons). Another factor to reckon with is the "neighbor effect." Because of historical links,

language homogeneity or simply territorial proximity, some nationalities are strongly over-represented among migrants in countries
across their borders. This is the case for the Irish in the U.K. (91.5
percent of Irish migrants in the EU are in Britain), but less so for
Britons (14.9 percent of those who reside in another EU country are
in Ireland, where they represent 75.3 percent of non–national EU
citizens). Finns account for 54.7 percent of EU foreigners in Sweden, and Swedes for 47.4 percent of EU foreigners in Finland. Although in lower proportions, similar two–ways migrations can be
found between Germany and Austria, Benelux countries (among
themselves and with Germany), Germany and France (25.6 percent
of the French EU migrants are in Germany, 18.8 percent of the Germans are in France), Spain and Portugal (but with lower numbers).
Finally, there are growing communities of northern Europeans living in the southern countries of the continent. The bulk of them
moved at a relatively late age in search of more favorable weather
and leisure conditions. German "retirement migrants" have mostly
settled in Spain, where they amount to 23.6 percent of non–Spanish
EU citizens, and Italy (24.8 percent of non–Italian EU citizens),
whereas Britons have an equally sizeable presence in Greece (30.4
percent of EU immigrants), Spain (26.4 percent) and Portugal (24.8
percent). Retirement migration seems to be a soaring trend currently
boosting internal migration in the EU (King, Warnes and Williams,
2000).

Overall, women make up 48.1 percent of intra–EU movers in 2001.
About half the 15 EU member states have a majority of male EU
migrants, and the other half a majority of female migrants. At the
extremes there are Finland (63.7 percent of men) and Italy (58.1
percent of women). In particular, men prevail in all EU national groupings settled in Finland. With the sole exception of the U.K., all countries of older immigration (i.e., central and northern European countries) host a majority of male non–national EU citizens. The reverse
is true for southern European countries (except Portugal), where
women from other EU member states are in larger numbers. Possibly, this can reflect migration for intermarriage as being more common than migration for work, inasmuch as residence choices depend on the family breadwinner's residence (and husbands more
frequently have better jobs than wives in their own home country at
marriage, making couples settle in that same country). In terms of
"national" orientations by gender, it can be noted that Greek mi-

Table 3.2
Stocks of non–national EU citizens in EU member states by nationality, 2001

	B	DK	D	EL	E	F	IRL	I	L	NL	P	FIN	S	UK	Total
B		520	23,494	1,183	18,272	66,666		5,208	13,200	25,860	2,115	116	629	8,230	165,493
DK	3,240		20,963	1,238	6,173	4,500		2,237	2,000	2,588	767	580	25,567	16,739	86,592
D	34,321	12,701		9,369	88,651	78,381		38,183	10,020	54,811	10,374	2,201	16,357	62,087	417,456
EL	18,386	660	365,438		866	5,768		13,538	1,250	5,692	143	312	4,407	26,307	442,767
E	45,917	1,802	129,471	670		161,762		14,867	2,910	17,155	12,189	533	3,320	46,560	437,156
F	107,240	3,296	110,173	5,094	46,376			29,713	16,530	13,326	7,186	859	4,709	85,592	430,094
IRL	3,295	1,094	15,690	495	3,413	5,314		2,204	930	3,990	446	218	1,146	411,834	450,069
I	200,281	2,833	619,060	5,493	27,874	201,670			19,890	18,248	3,031	774	4,512	97,230	1,200,896
L	4,353	18	5,981	40	354	3,640		257		312	85	11	26	544	15,621
NL	85,763	4,531	110,786	2,701	21,763	24,745		7,312	3,810		4,073	623	3,801	28,822	298,730
A	2,072	746	187,742	1,424	4,088	4,139		6,256	500	3,366	542	217	2,767	5,958	219,817
P	25,560	555	133,726	241	43,340	553,663		4,639	54,490	9,765		118	1,317	33,859	861,273
FIN	2,688	2,085	15,903	954	5,420	2,748		1,579	620	1,980	506		98,571	11,950	145,004
S	4,284	10,839	18,875	1,812	9,879	7,252		3,240	860	3,077	1,232	7,887		20,445	89,682
UK	26,156	12,630	115,353	13,394	99,017	75,250	77,320	24,592	4,400	41,404	14,094	2,207	13,062		518,879
Non-national EU citizens	563,556	54,310	1,872,655	44,108	375,486	1,195,498	102,655	153,825	131,410	201,574	56,783	16,656	180,191	856,156	

Country of residence

Source: Eurostat, New Cronos database (2001)
Note: B = 2000; EL

grants are disproportionately male in all EU countries (being 86 percent of the Greeks in Finland and 76 percent of the Greeks in Denmark), whereas Finnish women are a majority among Finns living in all other EU member states (being 84 percent and 76 percent of their nationals residing in Greece and Italy). Like Finns, Swedish and Danish women also outnumber their male co–nationals in every EU member state but Portugal and Finland.

It is well known "traditional" migrations tend to follow established tracks, especially because of network effects. Faced with the uncertainties of life in alien environments, migrants concentrate where nationals (and possibly kin or friends) have already settled. Is this true of intra–EU migrants also? While micro–level studies are certainly needed to answer this question in greater detail, Lieberson's (1969) index of diversity can be applied to the distribution of each nationality of European movers among EU member states to measure how much these people scatter in the continent. In short, the index reveal intra–EU migrants do not spread around at random (table 3.3). As we have already seen, some of them are, indeed, channeled to typical destinations. This is the case with the low index for the Irish, who disproportionately move to Great Britain, the Austrians who tend to migrate to Germany, and the Greeks who are also more likely to settle in Germany than any other country. The British, Germans, and Swedish, with high index figures migrants, show greater variability. In general terms, it seems more recent waves of migration (such as those from the latter countries) have more diverse destinations than traditional intra–EU migrations dating back to the 1950s and 1960s. This may well correspond to an individualization of migration choices, shaped independently from the preexisting presence of national communities abroad. On the other hand, another use of Lieberson's index is to measure the degree of diversity of EU migrants within each member state. Most EU countries show a quite high *mixité* of their immigrant population from Western Europe. The lowest level of diversity is shown by Sweden, due to the overwhelming presence of citizens from other Nordic countries—an effect of cultural proximity but also of legal facilitation for mobility across Scandinavian states since 1954.

Overall, in the wake of the twenty-first century, four main intra–EU migration patterns can be outlined:

Traditional South–North migration

While current EU movers no longer fit in the post–World War II migrants' portrait (male, young, illiterate, from rural areas), the di-

Table 3.3

Lieberson's index of immigrant population diversity per nationality and country of residence

	Per nationality	Per country of residence
DK	.81	.80
D	.86	.83
EL	.31	.82
E	.75	.83
F	.81	.73
IRL	.16	–
I	.67	.85
L	.72	.77
NL	.76	.84
A	.27	–
P	.55	.83
FIN	.52	.73
S	.86	.66
UK	.88	.73

Source: Author's re–elaboration from Eurostat, New Cronos database (2001)

versification of migration projects and trajectories has not entirely offset the traditional model. Still in 2004, the fact at least two different bus companies operate a weekly service between Sicily and Germany, catering for a larger public than old migrants visiting their home country, is testament to the rise in the number of Italian residents in Germany—10 percent between 1994 and 2001 (Recchi et al., 2003: 30). Another clue of the persistence of these flows comes from employment data. In 2000 there were 16,225 Italians among construction workers in Germany (about 15 percent of the total) in an employment sector which absorbs immigrant workers in the early stages of their migration experience (Dobson and Salt, 2002: 24). Work opportunities in the building and tourism industries of the richest Northern EU countries are, likewise, still sought after by a sizeable proportion of the migrant population from Southern Europe.

Cross–Border Migration

Research on cross–border commuting in different areas of the EU finds considerable variation in the propensity of Europeans physically located at small distances from other member states, taking advantage of free movement rights (Clasen, 2003). However, this form of migration does not hinge on geographical proximity alone, as cultural and linguistic closeness between countries also facilitates migration flows. EU citizens moving from and to Benelux, Scandinavia, Ireland and Britain, Germany and Austria benefit from lower barriers for social integration in the host country. Moreover, cross–border migration is likely to increase, as mobility to Austria and Germany was already very popular among Eastern Europeans before the 2004 enlargement that extended to them the right to move within the EU without a visa (Wallace, 2002; William and Baláž, 2002). Citizens of the states who joined the EU in 2004 (Latvia, Lithuania, Estonia, Poland, Czech Republic, Slovakia, Hungary, Slovenia, Cyprus and Malta) are free to travel and live in any other member state and also to deliver services abroad as company–holders or the self–employed. Yet they cannot take up jobs as employees in those states that did not adopt an open labor market policy explicitly (i.e., except in the U.K., Ireland and Sweden). This transition arrangement, which replicates the limits to free movement set in occasion of previous enlargements, will terminate in 2011 at the latest, probably sooner in many countries. As an exception, citizens of Cyprus and Malta were granted full mobility rights all over the European Union immediately in 2004.

Retirement and Resort Migration

As anticipated, by the end of the twentieth century flows of north–to–south migrants have contributed to the rise of international migration in Western Europe. Recent research on a Spanish coastal area shows pensioners activate some network effects on their friends and relatives, expanding and diversifying the scope of these flows (Alaminos, Santacreu and Albert, 2003). Perhaps, thus, for retirement one must associate resort migration to include the growing number of people who buy or rent a second home and live intermittently in another EU country—usually in southern Europe, as well as those in global cities, art towns, and resorts elsewhere in the EU. The boundaries between the two forms of migration are becoming blurred. What they probably share is subjective identification: retirement and resort movers are likely to restrain from calling themselves "migrants," but neither would they accept to be classified as "tourists."

Student Migration

The Erasmus scheme (in 1995 renamed Socrates) an EU–funded program launched in 1989 to encourage student mobility between universities in the European Union, looks likely to be the single-most successful EU activity to spread Europeanness in everyday life (see King and Ruiz-Gelices, 2003). Erasmus–Socrates targets higher education, while other smaller programs promote mobility for internships (Leonardo program), language teaching and learning (Lingua program), voluntary work (Youth for Europe program), and adult education (Grundtvig program). In the late 1990s, participation in the Erasmus/Socrates scheme was extended to citizens of candidate countries; Iceland, Norway and Liechtenstein citizens were entitled to apply from the start; Turkey joined in 2004. Spain and France are the most popular destinations, while the U.K. has the greatest net in-migration of EU moving students. The program has widened its scope enormously: from 3,200 participants in 1987 to 124,000 fifteen years later. In 2002, the symbolic threshold of one million participants was crossed. High as they can seem, these numbers lag behind the European Commission's goal of involving 10 percent of all students in higher education institutions in cross-border experiences.[4] Since such residence abroad can last from three to no more than twelve months, and registration rules vary from country to country, the incidence of Erasmus students among officially resident intra–EU migrants is hard to assess. For sure, however, it contributes to keep the average age of European movers low. On the basis of national statistics, Eurostat estimates among EU nationals moving between member states "37.5 percent of men and 43.5 percent of women were in their 20s in the 1995 to 1999 period" (Thorogood and Winqvist, 2003: 3).

Reluctance or False Expectations? Intra-EU Migrants and an "Ever Closer Union"

The European Union has two neatly distinct migration regimes: one for EU citizens and the other for TCNs. The first represents possibly the most open cross-state movement policy worldwide, to the point (almost) of turning international into internal migration. For EU citizens, political constraints to individual choices of relocation in another country of the Union are virtually non-existent. Also, legal barriers to integration in the host society are minimized. In contrast, the migration regime for non–EU nationals is definitely more severe. Although not so exclusionary as the rhetoric "fortress Europe" maintains (Favell and Hansen, 2002), gate–keeping measures, mostly defined at the nation–state level, make access to the EU for would–be migrants from less developed countries a troublesome venture. Equally, the rights of TCNs living in the EU remain closer to the "denizen" model than to the standards of anti–discrimination advocates. Queues for "EU–passport holders" and "Others" in European airports—and even more starkly in police stations issuing permits of stay on the continent—epitomize quite well the already different categorization of the people for whom the two distinct migration regimes are tailored: high-skilled vs. low-skilled persons split between primary and secondary labor market destinations. Although no available statistics permit a direct comparison of the educational and occupational profiles of these two migrant populations, without contest the average income and status of moving EU nationals are substantially higher than those of TCNs. While not the primary causes, citizenship and equal treatment rights widen the gulf between "internal" and "external" EU migrants in Europe, thus reinforcing the dual nature of the European migration policies.

This divergence mirrors the image and economic role assigned to the two groups of people by ruling elites and market actors. In public discourse, only moving Europeans are openly labeled as "wanted" migrants. In particular, EU institutions sustain intra-EU free movement on both economic and political grounds. From an economic viewpoint, intra–EU migration is framed as the labor market counterpart to monetary union. Workers' mobility is required in an optimally functioning single currency area to absorb local economic shocks due to the decline of some country–based production system. This argument won Robert Mundell, who first formulated it in a widely cited article (Mundell, 1961), the Nobel prize for economics in 1999, and stands as the major theoretical justification for the continued support of the free movement of market–oriented pundits and policymakers (e.g., Sapir et al., 2004). From a political viewpoint, on the other hand, free movement is cherished by EU institutions as an instrument to deepen European integration at the societal level. As has been observed, "the Union has not been totally 'agnostic' with respect to the Good. It tends to favor the way of life of mobile, well-resourced and well-educated Europeans, who have participated in Erasmus exchange programs and developed a cosmopolitan outlook" (Kostakopolou, 2001: 89). The rationale for this, as affirmed for instance in the *Action Plan for Mobility* (European Commission, 2002), is that those who have tasted free movement rights are led to appreciate EU citizenship and endorse European unification more vigorously. The point is made explicit by the most recent legislation consolidating and expanding free movement rights: "Enjoyment of permanent residence by Union citizens who have chosen to settle long term in the host member state would strengthen the feeling of Union citizenship and is a key element in promoting social cohesion, which is one of the fundamental objectives of the Union" (Directive 2004/38). In other words, there is the expectation movers may contribute to overcome national differences, fulfilling the vision of Euro–enthusiast intellectuals like Vaclav Havel: "If regulations on the movements of citizens disappear, we will see the sort of blending produced in the Austro–Hungarian Monarchy before the First World War. Subject came and went, married all over the place, tried their luck at many things, without any of the preceding impeding development of national cultures" (Havel, 1998: 119). From the viewpoint of sociological theory, this is not a trivial hypothesis. It implies that migratory *experiences* bring about *collective identities* based on acculturation and contacts occurring in the everyday life of another European country. It assumes that practices influence values more than the other way around—the reverse of socialization theories. In this scenario, the fusion of European societies would be greatly facilitated by burgeoning territorial mobility (see also Favell, 2004: 1).

To these two longstanding arguments in support of free movement, the EU has more recently added another: mobility as an "autarchic" response to demand at the higher end of the labor market (e.g., see European Commission, 2004). Ironically, this argument was reinforced by some member states'—notably Germany—inability in the late 1990s to attract IT specialists from India and other less developed countries with some sort of "green card" recruitment scheme (Favell and Hansen, 2002). While the free movement doctrine was born of the need to facilitate working class migration from the south in the 1950s, in the last decade or so it has been refocused on encouraging the knowledge economy through a more dynamic use of the educated workforce. The ambition is to promote an increased use of the brains of the continent as a means to support its (likely utopian) program to "make the EU the world's most dynamic and competitive economy," as stated in the so-called "Lisbon Agenda" of year 2000.[5] Basically, this equates to triggering the creation or the expansion of supra–national R&D structures, both in the public and the private sectors in the global struggle for competitiveness.

In the face of the Union's wishes and efforts to favor internal *qua* high–skilled mobility, data presented in this chapter shows that the stock of TCNs is still twice that of intra–EU migrants in the whole EU, about three times in Germany, and almost eight times in Italy. This evidence lends itself to contrasting interpretations. On the one hand, the difference in the size of the two foreign populations can be read as revealing a stronger demand of European economies for cheap low end workers than for highly educated and skilled professionals. Alternatively, the difference can be attributed to supply factors, pointing to the relative paucity of internal movers in the European Union. Since it downplays the persistence of backward and often informal areas of production, as well as the substitution role of non–EU migrants in a number of work sectors (e.g., construction, nursing, housekeeping services), that are politically sensitive for low–skilled natives, the latter explanation is the favorite official reading of this unbalance. As an EC top bureaucrat argues, in the EU "people do not seek to migrate unless there are compelling reasons. Frequently, in both member states and candidate countries, jobs in one part of a country fail to attract people from other parts; how much less is the attraction then in a wholly different linguistic and social environment?" (Glaser, 2001: 33). Europeans' alleged reluctance to move is thus imputed to a variety of supply–side causes. One is the ongoing reduction of cross–country differences in salaries due to economic convergence, although minimum wages do still range from 416 in Portugal to 1369 in Luxembourg (Clare and Paternoster, 2003: 2). On this point, existing studies on the effects of wage and unemployment differentials on workforce mobility within the EU show that intra–EU migration flows have a relatively low elasticity to changes in these two economic factors, in particular when compared to U.S. states (Ederveen and Bardsley, 2003). Other less precise reasons given include the deep–seated persistence of national identities and life habits, and geographical stability as a typical European value associated with well–being and affluence (Pastore, 2004: 76).

Whatever the reasons that migration flows of European citizens lie below economists' and Euro–enthusiasts' aspirations is an established fact. But are we really sure Europeans are so immobile? Statements like Glaser's quoted above circulate quite commonly in both political and academic discourse. They assume a *spatial* yardstick for comparison: internal migration in the EU is low vis–à–vis its U.S. counterpart. Annual cross–EU mobility flows—about 0.1 percent of the resident population—are compared to the cross–state mobility flow of the U.S., which amounts to 3.1 percent (European Commission, 2002: 29; Piracha and Vickerman, 2003: 5; for U.S. data Schachter, 2001: 1). Yet the correctness of this exercise seems questionable on many grounds. The United States is a federal, state whereas the European Union is not; the U.S. is a nation, whereas the EU not; and internal migration in the U.S. is a century–old phenomenon, whilst it is only a very recent possibility in the EU. Perhaps, when assessing the success of the free mobility policy in the European Union, a *temporal* yardstick is more appropriate. In this perspective, as shown before (figure 3.3), it must be acknowledged the number of moving EU citizens is, in fact, on the rise by the end of the twentieth century.

However, this is not all. There is room to believe the real size of intra–EU mobility is not entirely taken into account by existing statistics. Western Europeans are likely to be more mobile than censuses and other public records suggest. The point is their *movements* are becoming too volatile for the statistical eye. Paradoxically, elusive migrations are engendered by the very legislation on free movement, as EU citizens can relocate for temporary or intermittent stays, without any stringent necessity to register abroad. The emerging pattern of Europeans' mobility projects is perhaps "bite–and–go migration." Some major urban hubs (London, Paris, Berlin, Brussels, Barcelona) take the lion's share of these movements, as they enjoy inherent and persistent appeals. They also offer higher porosity in terms of access to temporary housing, employment arrangements, commercial niches, and specialized leisure tastes. If economic considerations contribute to shape individual migration projects, they obey far more subtle logics than the kind of disequilibria that explain traditional migration flows in neoclassical economic theory. For example, EU movers can accumulate different forms of cultural capital at lower costs and also faster than in their home countries. Indeed, recent analyses indicate changes in the economic outlook of EU–15 member states do not affect population movements between them significantly (Mouhoud and Oudinet, 2004). Intra–EU migrations are largely inertial. Year after year, movements in and out of each country repeat themselves with marginal variations regardless of variations in wage and unemployment differentials between member states. What is more, emigration and immigration in EU countries are highly correlated—that is, destinations with higher inflows have higher outflows as well (ibidem: 90). This is consistent with the hypothesis that the emerging form of migration across the EU has a short–term and circulatory character. *Guests come to stay* was the brilliant title of a study on post–World War II migration in Europe (Rogers, 1985). "Guests come to stay *and go*" could be its reprise to depict intra–EU movements in the early twenty-first century.

Although we may speculate this model of territorial mobility has some overrepresentation in middle to upper classes with a nomadic and globalizing lifestyle, it would be highly misleading to classify it as "elite migration." In fact, the opportunity to move around the EU without too many formalities is also appealing to lower–middle class individuals as a shortcut to capital accumulation—be it economic or cultural capital, or a mix of the two. An example is the myriads of young Europeans temporarily employed in the tourism business in London, trying to make some pocket money and improve their English at the same time. Among more stable workers, there are certainly the "golden migrations" of expatriate managers (Wagner, 1999), but also the wearying and lonesome commuting experiences of sales agents and technicians (Tarrius, 1992, 2000). They have little in common, except for the (still quite unusual) practice of mobility, which seems to be a growing criterion of social distinction in Western societies (Bauman, 1998). Should their number expand, we could even expect the rise of a new politico–identitarian cleavage based on multicultural mindsets for "movers" vs. monocultural frameworks prevailing among "stayers." *Grosso modo*, this outcome would reproduce the "local–cosmopolitan" divide—a dichotomy of reference group orientations dear to classic sociologists, yet unjustly forgotten (Merton, 1957: 368 ff.; Gouldner, 1957, 1958). Originally conceived as an integrative tool across national borders, EU citizenship could thus instead become the basis for emerging forms of social differentiation.

Notes

1. See http://www.ellisisland.com/indexinfo.html.
2. Somewhat different totals can be found in Bade (2000: 141-142), while a critical assessment of all calculations of historical migration flows is provided by Nugent (1996: 78-79).
3. Lastly, Directive 2004/38 has introduced "permanent residence" as a new right for intra–EU migrants with more than five year settlement in a member state, regardless of their current status.
4. All figures are taken from the official EU Erasmus–Socrates website (http://europa.eu.int/comm/education/programmes/socrates).
5. This widely quoted passage is taken from the EU website of the Lisbon agenda: http://europa.eu.int/comm/lisbon_strategy/index_en.html. Among the dozens of papers and reports commenting on the strategies to achieve the stated goal, Sapir et al. (2004) distinguishes itself for academic rigor and clarity.

Part Two

Highly Skilled Migration in the United States

4

"The Best and the Brightest": Immigrant Professionals in the U.S.

Jeanne Batalova and B. Lindsay Lowell

In the world of competitive, fast-moving, internationally-oriented business, employers rely on highly skilled workers to meet the challenges of a global economy. Both the traditional countries of immigration and many European countries have been actively promoting—or at least seriously considering—an increase in foreign labor flows, to meet the demands of their economies, keep up with the reach of multinational corporations, offset the adverse consequences of an aging population, stimulate R&D or promote entrepreneurship, and to expand foreign markets. While it is true the United States receives a lion's share of the global flow (i.e., about two-thirds of tertiary educated immigrants from developing countries), its dominant position is being challenged by a growing competition for the "best and the brightest" (Lowell, Findlay, and Stewart, 2004).

In the last decade there has been a proliferation of new schemes and policy measures directed to recruit and ease the entry of skilled immigrants on both a temporary and permanent basis (Lowell, 2004b; Mclaughlan and Salt, 2002; OECD, 2002). Some well-known examples are the introduction of the Highly Skilled Migrant Program in the United Kingdom (based on a point system), active recruitment of foreign students in both the U.K. and France; Germany's surprising, albeit unsuccessful, "Green Card" scheme for computer workers, a revamped point system for independent immigration in Australia and Canada, and fast-track work authorization in Ireland. Immigration, however, is not only a strategy for increasing the size of a country's labor force. Countries like India, China, Taiwan, Ireland, and Sweden have adopted policies to stimulate return migration, as well as encouraging the transnational ties of their highly skilled expatriates by creating business and investment opportunities; giving an option of dual citizenship; and providing tax incentives (Mclaughlan and Salt, 2002; OECD, 2002; O'Neil, 2003).

But who are these highly skilled workers whose skills and qualifications are in such a great demand? Here we provide a broad profile of the highly skilled in the United States, defined as workers in professional occupations at the end of the 1990s. In comparison, a far greater body of existing literature looks at the long-recognized challenge of low-skilled immigration. And what research exists on the highly skilled tends to focus either on scientists and engineers, the mobility of healthcare workers or, to a very much lesser extent, the business class. We look here at *all* professional workers, who fall under various policy regimes, because we wish to better understand the entire phenomenon and not just the given occupational classes. First, we provide a brief overview of immigration admission policy, focusing on the comparison of different groups of foreign-born admitted to the United States. Second, we discuss problems with definition and the identification of different ways used in research and immigration policies to operationalize the category 'highly skilled.' And third, we describe the highly skilled/professional immigrant labor force in terms of their demographic and socio-economic characteristics using data from the 2000 U.S. Census. We compare immigrants to natives on their human capital characteristics, their geographical and occupational distribution, and their labor market outcomes.

Immigration Admission Policy

The Immigration Act of 1965 is the architecture of today's U.S. immigration system. It divided the inflow into a predominantly family-based intake and a smaller employment-based one, established the practice of testing the labor market to protect domestic workers, and set the conditions for temporary workers under a variety of alphabetically named visas designed to accomplish different purposes. With the exception of reform on refugee policy, the next major legislation was the Immigration and Reform Act of 1986. It traded the amnesty of nearly 3 million formerly unauthorized immigrants for sanctions against employers who hire unauthorized workers. Having "closed the back door," Congress enacted the Immigration Act of 1990, which increased the overall number of permanent immigrants, nearly tripling the number of employment-based admissions. The 1990 Act also expanded the number of visas for skilled temporary workers, simplified some procedures, and made the transition from temporary to permanent immigrant easier.

Today, skilled foreign workers enter the United States under one of several admission statuses, often as "non-immigrant" temporary workers. Foreign scientists, engineers, and healthcare workers enter under a select set of temporary working visas. The well-known H-1B visa for specialty workers generally requires a baccalaureate or higher degree. Its major features have been, and remain, a six-year maximum duration of stay and a numerical limit of 65,000 temporary migrants to be admitted each year. During the boom years of the New Economy, the information technology industry lobbied hard for more H-1Bs, an effort analyzed by Freeman and Hill in this volume. The U.S. Congress passed higher caps in 1998 and again in 1999, but reverted to the original cap in 2003. Recently in 2004, an additional 20,000 visas exempted from the cap were awarded for graduates of U.S. colleges. The loosely similar L visa is for intracompany transferees employed by a multinational company. Both H-1B and L visa holders may adjust to permanent status and perhaps as many as half do so (Lowell, 2001a). Other temporary working visas include the H-2B visa for temporary non-agricultural workers, that permit entry for a small numbers of nonprofessionals who work in the science and engineering fields. The companion H-2A visa is for agricultural workers. Other temporary visas for professionals include the O visas for aliens with extraordinary abilities in the sciences, arts, education, business, or athletic fields, and for those assisting them. The P visas are for internationally recognized entertainers, athletes, or artists. The Q visas are for participants in international exchange programs. Restricted working rights are granted to foreign students (F visa) and cultural exchange visitors (J). The TN (Trade NAFTA) professional workers are citizens of Canada or Mexico who may stay for up to one year with no limit on the number of extensions.

Permanent resident admissions are given to several classes of immigrants, the two broadest of which, family-based and employment-based, are generated through the sponsorship by an immediate family member or an employer. Family-based admissions dominate the flow of immigrants. Any family-based immigrant may work in the United States. These categories do not require labor market tests or exceptional ability to contribute to the U.S. economy. As to the employment-based admissions, immigrants come under one of the five preference categories. Priority workers or first preference (EB-1) permanent immigrants include those with an extraordinary ability and/or outstanding professors or researchers. Professionals with advanced degrees or second preference (EB-2) immigrants are those with an exceptional ability who do not meet the criteria laid out for priority workers and are labor market tested. Skilled workers/professionals with baccalaureate degrees or third preference (EB-3) immigrants are those with at least two years of training or experience and are also labor market tested. The fourth preference (EB-4) is for certain special immigrants such as religious ministers and workers. Yet another employment visa, although little-used, applies to self-employed entrepreneurs (Papademetriou and Yale-Loehr, 1996).

One of the hotly debated issues in the United States concerns the economic success of family- vs. employment-based immigrants. Consider table 4.1 showing occupational distribution by broad classes of admission in the U.S. in 1996 and 2000. It shows family-based immigrants (family preferences and relatives of U.S. citizens) are unlikely to be in professional and management occupations, much less employed in the first place. Between 1996 and 2000 the share of family-based workers in professional jobs even declines somewhat, while the proportion of employment-based workers in the professions increases notably. Although numerically rather small, refugees are even less educated than family-based immigrants, while the diversity class, which requires a minimum of a high school degree, has education levels that are intermediate between the family and employment admission classes. The Immigration Act of 1990, by increasing the numerical cap and easing admissions, favorably impacted the skill composition of employment-based immigrants (Greenwood and Ziel, 1997). Still, the 4.5 to 1 ratio of family- to employment-based immigrants militates against a significant upward shift in education of the entire immigrant pool.

There is a strong argument to be made that immigration policy, in order to facilitate immigrant integration, should increase the relative share of immigrants who have high school and college education. Borjas (1995) argues that the Immigration Act of 1965, with its greater emphasis on family reunification, has resulted in a high inflow of

Table 4.1
Legal Immigrants by Class of Admission and Occupation, Ages 18 to 64[a]

	Family-Based	Employment-Based	Diversity	Refugees/Asylees
2000 - Fiscal Year of Admission				
Professional, Technical & Kindred, %	19.4	63.2	34.8	8.3
Executive, Administrative & Managerial, %	9.4	19.3	7.4	1.8
Other Occupations, %	70.9	17.5	57.8	89.9
Total with Occupation, %	99.7	100.0	100.0	100.0
Immigrants with an occupation	91,370	47,346	25,431	12,573
All Immigrants[b]	402,408	85,308	37,675	45,553
1996 - Fiscal Year of Admission				
Professional, Technical & Kindred, %	17.3	47.8	38.2	8.1
Executive, Administrative & Managerial, %	8.6	20.3	8.7	2.0
Other Occupations, %	74.2	31.9	53.1	90.5
Total with Occupation, %	100.1	100.0	100.0	100.7
Immigrants with an occupation	175,772	61,447	28,356	39,047
All Immigrants[b]	399,744	89,054	43,491	88,342

[a] Numbers reflect both new admissions and adjustments. Some classes of admission (e.g. IRCA legalization dependents) are not shown in the table

[b] The number of legal immigrants includes principal applicants and their dependents

Source: U.S. Department of Justice, Immigration and Naturalization Service. 1998. "Immigrants Admitted to the United States, 1996 [Computer files]. ICPSR version." 2000. "Immigrants Admitted to the United States, 1998 [Computer files]. ICPSR version." Washington, U.S. Dept. of Justice, Immigration and Naturalization Service [producer] Ann Arbor, MI: Inter-university Consortium for Political and Social Research [distributor].

low-skilled and poorly educated migrants. Consequently, it undermines the international competitiveness of the United States and imposes high costs on the welfare system. To be sure, a few studies—albeit using 1980 and 1990 Census data or based on fieldwork during that time—question the assumption that professional immigrants differ over the long run in their ability to assimilate in terms of their economic adaptation and impacts (Lowell, 1996; Sorensen, Bean, Ku, and Zimmermann, 1992). Even refugees may experience fast enough wage growth so that, after a decade or two, their earnings are equivalent to other similarly-educated workers (Lowell, 2004a). Yet, even if family-based immigrants eventually earn as much as "otherwise similar" native workers who also have little education, they are much less educated on average than most natives. Many family-based immigrants live in poverty after several years in the United States whereas rather few employment-based immigrants do. In the final analysis, better-educated workers assimilate more readily into the U.S. labor market.

Defining the "Highly Skilled"

Although the phrase "the best and the brightest" has become a mantra in public and policy discourses in recent years, there is no consistent definition or measurement of "highly skilled." Questions about the definition, size, and impacts of highly skilled migrants are, in part, unanswered due to the absence of appropriate data. The most readily available data sources are censuses and surveys. Although these sources have large sample sizes and employ standardized classifications, they are also cross-sectional and offer just a snapshot of social and economic experiences rather than a dynamic picture. More to the point, they often lack detailed information about immigrants such as their legal status, migration history, or place of education (Jasso. Massey, Rosenzweig and Smith, 2000; Rumbaut, 2004). Indeed, U.S. administrative data lack information on education altogether—either the level of schooling completed or the field of education—and the information on occupation is crude. Critical detail is also absent for informed policymaking: data is lacking on industry and there is nothing on the characteristics of the immigrants' employers who are the linchpin of the admissions system (Lowell, 2001b).

Another set of problems has methodological and conceptual roots. Different policy and philosophical approaches on managing migration make it unclear who the highly skilled are in various contexts. (Mclaughlan and Salt, 2002; OECD, 2002; Solimano and Pollack, 2004). Recognition of qualifications of skilled workers varies across countries, making comparative research using international migration statistics difficult. Moreover, definitions vary over time reflecting the changes in economic and labor market structures of national and global economies. The term "skilled," which often is used interchangeably with professional and highly skilled, does not have the same meaning in different contexts.

The most obvious markers of "skill" are either education or occupation, with economists often opting for education, while demographic and sociological researchers almost always opts for occupation (Borjas, 2003; Bouvier and Simcox, 1994). Which definition is applied often depends on what one is trying to accomplish and what data are available. A common international definition of highly skilled tends to be persons with a tertiary education, typically meaning adult age persons who have completed a formal two-year college degree or more. This is also the most readily available international statistic and so, by default, the most widely studied measure (Dumont and George, 2004). When possible it is preferable to have additional information about baccalaureate degree holdings and even graduate or professional degrees. Indeed, information about detailed levels of education is almost always invaluable, as can be readily seen when occupation alone is used to proxy for skill. For example, Bouvier and Martin (1995) found in 1990 a surprising 15 percent of immigrant engineers and 23 percent of mathematicians and computer scientists did not have a college degree. Conversely, many had graduate degrees.

For research purposes, and perhaps even more so for government policy, highly skilled immigrants are preferably classified not in terms of either/or, but in terms of both education and occupation (Mclaughlan and Salt, 2002). One example is the Canberra Manuel definition of Human Resources in Science and Technology (HRST). This measure, collaboratively constructed by the OECD and the European Commission with Eurostat, is based on both qualification (tertiary level or better education) and occupation (training/employment in a science and technology occupations) (Auriol and Sexton, 2002; OECD, 1995). According to the manual, HRST are individuals who satisfy one or the other of two requirements: 1) successfully completed education at the third level in the field of Science & Technology (S&T); or 2) not formally educated/qualified as above, but employed in an S&T occupation where the above qualifications are normally required. In fact, the definition of highly skilled is best served by both an educational component and a threshold defining the minimum competence in a knowledge-based field or society. Additionally, the Canberra Manuel allows for a narrow (including only natural sciences) or broad definition (engineering and technology, natural and social sciences as well as medical sciences and humanities). Occupation is important not only because by its nature it excludes workers with little education, but also because it targets skills that tend to be highly productive. The S&T occupations in the Canberra definitions can be seen as uniquely embodying technical skills that are crucial for knowledge economies.

Yet, restricting the meaning of highly skilled to S&T occupations arguably makes the Canberra Manual rather narrow insofar as it disregards other highly skilled categories that are in high demand, such as businessmen, managers, teachers, and healthcare providers. And one can even add writers and artists to a "creative class" of workers (Florida, 2002). Even if education and occupation are the most readily available benchmarks of skill, such an alternative definition raises an interesting point about what is most important in today's knowledge-based society? At the very least, our interest here is broader than just S&T occupations as we wish to know something about immigrants in a variety of U.S. professions.

Note on Methods

The definition of "highly skilled" workers may be met in a number of ways. Defining highly skilled by a *combination of occupation and education*, as Lofstrom (2001) does, generates a lower bound number. Using, 2000 Census data, we select only detailed 3-digit occupations that have a preponderance of college-educated workers arriving, thereby, at 23.3 million highly skilled workers, 11.9 percent of whom are foreign-born (authors' tabulations, see discussion below). A larger number is arrived at using just *college education* as the definition of highly skilled that generates 33.2 million workers, 13 percent of whom are foreign-born. The most liberal estimate of highly skilled is arrived at using just *professional occupations* that generates 39.9 million workers, of whom the foreign-born represent 11 percent.

Because we wish to examine the characteristics of highly skilled immigrants in the most general sense, we define highly skilled in terms of occupation. Professional occupations are typically thought of as highly skilled by most researchers and so readily accord with our general focus. Although it is worthwhile pursuing alternative analyses using just college education or a combination of education and occupation, our focus is on the occupational definition. In turn, we examine educational qualifications within those occupations in order to better our understanding of how comparatively "skilled" native and immigrant professionals are.

We consider the following professional occupations to be highly skilled (see the tables that follow): management, business/finance operations, information technology (computer scientists, programmers, engineers, and technical support), math science and engineering, architecture and engineering, life and physical sciences, social sciences, science technicians of all sorts, the healthcare professions such as physicians, registered nurses, and healthcare technicians; teachers and educators; and other professional occupations such as legal, community service, arts, sports and entertainment occupations. These are, in fact, somewhat aggregated groupings. But while a detailed breakdown of occupations would be of undoubted interest, it is necessary to group some occupations to obtain reliable sample estimates.

The tables that follow are based on the authors' tabulations of the 2000 Census 5 percent Public Use Micro-Sample (PUMS) file (U.S. Census, 2003) and are restricted to the civilian labor force with an occupation in the ages twenty-five to sixty-four. Our interest in the civilian labor force is dictated by our interest in the workforce where the bulk of immigrants are found. We restrict our focus to the adult working population because our overlapping interest in completed education dictates that adults are the relevant age group. Degree holding captures the most essential element of education and tends to confer higher earnings on workers (Betts and Lofstrom, 2000).

A Demographic and Socio-Economic Profile of Professionals

The 39.9 million U.S. workers in our professional occupations represent about 36.2 percent of the civilian labor force between the ages of twenty-five and sixty-four. The foreign-born represent 11 percent of these professionals, which is a little less than their 13.5 percent share of the total civilian labor force. This suggests immigrants are somewhat under-represented in professional occupations relative to their share of all workers. Yet, we also know immigrants tend to cluster in a few states and immigrants' share of U.S. professionals, as a grouping, also varies significantly across states.

Map 4.1 depicts the foreign-born as a percentage of professional workers in the fifty states and Washington, DC. Immigrants represent only about one out of twenty professionals in a significant number of states (mostly central and midwest areas). Similarly, the overall foreign-born population of these states is relatively small both in absolute and relative terms (Bean, Lee, Batalova, and Leach, 2004). On the other hand, in traditional immigrant-receiving states such as California, New York, Florida, and New Jersey, almost one out of five, professionals are foreign-born. For the last several decades these states have received the lion's share of all immigrants and, while immigrant professionals unsurprisingly cluster in these traditional-receiving states, they are yet more concentrated in those states than

Map 4.1
Foreign Born Among Professionals by State, 2000

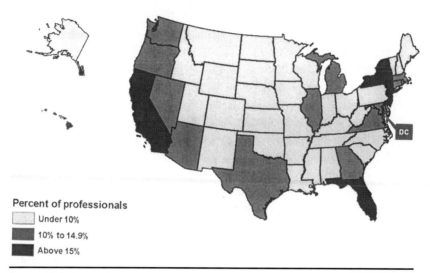

Percent of professionals

☐ Under 10%

■ 10% to 14.9%

■ Above 15%

Source: U. S. Census 2000

are other immigrants. They also are a disproportionate share of the professional occupations in these traditional states.

Table 4.2 shows the concentration of immigrants within professional occupations nationally, as well as their educational completion relative to natives within each occupation. Immigrant professionals are most often found among information technology (IT) workers, life and physical scientists and, especially, in medical professions. One quarter of all physicians and surgeons, as well as, computer programmers/engineers are foreign-born. On the other hand, the foreign-born are underrepresented among all educators (particularly primary and secondary teachers).

Furthermore, table 4.2 indicates the foreign-born tend to be better educated than natives. For example, within practically all professional occupations, immigrants are much more likely to possess a doctorate or a professional degree. All immigrant professionals (14.8 percent) are almost twice as likely than natives (8.3 percent) to hold a doctorate or professional degree. Indeed, while underrepresented among all educators, immigrant educators are nearly three times more likely than native educators to hold a doctorate degree. Among math

Table 4.2
Percent of Professionals Within Occupational Workforces and by Education and Nativity

	Total		Percent of Natives				Percent of Foreign Born			
	Number of workers ('000s)	Percent foreign born	No college	Bachelor	Master	PhD / Professional	No college	Bachelor	Master	PhD / Professional
Total	39,938.2	11.1	40.4	34.7	16.7	8.3	32.1	33.2	19.9	14.8
Management	11,114.5	9.9	51.0	31.9	14.2	2.9	47.2	29.3	17.3	6.3
Business/finance	5,096.4	10.1	44.4	41.2	12.2	2.3	34.3	43.2	17.8	4.7
Information Technology workers										
Computer scientists	625.3	16.7	42.4	42.3	13.2	2.2	20.8	43.9	29.0	6.3
Computer programmers/engineers	1,260.8	24.7	33.9	49.4	14.8	1.9	11.2	43.0	39.3	6.5
Computer technical support	863.7	12.0	54.7	35.9	8.2	1.2	33.0	42.4	21.5	3.1
Math scientists & engineers	142.7	12.2	29.0	41.3	22.8	7.0	17.1	33.6	30.6	18.7
Architects & engineers	2,468.0	15.4	43.6	40.6	13.4	2.5	23.4	38.8	28.1	9.7
Life & physical scientists	541.7	25.1	8.6	41.0	26.4	24.1	2.2	16.2	21.6	60.0
Social scientists	318.2	10.1	9.0	22.6	39.1	29.4	6.7	20.9	36.8	35.6
Life, physical, and social science technicians/assistants	231.7	13.3	69.8	23.5	5.0	1.7	41.0	32.4	13.9	12.7
Healthcare workers										
Physicians & surgeons	669.7	26.1	0.2	2.8	2.4	94.6	0.5	2.5	1.4	95.6
Registered nurses	2,158.6	12.0	49.6	37.0	8.5	4.9	36.6	50.6	7.5	5.3
Other health practitioners	1,064.5	11.2	15.1	30.3	20.5	34.1	13.2	34.3	12.4	40.2
Healthcare technicians	1,688.5	10.0	78.8	15.8	2.3	3.2	61.7	27.1	4.9	6.3
Teachers and other educators	5,501.4	7.8	12.0	44.0	36.3	7.7	15.7	31.6	30.8	21.9
Other professionals	6,192.7	9.0	38.9	28.6	16.1	16.5	44.3	28.0	16.5	11.2

Source: Authors' tabulations from U.S. Census 2000 microdata.

scientists and engineers, as well as computer scientists, programmers, and engineers, the foreign-born are about three times more likely than natives to possess a PhD degree. Among life and physical science technicians and assistants, the likelihood for immigrants to have advanced degree is even greater; they are seven times more likely than natives to hold a doctorate degree. It is probably the case immigrants are better educated than natives because they are the cream of the crop of graduates from U.S. and foreign institutions, and because only better educated immigrants are able to clear formal and informal employment barriers. Thus, immigrants tend to constitute a large share of specific occupations, within which they also represent the best educated workers of that occupation. This is particularly the case in occupations in which a high degree (i.e., MDs) is not, itself, a requirement for employment.

The figures in table 4.3 reinforce the observation immigrants are much more likely to find employment in certain occupations. The table also makes this comparison by both nativity and sex. Nativity differences are particularly striking in the IT occupations where the foreign-born are almost twice as likely to work in computer related occupations as are natives (11.7 percent versus 6.3 percent). And immigrants are more than 2.5 times more likely to be physicians/surgeons and life and physical scientists than are natives. As shown in table 4.2, these occupations tend to have a large representation (more than a quarter) of immigrants. Conversely, immigrants constitute a small share of all educators (7.8 percent). In fact, they are much less likely than natives to be employed as educators in the first place (9.7 versus 14.3 percent). While a low likelihood of occupational employment does not necessarily mean immigrants are a small share of an occupational workforce, such a finding is not surprising. Otherwise, table 4.3 shows differences in occupational employment by sex follow historical patterns. Regardless of nativity, men predominate as managers, information technologists, scientists and engineers (except social sciences), physicians and surgeons; yet, women are over-represented among nurses and teachers.

The 1990s saw a boom in immigration with 40 percent of *all* immigrants arriving in that decade and 22 percent arriving in just the last five years of the decade (U.S. Census, 2000). In contrast, as table 4.4 shows, a lesser 32 percent of immigrants in the subset of professional occupations arrived in the decade of the nineties. This reflects the fact relatively fewer professionals emigrate compared to

Table 4.3
Percent of Professionals in Occupations by Nativity and Sex

	Native-born Percentage			Foreign-born Percentage		
	Male	Female	Total	Male	Female	Total
Number ('000s)	17,331.2	18,164.4	35,495.6	2,463.5	1,979.1	4,442.5
Total Percent	100.0	100.0	100.0	100.0	100.0	100.0
Management	36.5	20.3	28.2	30.2	18.1	24.8
Business/finance	12.0	13.7	12.9	9.4	14.2	11.6
Information Technology workers						
Computer scientists	2.0	1.0	1.5	3.1	1.5	2.4
Computer programmers/engineers	4.0	1.4	2.7	9.2	4.3	7.0
Computer technical support	3.0	1.4	2.1	3.2	1.3	2.3
Math scientists & engineers	0.4	0.3	0.4	0.4	0.4	0.4
Architects & engineers	10.5	1.5	5.9	13.1	2.9	8.5
Life & physical scientists	1.6	0.7	1.1	3.5	2.6	3.1
Social scientists	0.7	0.9	0.8	0.7	0.8	0.7
Life, physical, and social science technicians/assistants	0.7	0.4	0.6	0.7	0.7	0.7
Healthcare workers						
Physicians & surgeons	2.1	0.7	1.4	4.9	2.7	3.9
Registered nurses	0.8	9.7	5.4	1.1	11.7	5.8
Other health practitioners	2.3	3.0	2.7	2.1	3.4	2.7
Healthcare technicians	1.8	6.7	4.3	2.0	6.1	3.8
Teachers and other educators	8.1	20.2	14.3	6.8	13.3	9.7
Other professionals	13.5	18.2	15.9	9.9	16.0	12.6

Source: Authors' tabulations from U.S. Census 2000 microdata.

lesser skilled immigrants. In addition, professionals are a small portion of the overall inflow of immigrants to the United States and so could not accumulate as great a relative number. Yet, there are significant occupational differences: about half of immigrants in both information technology and life and physical sciences have arrived in the nineties. In fact, over a third of all foreign-born professionals who arrived between 1990 and 2000 were IT workers or scientists and engineers. This reflects the well-known fact information technology led the "New Economy" and employment growth during the decade. So the greatest demand, and a relatively new demand at that, was for immigrant IT workers, many of whom came first as temporary H-1B workers. The significant growth of immigrant workers in life and physical sciences, however, is not as clear, as life sciences faced a glut of U.S. graduate students in the nineties.

In turn, table 4.5 has a schematic presentation in the shift in the national origins of workers in professional occupations by period of

Table 4.4
Percent of Foreign Born Professionals by Year of Arrival

	Number ('000s)	Percent within Occupation Arriving by Period					
		Before 1950	1950-1959	1960-1969	1970-1979	1980-1989	1990-2000
Total	4,442.5	0.8	4.4	11.6	22.6	28.7	31.9
Management	1,101.6	0.9	5.4	13.8	24.0	29.5	26.5
Business/finance	513.0	0.7	4.7	12.2	25.4	30.4	26.6
Information Technology workers							
Computer scientists	104.6	0.4	2.5	6.7	17.5	24.8	48.1
Computer programmers/engineers	311.5	0.3	1.3	4.2	14.1	25.3	54.8
Computer technical support	103.9	0.3	2.5	6.9	21.4	29.4	39.6
Math scientists & engineers	17.4	0.8	3.4	10.3	23.1	27.8	34.5
Architects & engineers	379.5	0.6	3.6	10.8	24.0	29.7	31.3
Life & physical scientists	136.1	0.3	2.0	5.9	13.2	25.3	53.4
Social scientists	32.2	2.0	5.4	14.2	18.6	24.3	35.5
Life, physical, and social science technicians/assistants	30.9	0.3	2.6	6.8	21.7	25.7	43.0
Healthcare workers							
Physicians & surgeons	174.6	0.6	2.5	14.4	28.7	24.1	29.7
Registered nurses	258.2	0.7	3.5	11.8	25.0	31.4	27.6
Other health practitioners	119.6	0.8	3.6	10.4	25.9	30.9	28.4
Healthcare technicians	169.4	0.5	3.7	12.3	23.3	33.7	26.5
Teachers and other educators	430.7	1.4	6.7	12.6	20.2	26.3	32.9
Other professionals	559.2	1.2	5.7	12.8	23.1	28.5	28.7

Source: Authors' tabulations from U.S. Census 2000 microdata.

arrival, which is, in turn, a reflection of the changing nature of immigration since World War II. The top sending country in each decade changed, namely there was shift from a predominance of Europeans to a diversification and predominance of non-European newcomers. Whereas before 1970, Western Europeans (especially Germans) dominated practically all skilled occupations, from 1965 on the foreign-born working in emerging information technology industries and hard sciences in general were mainly of Asian (often Chinese) origin. In the last decade, computer programmers, engineers, and scientists from India joined the Chinese as the most significant group. Filipinos, Middle Easterners, and Indians replaced Western Europeans in medical professions as well, with Filipino immigrants concentrated in nursing, Middle Easterners, among general health practitioners, and Indians among physicians and surgeons. Western Europeans remained well-represented in management, business, and finance operations occupations. Even though between 1970 and 1990 they were pushed aside by immigrants from Mexico, Philippines, and Central and South America, in the 1990s, Europeans

Table 4.5
Dominant National Origin of Professionals by Period of Arrival

	Before 1950	1950-1959	1960-1969	1970-1979	1980-1989	1990-2000
Number ('000s)	36.2	196.5	513.6	1,006.0	1,273.8	1,416.4
Management	W.Europe	W.Europe	W.Europe	Mexico	Centr./So. America*	W.Europe
Business/finance	W.Europe	W.Europe	W.Europe	Philippines	China/Taiwan	W.Europe
Information Technology workers						
Computer scientists	NA	W.Europe	China/Taiwan	China/Taiwan	China/Taiwan	India
Computer programmers/engineers	NA	W.Europe	China/Taiwan	China/Taiwan	China/Taiwan	India
Computer technical support	NA	Canada	W.Europe	China/Taiwan	China/Taiwan	India
Math scientists & engineers	NA	NA	Centr./So. America*	China/Taiwan	China/Taiwan	China/Taiwan
Architects & engineers	W.Europe	W.Europe	W.Europe	Middle Eastern	China/Taiwan	China/Taiwan
Life & physical scientists	NA	W.Europe	China/Taiwan	India	China/Taiwan	China/Taiwan
Social scientists	NA	W.Europe	W.Europe	W.Europe	Centr./So. America*	China/Taiwan
Life, physical, and social science technicians/assistants	NA	NA	Mexico	Mexico	Mexico	China/Taiwan
Healthcare workers						
Physicians & surgeons	NA	W.Europe	Philippines	India	India	India
Registered nurses	Canada	W.Europe	Philippines	Philippines	Philippines	Philippines
Other health practitioners	NA	W.Europe	W.Europe	Middle Eastern	Middle Eastern	Philippines
Healthcare technicians	NA	W.Europe	W.Europe	Philippines	Philippines	Philippines
Teachers and other educators	W.Europe	W.Europe	W.Europe	Mexico	Centr./So. America*	China/Taiwan
Other professionals	W.Europe	W.Europe	W.Europe	Mexico	Centr./So. America*	W.Europe

Notes: NA-small number of cases (fewer than 50 data points)
*Central and South America excluding Mexico and Cuba

(mainly those from Great Britain and Germany) predominated in management and finance.

As seen in table 4.6, these shifts in origin are reflected in the significant differences in the racial and ethnic composition of native and foreign workers. Following the approach offered by Bean et al. (2004), we combine race and ethnicity information to force mutual exclusivity of four racial-ethnic categories. Unsurprisingly, the overwhelming majority of native-born professionals (86 percent), are white, while race/ethnic minorities are underrepresented relative to their share of the total labor force. Of course, working-age Asian and Latino groups are primarily first-generation and their shares of just the foreign-born professionals are correspondingly higher. Somewhat surprisingly, though expected, Asians, alone, makeup 38.2 percent of all foreign-born professionals and Latinos another 20.7 percent. Whites, primarily of European descent, make up an additional 31.1 percent of foreign-born professionals.

Otherwise, there is a wide variation in the specific professional occupations in which race/ethnic groups concentrate. Native and foreign-born Asians alike (mainly Indians and Chinese) concentrate in IT occupations, as well as in sciences and engineering. More than 30 percent of foreign-born Asians and 20 percent of native Asians work as IT workers, scientists and engineers, while only 10.6 percent of native blacks and Latinos work in these occupations. Asians and whites, regardless of their nativity, are more likely to be physicians and surgeons than other groups. Interestingly, foreign-born blacks concentrate in nursing and other healthcare support occupations (25.9 percent), perhaps due to the well-known employment of Caribbean nurses and technicians. Foreign-born Asians and blacks are less likely to be found among managers than are other immigrants, while Latino immigrants are well-represented in management occupations.

Table 4.7 presents a demographic and labor force profile of native and foreign-born workers. It shows foreign-born workers are, on average, not quite two years younger than natives. The youngest workers, regardless of their nativity, are in IT occupations. Similarly, the IT and engineering occupations tend to be heavily male-dominated, especially among the foreign-born. Compared to their native counterparts, immigrant physicians, life and physical scientists and technicians are somewhat more likely to be female. On the other hand, immigrant women are less likely than natives to be working as managers, social scientists, healthcare technicians, or teachers.

Table 4.6
Percent of Professionals in Occupations by Nativity and Race/Ethnicity

	Native-born					Foreign-born				
	White	Black	Asian	Other	Latino	White	Black	Asian	Other	Latino
Number ('000s)	30,666	2,760	441	399	1,230	1,384	371	1,698	71	920
Percent Race/Ethnicity within Nativity	86.4	7.8	1.2	1.1	3.5	31.1	8.3	38.2	1.6	20.7
Total Percent	100.0	100.0	100.0	100.0	100.0	100.0	100.0	100.0	100.0	100.0
Management	29.0	22.0	22.4	27.0	25.9	28.9	17.4	19.5	29.7	31.0
Business/finance	12.7	15.1	14.6	12.1	14.0	10.1	14.1	11.8	10.6	12.4
Information Technology workers										
Computer scientists	1.5	1.6	2.1	1.3	1.4	1.9	1.8	3.5	1.5	1.2
Computer programmers/engineers	2.7	2.1	4.7	2.0	1.9	5.8	2.7	11.6	5.5	2.2
Computer technical support	2.1	2.4	3.3	2.5	2.4	2.0	2.2	2.9	2.4	1.8
Math scientists & engineers	0.4	0.4	0.5	0.3	0.3	0.3	0.5	0.5	0.2	0.2
Architects & engineers	6.1	3.5	7.9	5.3	5.2	8.6	5.0	10.8	8.2	5.8
Life & physical scientists	1.2	0.5	1.9	1.1	0.7	3.3	1.3	4.4	1.8	1.1
Social scientists	0.9	0.5	0.8	0.8	0.6	1.0	0.6	0.6	0.7	0.6
Life, physical, and social science technicians/assistants	0.5	0.8	0.6	0.9	0.7	0.5	0.5	0.8	0.5	0.8
Healthcare workers										
Physicians & surgeons	1.4	0.9	4.1	0.7	1.0	3.6	2.7	5.3	3.4	2.4
Registered nurses	5.5	5.2	3.5	4.9	3.6	4.3	13.8	7.0	3.4	2.8
Other health practitioners	2.8	1.9	4.1	2.1	2.0	2.6	3.1	3.1	2.6	1.8
Healthcare technicians	4.0	7.3	3.2	5.4	5.2	2.6	9.0	3.6	4.1	4.0
Teachers and other educators	14.2	15.7	11.1	14.0	14.9	11.2	10.6	6.9	10.0	12.3
Other professionals	15.3	20.1	15.1	19.7	20.2	13.2	14.8	7.6	15.3	19.7

Source: Authors' tabulations from U.S. Census 2000 microdata.

In terms of labor force characteristics, immigrant professionals are slightly less likely to work full-time and are more likely to be unemployed. The foreign-born are less likely to be employed full-time if they are educators, while natives are less likely to be working full-time if they are healthcare technicians. In terms of propensity to be self-employed, there are no overall nativity differences. However, natives and immigrants vary substantially within and across occupational groups. Not surprisingly, for both groups, physicians and other health practitioners are more likely to be self-employed than any other occupational group. For example, a third of natives and 28 percent of foreign-born physicians are self-employed. Workers in nursing, healthcare technical, and life and physical assistant occupations are the least likely to be self-employed. Among scientists and engineers, natives are somewhat more likely to work for themselves that their foreign-born counterparts.

As to earnings outcomes, previous studies indicate foreign-born professionals have higher nominal earnings than the native born (Bouvier and Martin, 1995). However, an analysis that takes into

Table 4.7
Selected Labor Force Characteristics in Occupations by Navtivity

	Average Age		Percent female		Percent employed full-time		Percent unemployed		Percent self-employed	
	Native	Foreign	Native	Foreign	Native	Foreign	Native	Foreign	Native	Foreign
Total	42.3	40.7	51.2	44.6	87.1	86.5	1.9	2.8	11.3	11.3
Management	43.2	42.1	36.9	32.6	93.3	92.1	1.9	3.0	17.0	20.3
Business/finance	41.7	40.4	54.5	54.8	90.4	89.5	2.1	3.3	11.5	10.3
Information Technology workers										
Computer scientists	40.5	37.0	35.2	27.4	94.1	94.1	2.3	2.3	7.4	6.2
Computer programmers/ engineers	39.7	35.9	26.2	27.5	95.1	94.4	2.1	2.3	5.6	3.3
Computer technical support	38.4	35.9	32.5	24.9	94.0	91.5	2.1	2.8	4.5	3.9
Math scientists & engineers	42.0	39.6	45.3	40.7	93.2	91.8	1.6	1.8	3.7	2.9
Architects & engineers	41.6	41.0	12.6	15.1	96.2	95.3	1.9	2.5	5.9	4.3
Life & physical scientists	40.8	39.4	31.5	37.2	93.0	91.5	1.8	1.6	4.7	1.5
Social scientists	43.3	41.1	55.0	50.3	81.3	84.1	1.5	3.1	23.2	14.5
Life, physical, and social science technicians/assistants	40.8	38.5	39.3	45.0	90.8	85.2	3.3	4.7	1.9	2.0
Healthcare workers										
Physicians & surgeons	43.1	43.1	26.4	31.0	92.2	92.0	0.5	1.5	31.9	28.4
Registered nurses	42.8	42.5	92.7	89.8	73.5	83.2	1.4	1.7	1.2	1.6
Other health practitioners	41.0	39.4	58.1	56.6	78.6	80.6	1.1	1.5	24.4	21.7
Healthcare technicians	40.8	41.4	80.0	71.4	77.8	82.0	2.3	3.1	1.7	2.4
Teachers and other educators	43.0	41.4	72.2	61.2	81.3	68.5	1.1	2.7	2.5	3.2
Other professionals	42.1	40.9	58.5	56.5	80.2	75.6	2.4	4.1	15.8	14.6

Source: Authors' tabulations from U.S. Census 2000 microdata.

Table 4.8
Median Income of Professionals in Occupations by Nativity ($)*

	Native-born	Earlier Immigrants	Recent Immigrants
Management	50,000	50,000	50,000
Business/finance	40,000	39,000	36,500
Information Technology workers			
Computer scientists	52,000	55,000	58,000
Computer programmers/engineers	58,000	63,000	56,000
Computer technical support	45,000	49,000	48,000
Math scientists & engineers	53,000	56,000	50,000
Architects & engineers	51,000	55,000	48,000
Life & physical scientists	48,000	50,000	30,000
Social scientists	48,000	53,000	54,000
Life, physical, and social science technicians/assistants	35,000	33,900	25,000
Healthcare workers			
Physicians & surgeons	110,000	100,000	38,500
Registered nurses	41,000	50,000	40,000
Other health practitioners	45,000	50,000	43,000
Healthcare technicians	29,000	32,000	24,800
Teachers and other educators	36,000	38,000	24,000
Other professionals	34,000	32,000	28,000

*Excluding self-employed and those who did not work full-time
Earlier Immigrants are those who arrived to the United States before 1995;
Recent Immigrants are those who arrived between 1995 and 2000

account immigrants' length of stay, e.g., their assimilation premium, indicates immigrants' higher nominal wages primarily reflects their better education compared with natives. We consider here "recent immigrants" as those who arrived between 1995 and 2000, while "earlier immigrants" are those who came to the United States before 1995. Batalova (2005) finds the higher education of recent immigrants does not necessarily translate to better achievement in the labor market. The recently arrived are significantly more likely to be unemployed as well as less likely to work full-time than either earlier immigrants or natives (results are not shown here).

Indeed, table 4.8 demonstrates with respect to the annual earnings of full-time employees (not self-employed), recent immigrants are outperformed by both natives and immigrants with a longer duration of stay. The largest earning differentials are among physicians. Earlier immigrants are better paid, on the average, than native professionals in all occupations but business/finance, physicians/surgeons, and "other" professional occupations. A wide variation in earnings exists along gender and racial-ethnic lines (the results are not shown here). For example, female professionals are paid much less than their male counterparts. Overall, recent immigrant minority women fare the worst, while white and Asian earlier immigrant women are doing better than other women. So better education does not, by and of itself, ensure higher wages for immigrants. Rather, immigrants need to accumulate U.S. labor market experience that tends to bring them nominal earnings that are higher or equal to those of natives. But the worlds of business and healthcare, apparently, do not afford immigrant professional the same earnings opportunities relative to natives.

Conclusions

The presented profile of foreign-born professionals has reinforced the image of these immigrants as being among the "best and the brightest" as well as being uniquely concentrated in certain occupations and places. First, immigrant workers in almost all professional occupations are better educated, e.g., hold higher degrees than their native counterparts. The occupations where that is not true, e.g., physicians and surgeons, have minimal educational standards which are quite high and, at least with these data, do not permit us to capture any possible differences in the quality or quantity of education. Immigrants are also much more likely to hold some of the most competitive professional occupations, being twice as likely as natives to be among computer scientists, computer engineers, and physicians; and three times as likely to be found in life and physical science jobs. Second, immigrants makeup disproportionate shares of these workforces being one-quarter of IT workers, physicians and life and physical science workers. Furthermore, while being just 11 percent of all professional workers nationwide and less than five percent in central and midwest states, the foreign-born constitute almost one-fifth of professionals in the traditional immigrant-receiving states such as California, New York, Florida, and New Jersey.

Surprisingly little is known about how these patterns of education and occupational/geographic concentration play out for immigrants. Our look at the data certainly shows immigrant professionals do not escape the assimilation costs of employment in a foreign nation. It takes time before their educational premium translates into improved earnings vis-a-vis natives. And not all professionals, apparently, face the same opportunities: immigrant physicians, on average, earn less than natives, even after a significant number of years in the United

States. We have also not examined place of education in this regard, although evidence suggests completed education in the United States better prepares immigrants for the U.S. labor market, so that their earnings are equal to natives at the outset of their working careers (Lowell, 2004b).

Surely the differential concentration of immigrants has yet a further conditioning effect on natives' and immigrants' labor market outcomes (Batalova, 2005). With certain occupations heavily impacted by a ready supply of immigrants, it raises questions about their impact on earnings and, if that impact re-sets the starting conditions for newcomers, it may send adverse market signals down the chain of supply to students in U.S. higher education. Such a chain of events could reinforce the demand for immigrants. Then again, the heavy concentration of immigrants in geographically bound labor markets may well create locally concentrated occupational niches with also mostly unexamined impacts. Nor would we conclude that concentration necessarily translates into adverse outcomes for U.S. domestic workers. Indeed, immigrant professionals may well provide the fodder for the most "frothy" labor markets as they do in IT's Silicon Valley that drove the booming "New Economy." But convincing answers to these types of questions need to be forthcoming if policymakers are to adequately understand and design immigration and labor market policies in an increasingly competitive global market for highly skilled workers.

5

Disaggregating Immigration Policy: The Politics of Skilled Labor Recruitment in the U.S.

Gary P. Freeman and David K. Hill

Generalizations about the politics of immigration policy writ large are suspect. Migration flows are multi-faceted. Different sorts of migrants create distinct migratory flows and produce diverse consequences. The migration control and recruitment programs of the leading democratic societies are, in turn, highly complex, reflecting the underlying heterogeneity of migrants and migration processes. Diverse migratory processes and the migration policies that seek to organize and control them produce diverse modes of politics.

We seek to contribute to building the theoretical and empirical base necessary to test the above propositions through a close examination of the politics of skilled labor migration programs in the United States. We focus on the recruitment of temporary, non-immigrant skilled workers in the H-1B and L-1 visa categories as well as employment-based visas available under the immigrant settlement program. Workers in both of the non-immigrant categories tend to be concentrated in the information technology sector; following that sector's rapid growth in the 1990s, temporary migration programs became sources of contention leading to the formation of novel political coalitions. The work-based categories within the immigrant settlement program, on the other hand, did not generate controversy with the same interest group configurations. We begin with an overview of the features of the main visa programs for skilled workers and show how these programs were modified in response to broad concerns over the role of skilled labor in contemporary capitalism. Next, we elaborate a theoretical framework for delineating peculiar features of different kinds of migration flows and the policies designed to manage them. Finally, we employ the framework to help account for the political processes attached to each of the three skilled migration programs.

Skilled Migration Programs in the United States

Millions of persons have migrated to the United States since the colonial period. Although their hands provided the work needed to settle a continent and build a modern economy, most were not deliberately recruited on the basis of their occupational talents or skills. However, American immigration policy has gradually shifted to emphasize the labor market qualifications of potential migrants. It currently provides for the annual admission of skilled migrants in two classifications: (a) the immigrant settlement program for individuals and their families admitted as permanent residents and (b) non-immigrant visas for temporary work in stipulated positions.

Permanent Residence Visas

The focus of American permanent residence policy has changed dramatically in the last half-century. The Immigration and Nationality Act of 1952, the first serious attempt to select immigrants on the basis of skill, introduced two innovations into U.S. policy: the preference system and the labor certification process. The preference system consists of a series of categories of immigrants, ranked according to priority and allocated different annual quotas. The first preference in the 1952 legislation reserved half of all visas annually for those with the education, technical training, special experience or exceptional abilities that were designated by the Attorney General to be beneficial to the United States. The law also authorized the Secretary of Labor to certify that the admission of non-family-related immigrants would not adversely affect the wages and working conditions of native workers who were similarly employed, although implementation of this feature was erratic (Briggs, 1996: 103).

Emphasis on employment-based visas was reduced when the immigration amendments of 1965 reordered the preference system to favor family reunification. The previous employment-based first preference was split into two parts and downgraded to the third and sixth preferences. By the time the Immigration Act of 1990 (IMMACT) was under consideration however, there was growing concern over the consequences of the family-dominated admissions program.

Worries over potential labor shortages emerged as unemployment fell, birth rates dropped below replacement and the 1986 Immigration Reform and Control Act (IRCA) threatened to shut off easy access to illegal workers. Employers complained of the 18-month wait for workers receiving permanent residency visas under the work-based third preference for professional and highly skilled workers. They also objected to   the two and one-half year wait for those entering under the sixth preference for other skilled and unskilled workers (Usdansky and Espenshade, 2001: 46). Proponents also argued that immigration reform was necessary to redress the fall in average skill level of immigrants following the 1965 legislation. They called for the recruitment of immigrants with the scientific and technical knowledge essential to the health of a modern post-industrial economy (Hudson Institute, 1987; National Center on Education and the Economy, 1990; Commission on Workforce Quality and Labor Market Efficiency, 1989). The IMMACT increased employment-based visas for permanent residence nearly three-fold to 140,000 annually plus the unused family-sponsored preference visas in the previous year. Under the IMMACT, visas are distributed across five employment categories, increasing the share going to highly skilled immigrants and their spouses and children.[1] Most immigrants in the second and third employment-based preference categories require certification from the Secretary of Labor that their arrival will not adversely affect wages and conditions of U.S. workers in the same jobs.

Employment-based entries as a share of all admissions quadrupled from 1991 to 1992 and increased again in 1993 to 16 percent. The number of employment-based visas fluctuated during 1994 to 1999, never exceeding the peak year of 1993 but still accounting for nearly 17 percent of total admissions in both 2001 and 2002. In 2003, these visas plummeted to just 82,137, or 11.6 percent of all admissions. Because dependents are counted in the skill category however, active skilled migrants made up only about half of the total of employment-based entries. (http://www.uscis.gov/graphics/shared/aboutus/statistics/Immigs.htm).

H-1B Non-immigrant Visas

The most important category of non-immigrant skilled migration, the H-1B visa, took its contemporary form after IMMACT altered the preexisting H-1 program.[2] The H-1B visa pertains solely to "spe-

cialty workers" who must have at least a bachelor's degree or equivalent experience. This visa is issued initially for a maximum of three
years and can be renewed once. As originally conceived, H-1 visa
holders could work only in positions that were themselves designated as temporary and were required to possess a domicile in their
country of origin. In 1970, Congress removed the word "temporary" before services, thus permitting H-1 workers to temporarily
take up work in permanent positions (Lowell, 2001a: 137). Currently, employers may hire H-1B workers by filing a labor condition
application with the Department of Labor (DOL) specifying the type
of work to be done and attesting they will pay the prevailing wage.

Critics charge that many of the protections for American workers
are illusory because they only apply to "H-1B dependent" firms` in
which H-1B holders make up at least 15 percent of the workforce.
Because these stipulations are based on the proportion rather than
the number of H-1B workers employed by a given company, very
large firms escape the regulations. Similarly, in the eyes of critics, this
permits the majority of firms to lawfully hire H-1Bs without properly
searching for U.S. workers in order to avoid paying temporary workers the prevailing wage and to lay off U.S. workers and replace them
with H-1B temporary workers (Matloff, 2003: 5; 2004). Because H-
1B visas are tied to the specific firms for which they are granted, if H-
1B workers wish to change jobs, they must apply for new visas. This
all but pre-empts H-1B workers from bargaining with employers over
wages, hours or working conditions. Although H-1B visa holders may
apply for permanent residence status during their term and may use
their temporary work experience to qualify for permanent residency,
H-1B holders must go through the same adjustment process as other
applicants for legal permanent residence. As the number of H-1Bs
increases, so does the processing time; and because the H-1B visa
must expire after six years, time sometimes runs out. Approved applications for legal permanent residence remain subject to the 140,000
annual limit on employment-based visas.

Many H-1B recipients work in so-called "job shops" or "body
shops" that recruit foreign workers in order to contract them out to
other American firms. Because H-1Bs constitute over 15 percent of
the workforce of such enterprises, employers must certify that they
did not lay off U.S. workers to open jobs for the H-1Bs they are
requesting and that they are paying the prevailing wage. DOL is
charged with investigating firms that bring H-1Bs into the US with-

out jobs and then fail to pay them when they have no work. Congress outlawed this practice (known as "benching") in 1998 but DOL did not issue regulations implementing the provision until January 2001 (*Migration News,* September 2002).

IMMACT imposed a 65,000 per annum cap on new H-1Bs that was not met until 1997.[3] In 1998, Senator Spencer Abraham (R-MI), the chair of the Immigration Sub-Committee of the Judiciary Committee, sparked serious opposition in the House and Senate when he introduced legislation to raise the cap. Meanwhile, the Clinton administration proposed an employer tax of $3,000 on H-1B visas with the proceeds going into worker education programs. Ultimately, Abraham managed to attach provisions to an omnibus spending bill, the American Competitiveness and Workforce Improvement Act of 1998 (ACWIA) that successfully raised the annual number of new H-1B visas from 65,000 to 115,000 in 1999 and 2000, and 107,000 in 2001, after which it was to revert to 65,000. ACWIA also instituted a $500 per visa fee to be paid by employers with the proceeds designated to support training of American workers.

The new quota was quickly filled, a backlog of petitions developed and within the year Congress heard renewed calls for expansion. Initially, there was little enthusiasm on Capitol Hill for another fight on the issue; for instance, Rep. Lamar Smith (R-TX), chair of the House Immigration Subcommittee, argued that the H-1B program was "plagued by growing fraud and that America should concentrate on producing 'more well-educated workers'" (Branigin, 1999). Yet as the 2000 election approached and support for expansion gathered, the lines of dispute shifted from whether to raise the caps, to what U.S. worker protections should be attached to the new round of visas. The White House proposed that the cap be set at 200,000 for three years, with 10,000 of that total designated for research and higher education institutions; the fee per visa would be raised to $2,000 for most companies and $3,000 for H-1B dependent firms. The proceeds would be split between worker training and education and beefing up enforcement activities of the Immigration and Naturalization Service (*Wall Street Journal,* May 12, 2000).

Representatives Zoe Lofgren (D-CA) and David Dreier (R-CA), both of whom represented IT-heavy districts, co-sponsored a bipartisan bill in the House that would raise the cap to 200,000 for three years and set the visa fee at $1,000 to fund science scholarships and worker training programs (*Wall Street Journal,* June 30, 2000). Smith, still chair of the Immigration Subcommittee, offered a less expansive alternative bill. Meanwhile, the Senate passed another Abraham authored industry-friendly bill by a wide margin. In a series of bizarre moves, the Conference Committee and the House adopted the Senate bill in its entirety, and in the process effectively chose the Lofgren-Dreier proposals over those of the Immigration Subcommittee chair. The resulting legislation, the American Competitiveness in the Twenty-first Century Act, lifted the ceiling for new H-1Bs from 115,000 to 195,000 for three years.

Due to the contraction of high technology industries in 2000, the additional visas under the new cap were not fully utilized. Between October 1999 and March 2000 about 100,000 applications were lodged, but the same period in 2001 saw only 72,000 applications. In addition, many large technology firms announced they would make substantial cuts in both permanent and temporary positions in the next year (Johnson, 2001). Similarly, although numbers rose slightly between FY 2000 and 2001, by 2003 both applications and approvals had declined by 40 percent (USDHS, 2003a: 3-4). Numbers rebounded slightly in 2003; 231,030 petitions were filed and 217,340 were approved. However, the 195,000 cap was not reached because almost all those approved for continuing employment (112,026) were not counted toward the limit (USDHS, 2003b). In October 2003, the expanded caps expired and reverted to 65,000; fees fell to $130 per visa as well. Political activity on the H-1B front declined temporarily along with the number of new applications. Harris Miller, president of the Information Technology Association of America (ITAA), a trade group representing employers, said "we don't think this is a good time for members [of Congress] to be voting on immigration matters. We hope the economy will be a lot stronger in the spring. . . . It's much easier to have a rational, fact-based conversation when the economy is stronger and unemployment is going down" (McCarthy, 2003). Instead of asking the ceiling be lifted, many high-tech firms sought wider exemptions from the ceiling. For example, it was suggested only H1-B dependent firms be subject to the annual ceiling (*Migration News,* January 2003).

In February 2004, the Department of Homeland Security (DHS) announced it had received enough H-1B petitions to fill the 65,000 cap for new workers for FY 2004 (USDHS, 2004). In an unprecedented development, the cap for FY 2005 was filled on the first day of the fiscal year (leaving small companies and start-ups in the lurch). The Omnibus Appropriations Act for FY 2005, signed by President Bush in December 2004, reinstituted the ACWIA fee and raised it to $1500, although firms hiring fewer than twenty-five employees could submit a reduced fee. Additionally, the law attached a $500 Fraud Prevention and Detection Fee to every new H-lB application or change in a beneficiary's classification. The law also exempted from the annual cap the first 20,000 H-lB beneficiaries who had earned a master's degree or higher from a U.S. institution (USCIS, 2004a).

L-1 Visas

The L-1 visa also plays prominently in discussions of temporary skilled workers. Originally established in 1970 as a means by which foreign companies with affiliates in the United States could temporarily transfer their executives to the USA, the L-1 visa was never subject to an annual cap. Generally, L-1 recipients must have been employed outside the US for at least one of the prior three years in an executive, managerial or specialized knowledge position for a qualifying related business entity. They may only seek temporary work in a similar capacity. Prior to 1990, L-visa holders were required to establish continuing non-immigrant intent; relaxation of this policy eased the path to converting their temporary status into permanent residency. The L-1 visa is good for five years if the individual is an employee with specialized knowledge, or seven years if he or she is an executive or a manager. Employers of L-1 visa holders do not have to pay the same fees required for H-1B visa holders; nor do they have to promise to pay the prevailing wage.

As demand for skilled workers put pressure on the H-1B program, companies began to resort to the L-1 category to obtain foreign skilled labor. The number of new L-1 visas increased by 50 percent from 1998 to 2002. In 2001 there were nearly as many L-1 visa holders in the US (329,000) as H-1Bs (384,000). Some critics argued that the L-1 had become "the work visa of choice" for American businesses (Endelman, 2003: 1; Esposito, 1999). The INS launched a number of investigations into firms suspected of misusing the L-1 visa (*Migration News,* July 2003). At the end of 2004, the Omnibus Appropriations Act for FY 2005 generally prohibited L-1s from working primarily at a worksite other than that of their petitioning employer. The prohibition applies only if the work in question is supervised by a different employer or if the off-site arrangement is essentially to provide labor for hire (rather than services related to the specialized knowledge of the original petitioning employer). The law also imposed a new Fraud Prevention and Detection Fee of $500 for initial L visa workers or petitions for changing an L-1's status (USCIS, 2004b).

A Framework for Analyzing Immigration Politics

How can we best make sense of the evolving politics of skilled migration? Our central premise is that specific components of large and heterogeneous immigration programs are associated with different styles of politics. We, therefore, need an analytical framework that contributes to elucidating relevant types of immigration policy. In an earlier article Freeman (1995) applied a four-part typology developed by James Q. Wilson (1973, 1980) to immigration politics, arguing that immigration tends to produce concentrated benefits and diffuse costs, yielding what Wilson terms client politics. This exposition was unsatisfactory on at least two counts (cf. Brubaker, 1995; Perlmutter, 1996; Joppke, 1998 for other criticisms). First, it failed to provide a theoretically grounded account of how immigration produces particular allocations of costs and benefits. As this deficiency is addressed in part elsewhere (Freeman, 2002), here we deal with the second problem, namely the tendency to treat immigration policy as a seamless whole, neglecting the various types of migration and the distinctive policies regulating them (cf. Meyers, 2004: 10). We undertake to remedy this problem by supplementing Wilson's framework, which already lends itself to addressing this issue, with that of Theodore Lowi (1964a).

Both Wilson and Lowi assert that different types of policy produce distinct patterns of benefit/cost allocations that, in turn, yield distinct modes of politics. The question is whether immigration policy can be meaningfully disaggregated along the lines their models suggest. Although Wilson's typology was originally intended to address only regulation, we believe its utility extends to the full range of policies explicitly described by Lowi's typology. Lowi (1964b) also deals extensively with the question of the arena in which policy decisions are made. The decision-making arena may serve to broaden or narrow the scope of conflict by affecting the interest or ability of societal interests to organize, participate and make themselves heard (Schattschneider, 1960). That various immigration policies may be formally formulated and implemented in different arenas is an idiosyncratic feature of the American case. This implies that theories stressing the importance of the political arena or "venue shopping" (Guiraudon, 2000) are likely to be particularly fruitful starting points for explaining the resultant modes of politics.

Wilson identifies four policy types based on their benefit/cost distributions that yield different modes of politics: (1) concentrated benefits and costs/*interest group politics*; (2) concentrated benefits and diffuse costs/*client politics*; (3) diffuse benefits and concentrated costs/*entrepreneurial politics*, and (4) diffuse benefits and costs/ *majoritarian politics*. Lowi's tri-partite typology includes distributive, redistributive and regulatory policies. We split Lowi's distributive category into two parts, depending on whether they entail diffuse or concentrated benefits. Concentrated distributive policies yield client politics; diffuse distributive policies yield majoritarian politics. Lowi's redistributive category closely resembles Wilson's interest group rubric, and his regulatory category fits Wilson's entrepreneurial rubric. The resulting typology is given in Table 5.1.

Wilson tends to assume the more or less direct translation of particular distributions of benefits/costs into particular modes of politics. His model, once the benefit/cost pattern is determined, generates specific testable hypotheses. Lowi takes a more constructivist view; for him, the perceptions of the main actors as to the incidence of benefits/costs are as important as empirically demonstrable effects. In the framing of political issues and the use of political rheto-

Table 5.1
A Typology of Public Policies

Benefit/Cost Allocation	Policy Type	Mode of Politics
Diffuse benefits and costs	Diffuse Distributive Policy	Majoritarian Politics
Concentrated Benefits and Diffuse Costs	Concentrated Distributive Policy	Client Politics
Concentrated Benefits and Costs	Redistributive Policy	Interest Group Politics
Diffuse Benefits and Concentrated Costs	Regulatory Policy	Entrepreneurial Politics

ric, perceptions of who is winning and who is losing from a particular policy, may change over time and may depart from expert or official judgments about the actual incidence of policies (although we assume the gap between "reality" and "perception" should not be overly large nor survive in the long run). For instance, a policy that produces client politics at one point may produce interest group politics at another. Moreover, given the obstacles to collecting the kind of data necessary to assess the consequences of public policies and the inevitability of conflicting expert claims, we examine the political dynamics around the policy and reason backwards, so to speak, to the matter of who wins or loses from the policy. Discourse over public policies often frames policy in a language of contestation. Thus, by focusing precisely on the question of winners and losers, we are afforded both a window onto the perceptions of the principal actors regarding the policy consequences and an opportunity to directly deploy, rather than impute, those perceptions in our analysis.

Specific immigration policies may display characteristics of more than one policy type simultaneously or over time. In a sense, this is true of all immigration policy components. Permanent residence visa policy may be mostly a matter of distribution but it entails some regulation as well. If family- and work-based visas are pitted against one another during legislative debate, the programs take on the qualities of redistributive politics. Because the mode of politics stimulated by a policy is dependent on changeable perceptions of key actors, our framework serves more as a device for tracking and interpreting the evolution of immigration politics than as a predictive mechanism.

One reason we focus on skilled migration, a relatively small subset of immigration policies for a relatively small sub set of migrants, is its substantive importance in the immigration politics of capitalist societies (see Lavanex, this volume; Freeman, 1999). Another reason however, is skilled migration programs present a particularly challenging case for our thesis. Few would challenge the claim asylum seeking and family reunification immigration spark substantially different political conflicts; whether the same is true for temporary and permanent skilled migration is much more debatable. We propose skill-based immigrant visas for permanent residence will tend to produce a mode of politics distinct from the temporary labor visas under discussion. We identify four key differences between these visa classes that should affect the incidence of benefits and costs: *duration* (temporary versus permanent), *specificity* (the extent to which they are targeted at particular industrial sectors), *flexibility* (how quickly and effectively they can be modified in light of changing economic circumstances), and *size*.

Work-based immigrant visas are for permanent residence. They are targeted to particular skill categories but not to specific industries or sectors. They are relatively inflexible in the sense they are infrequently modified in character or number. This occurs only within the context of a major overhaul of national immigration legislation. The program cannot be easily adapted to meet immediate labor market demand and is, therefore, presumably less easily manipulated to undercut industrial wages. Although the numbers allocated to work-based visas (140,000 annually) are roughly equivalent to those provided for temporary skilled migrants, many of the persons in the work-based immigrant category are non-working dependents of visa recipients.

The H-1B and L-1 visas are for fixed, renewable terms and do not automatically convert into permanent residence. Compared to work-based immigrant visas, the H-1B and L-1 visas are targeted to specific occupational sectors (information technology foremost but also the scientific, engineering, medical research and university sectors). As the legislative record since the mid-1990s suggests, these non-immigrant visas are more easily modified and are distributed in larger numbers than immigrant visas. Because dependents are not counted against caps, all visas go to actual workers and new entries each year must be added to those visa holders already in the country.

What are the implications of these differences for the benefit/cost consequences of these two sorts of skilled labor programs? These are not, to say the least, perfectly obvious. Duration is especially indeterminant, in our view. One might expect that visas for permanent settlement would be more controversial than those for temporary stays. In Western Europe, popular acquiescence to large-scale labor migration in the post-war period was purchased via assurances the migrants would not stay on permanently; comparable programs granting permanent residence visas would have been politically untenable (Messina, 1990). Since the cessation of the major guest worker programs, more limited temporary skilled recruitment programs in Europe have passed with relatively little public protest. On the other hand, if temporary workers are perceived by relevant sections of the public as more dispensable and easily manipulated than permanent workers, proposed increases in temporary work visas could well provoke opposition that would not apply to permanent programs. We assume programs narrowly targeted to particular skill groups or industries are more controversial than visa programs of a more general nature. Furthermore, the greater flexibility of temporary programs could make them more or less palatable, depending on whose interest is considered. To the extent the size of temporary inflows expanded during the period under consideration, this characteristic should lend controversy to those visa programs. In all, there seems some reason to anticipate that employment-based visas for permanent settlement will yield concentrated distributive policy and client politics, whereas non-immigrant visas for work should produce redistributive policy and interest group politics. These are weak predictions however, and we anticipate that whatever pattern emerges will be unstable.

Modes of Politics and Skilled Labor Migration

We turn now to the interpretation of the political dynamics of the skilled migration programs previously described. We begin with the specification of the arena in which policy is made. We consider, next, explicit discussions of the benefit/cost consequences of skilled migration, particularly as they are thought to reflect the supply of skilled labor. Perceptions of benefit/cost allocations are further documented through the analysis of trends in public opinion, the mobilization of organized groups and their aggregation by the political parties.

Decision-Making Arena

American immigration policies are generally formulated in the legislative arena. Immigration policy is laid out in statutes in highly specific language. Statutes stipulate the types of migrants who can enter the country, the procedures for issuing visas and the numbers that may be admitted. Changes in the annual quotas must be made by Congress, which has jealously guarded its prerogatives, leaving the executive much less flexibility to adjust the program to changing economic circumstances than is enjoyed by the governments of most other democracies. Within the House and Senate, authority over legislative matters is delegated to specialized committees. In the case of immigration, the Judiciary Committees have jurisdiction. They, in turn, delegate responsibility for initiating new legislation to sub-committees on immigration matters. These committees exercise substantial control over the legislative agenda with respect to immigration and decisive power over whether bills will reach the floor (Gimpel and Edwards, 1999; Oleszek, 2004).

Congressional dominance over immigration policy leads to a decision-making process that gives a prominent role to individual committee and subcommittee chairs and opens legislators to intense lobbying and to campaign contributions from interested parties. Skilled migration is neither the sole, or the most important part,of the larger immigration program and is often marginalized when Congress debates complicated immigration bills. The 1990s were unusual in that Congress addressed specific pieces of legislation dealing with skilled migration rather than rolling it into omnibus immigration legislation. This anomaly works to our advantage as policy processes that deal specifically or exclusively with skilled temporary migration present a more transparent indication of the issues and interests involved.

During recent decades, as immigration has grown in size and political salience, the White House has been drawn into immigration debates more often than in the past. Both presidents Clinton and George W. Bush have become embroiled in immigration debates. President Clinton, at first, generally endorsed the recommendations of the U.S. Commission on Immigration Reform (see below) but, under Congressional pressure, backed away from many of them. On the H-1B front, Clinton generally proposed modest protections for American workers in the form of equally modest employer fees, only some of which were adopted, in return for supporting increases in the H-1B ceiling. Soon after his 2000 election, President Bush proposed major reforms on Mexican migration and temporary worker programs. These initiatives were delayed by the events of September 11, 2001, but in the run-up to the 2004 election, he laid out bold proposals for a potentially vast, industry-friendly guest worker system alongside a liberal path to legal status for many of the estimated 8 to 12 million undocumented immigrants in the United States. Even so, immigration played almost no overt role in the presidential campaigns of the two major parties.

Other executive branch departments exercise formal authority over various aspects of the immigration program but play limited roles in the initiation or formulation of policy. Chronically under-funded and under-staffed, the Immigration and Naturalization Service (INS) has long been one of the weakest agencies in Washington, DC. Located in the Justice Department (DOJ), the agency lacked the visibility, clout and central policymaking role of the cabinet-level departments in Australia and Canada. The recent creation of the Department of Homeland Security (DHS) resulted in the duties of the INS being split between immigration control, now under the DHS, and naturalization and immigrant services which remain within DOJ. Employment-based visas begin life as petitions to the INS, which sends those it approves to the State Department for the issuance of visas. This sometimes produces intra-executive disagreement. In 1999, to give just one example, a representative of the Directorate for Visa Services in the State Department complained to the House Judiciary Committee the INS was approving unqualified candidates for L-1 and H-1B visas and the sponsoring companies existed only on paper (Esposito, 1999). As the agency that enforces labor market protection features of the law, the Department of Labor's certification office also participates in the process.

A notable feature of the immigration policy arena is the establishment of special commissions by Congress. The recommendations of the Select Committee on Immigration and Refugee Policy (SCIRP) in 1981 set the early agenda that eventually produced the 1986 Immigration Reform and Control Act (IRCA). As mandated by the 1990 IMMACT, the US Commission on Immigration Reform produced several influential reports. However, due to outside events and changes in the political mood, Congress never enacted the Commission's main recommendations calling for: reducing the number of annual legal immigrants; creating a national identity card and stepping up enforcement of employer sanctions to reduce illegal immigration; eliminating some family preference categories; imposing labor market tests for most skilled immigrants; and eliminating immigrant visas for unskilled workers (USCIR, 1994, 1995, 1997). With respect to temporary workers, the Commission proposed reorganizing visa categories to submit more non-immigrant workers to extensive and tough "specified labor market protection standards" (USCIR, 1997: 89). Some of these issues were at the center of Congressional debates over the H-1B visa program in the late-1990s.

The courts have played a contradictory role in the evolution of U.S. immigration policy. On the one hand, the Supreme Court has held that the Congress enjoys plenary powers over immigration matters and, following that principle, the courts have given Congress wide latitude to make policy. On the other hand, the detailed nature of immigration statutes limits administrative discretion and encourages litigation on behalf of individuals who believe particular policies or individual decisions are inconsistent with statutory requirements. A large, engaged immigration bar affects policy via lawsuits and also through active lobbying for reform (Schuck, 1998). The courts were not seriously involved in the skilled labor controversies we consider.

Benefit/Cost Allocation and Issue Definition

Who wins and who loses when foreigners are given permanent residency visas under the employment preference or receive nonimmigrant visas under the H-1B or L-1 programs? This question is central to the Wilson/Lowi framework but not readily answered. Economists have long debated whether foreign labor is a substitute for, or a complement to, national labor (Ethier, 1996; on the impact of H-1B workers on the employment and wages of native workers, see Gurcak, et al., 2001; Booz, Allen, and Hamilton, Inc., 1988; Borjas, 2004). Sorting out the differences between the various camps in this controversy is beyond the scope of this paper. Instead, we address the political dynamics of the debate over the supply and demand for skilled labor and the benefits, costs and consequences of skilled migration in the United States.

Whether there is a shortage of scientists and engineers in the US is a question that goes back at least to the 1950s with the launching of the Soviet satellite, Sputnik. The shock of that event led to national soul-searching and a renewed emphasis on spending on education in the sciences and engineering. Discussion of educational decline and skills shortages gathered steam again in the 1980s with the release of a study by the National Commission on Excellence in Education (1983) that identified glaring inadequacies in the training of American scientists and engineers. In addition, the National Science Foundation (NSF) began to issue forecasts of major shortfalls of scientists and engineers over the next decade. In 1992, a Congressional Subcommittee held hearings on the predictions; its Chair, Howard Wolpe (D-MI), sharply criticized the office in the NSF responsible for the studies (U.S. Congress, 1992). Teitelbaum (2003) has recently extended these critiques, charging the initial studies (e.g., NSF, 1987) were not only riddled with methodological errors but also based on faulty data. In the late-1990s, nevertheless, new studies trumpeting current or projected shortages began to appear. In 2002, an Information Technology Association of America (ITAA) study found that, notwithstanding that the economic downturn of the late 1990s resulted in IT firms losing 15 percent of their IT workers in 2001, there would be 578,711 unfilled positions in 2002 because of a lack of qualified workers (ITAA, 2002; cf. Kazmierczak, 2005; United States Department of Commerce, 1998). In contrast, a 2004 Rand Corporation survey of existing research concluded: "Despite recurring concerns about potential shortages of (scientific, technical, engineering and mathematics) personnel in the U.S. workforce, particularly in engineering and information technology, we did not find evidence that such shortages have existed at least since 1990, nor that they are on the horizon" (Butz, et al., 2004: Summary xv). A Congressionally commissioned National Research Council study reached more or less the same conclusions (National Research Council, 2000; cf. Hira, 2005).

In addition to empirical disagreements and methodological complaints, critics of labor shortage claims point to the questionable provenance of many of the studies finding acute shortages. Teitelbaum (2003) observes that "Most of the assertions of current or impending shortages, gaps or shortfalls have originated from four sources: university administrators and associations; government agencies that finance basic and applied research; corporate employers of scientists and engineers and their associations; and immigration lawyers and their associations." These groups, he notes, have a "broad commonality of interests" in keeping the supply of scientists and engineers in surplus in order to keep the costs of their payrolls down (cf. Weinstein, nd). One of the most important players is the Government-University-Industry-Research Roundtable (GUIRR), a creature of the National Academies of Science, Engineering, and Medicine, that brings together leaders in business, higher education and government (Jackson, 2003).[4]

Debates over shortages, whatever their empirical merit, are almost always won by those claiming shortfalls. A reading of the history of discussions of skill shortages in the U.S. leaves the impression that they are less a scientific question to be determined by demographic and economic analysis, than a political question to be resolved through rhetorical and institutional means. As Cornelius and his colleagues (2001: 8) observe: "What cannot be questioned is that, in the United States and virtually all other major labor importing countries today, the political process invariably operates to legitimize employer demand for high–skilled foreign labor..." Employers, whether in industry, government or universities, are better situated to marshal data and attract an audience.

Arrayed against these interests are influential intellectuals like Teitelbaum; professional associations representing high-tech workers; a few maverick professors (Weinstein, nd; Matloff, 2003, 2004); a handful of immigration study centers like the Center for Immigration Studies (Camarota, 2001); a few organizations critical of U.S. immigration policy such as the Federation of American Immigration Reform; and some highly engaged websites spawned by laid-off tech workers such as zazona.com.

Disagreements about potential shortages are simply prologue however, to fights over what to do about them. Most major studies finding shortages call for greater investment in national education to attract more native students to scientific and engineering careers. They stress the need to nourish the talents of women and underrepresented minorities but they also advocate drawing on the international supply of scientists and engineers through the recruitment of foreigners. Migration is perhaps the most obvious and direct remedy for a shortage of skilled labor. Migration is also a solution to skill shortages that does not require raising the pay of professionals. Whether foreign workers displace or compete with native workers, or complement them, depends on labor market dynamics and whether there is a shortage of particular skills at a given time. If shortages are real, as one scenario has it, employers will be unable to find the workers they need, production will suffer and native workers could feel the negative effects. Imported labor, therefore, may complement native workers. If shortages are real, according to another scenario, absent immigration, employers will raise the wages of skilled workers, eventually attracting more natives to acquire those skills in demand. In yet another scenario, regardless of whether shortages are real or bogus, the importation of foreign workers could have the effect of displacing native workers and/or holding down wages and working conditions and, in the process, discouraging investments in education and training. For some economists, there can be no significant long-term shortage of particular skills if the market for labor is allowed to operate; rising wages will draw persons to the fields where demand is strong. For employers, the inability to find workers as soon as they are needed constitutes de facto evidence of a shortage; for them, the supply of skilled workers is never large enough. These shifting and multi-faceted arguments formed the intellectual backdrop to Congressional debate over the IMMACT in 1990 and shaped perceptions of a potential skills crisis (Lowell, 2001a: 149).

Public Opinion and Organized Interests

Public opinion on immigration policy in the United States has been relatively stable for many years. Although data on public attitudes is thin—the questions posed are simple and there is little continuity across time in their wording—one is safe in saying that most Americans think either that current levels of immigration are too high or about right; only small minorities support increasing migration (Lynch and Simon, 2003; Fetzer, 2000; NPR, 2004). More detailed information about attitudes on specific types of migration is generally unavailable. Gimpel and Edwards (1999) provide a good summary of American views of immigration policy choices in the 1990s. They conclude, first, that from 1992 to 1994 the country moved toward a consensus favoring reductions in the numbers of legal immigrants admitted annually (p. 37). Second, the less educated and the less skilled were more likely to fear the economic consequences of immigration than those better placed in the job market (p. 39), giving attitudes toward immigration a class dimension. Third, and for our purposes, most importantly, although Americans typically had skeptical views about immigration, it was not an issue that drove individual decisions at the ballot box (pp. 41-45). This helps account for the otherwise puzzling fact that despite an absence of public support for increased levels of immigration, Congress has repeatedly passed expansive legislation over the last forty years. In part because immigration is absent from the agendas of electoral campaigns at the national level, the public has scant opportunity to affect the policy process between elections. Generally, opinion on immigration constitutes a modestly constraining framework within which politicians operate.

Despite this general pattern, in certain circumstances popular discontent with the immigration policy decisions of elected representatives can be activated in state or local races. Several of the principal actors in the H-1B debate faced such challenges. In 2000, Senator Spencer Abraham (R-MI) was unseated in a campaign that attracted well-organized opposition, and major contributions from out of state, that targeted Abraham as a pro-immigration zealot. The campaign was led by individuals and organizations associated with Dr. John Tanton, the founder of the Federation for American Immigration Reform (Zogby, 2000). In 2004, Representative David Dreier (R-CA) was selected by a popular Los Angeles talk show to be a "Political Human Sacrifice" because of his liberal votes on immigration matters, resulting in his narrowly winning re-election (http://www.johnandkenshow.com/). On the other side, Rep. Tom Tancredo (R-CO) was targeted by a 527 committee (Coloradans for Plain Talk) because of his outspoken advocacy of tougher immigration controls which, the group claimed, "crossed the line from politics of the far right to the politics of racism" (*Denver Post*, October 20, 2004). Tancredo won re-election but with a reduced margin.

More relevant than mass attitudes are the activities of organized groups seeking to influence both public opinion and public officials. Following the Wilson/Lowi framework, there are four possible patterns of immigration politics: client, majoritarian, interest group and entrepreneurial politics. Freeman (1995) argues elsewhere that given low public salience, collective action problems and avid interest on the part of groups supporting various aspects of the U.S. program, there is a general tendency for immigration politics in the United States to follow the client pattern. Nonetheless, there was evidence in the mid-1990s of a shift toward entrepreneurial/populist politics concerning illegal migration and the attendant welfare costs intruded into the system (Freeman, 2001). How does the pattern of political contestation over employment-based visas since the late 1980s fit into these categories?

One of the most important legacies of the fight over IMMACT was the creation of a new political coalition promoting expansionist immigration policies that remained robust throughout the 1990s and played a major role in the H-1B conflicts. The key characteristic of the coalition members was that they came from both the left and right of the political spectrum, joining Republicans and Democrats who might normally be on opposing sides of political issues. On the left, the coalition was composed of liberal-labor groups supporting family immigration, refugee advocacy organizations, civil libertarians (e.g., the ACLU) and ethnic-specific civil rights groups such as the Mexican American Legal Defense and Educational Fund (MALDEF) and La Raza Unida. On the right, it consisted of influen-

tial business organizations such as the National Association of Manu-
facturers (NAM), the National Chamber of Commerce, the American Business Roundtable, the American Council on International
Personnel (Fragomen, 1999), the Semiconductor Industry Association (Hatano, 1998), economic libertarians such as scholars at the
Cato Institute and Christian conservatives. The nation's research and
educational institutions were also actively engaged in efforts to retain, expand and adapt the H-1B program. These included the American Council on Education, the Association of American Universities, the College and University Personnel Association, the Association of International Educators, the Council of Graduate Schools and
the National Association of State Universities and Land-Grant Colleges (Lariviere, 1998).

That immigration politics produces strange bedfellows is hardly a
novel observation (Tichenor, 2002: 8-9; Krikorian, 2004). But, while
immigration politics routinely produces coalitions cutting across
partisan and ideological lines, each new manifestation of this tendency involves new players and mixtures of interest, party and ideology. The battle over immigration reform in the 102nd through the
104th Congresses (1991 to 1996) and the H1-B controversies which
began in earnest in 1997 were closely connected to the high-tech
boom which marked the entrance of the technology sector into immigration policy advocacy. This broadened considerably the range
of business interests actively engaged in immigration policy debates.
At first a temporary operation launched by a few high-tech companies, the high-tech lobby is now institutionalized and appears to have
become a permanent feature of the immigration policy landscape.

At the center of the new left-right coalition were Frank Sharry and
Rick Swartz. Sharry was the Executive Director of the National Immigration Forum, a pro-immigration lobby Swartz had founded in
1982 and on whose board he sat. By the mid-1990s, Swartz was an
influential Washington lobbyist who headed his own firm and was
also president of Public Strategies, Inc. These old friends and their
associates were able to mobilize high-tech industries that had previously shown little interest in Washington, DC, let alone in lobbying
Congress. Their chief organizational vehicle was a newly created
organization called American Business for Legal Immigration
(ABLI).[5] This group was supported by such firms as Microsoft,
Intel, Sun Microsystems, Motorola and Texas Instruments (Gimpel
and Edwards, 1999: 243-244). Jennifer Eisen, formerly with the

American Immigration Lawyers Association (AILA) moved over to spearhead this group. In 1996, the coalition was instrumental in the successful effort to split the Smith/Simpson immigration reform bill that had sought to deal with both legal and illegal immigration. This decision was critical to defeating the bill's most restrictive proposals with regard to legal immigration (Heileman, 1996).

High-tech interests were aided by the unusual influence that India and Indian-Americans exercise in the Congress though the bi-partisan Congressional Caucus on India & Indian-Americans. In 2002 Indians made up half of all H-1Bs and 90 percent of computer-related H-1Bs (*Migration News*, November 2002) and the India Caucus, founded in the House in 1993, was the largest in Congress. The Caucus was chaired in the 108th Congress by a New York Democrat and a South Carolina Republican. In March 2004, the Senate established its own India Caucus with co-chairs Hillary Rodham Clinton (D-NY) and John Cornyn (R-TX). Transnational influence is not limited to the India Caucuses; the National Association of Software and Service Companies (NASSCOM), an Indian trade association, also lobbied Congress actively on the H-1B issue (Bagchi, 2004).

Although those in favor of expanding access to foreign labor through either permanent residence visas or temporary admission won the day, they did so only after several near defeats. The pro-immigration side enjoyed the advantages of well-heeled corporations and highly organized and effective lobbying operations with long-standing relationships on Capitol Hill.[6] Opposition was much less well situated and coordinated but benefited from the large number of conservative Republicans in the Congress, both chambers of which the party controlled after 1994. However, the Republicans were, themselves, badly split on immigration.

Traditionally, the trade union movement was at the forefront of those interests opposing more liberal immigration policies, yet, by the 1990s, this, too, had begun to change. In the face of declining membership, unions representing sectors with large numbers of undocumented immigrants began to push the leadership of the AFL-CIO toward rethinking their strategy and, in February 2000, the labor federation did just that. It announced support for the abolition of employer sanctions against employers knowingly hiring unauthorized workers and called for a blanket amnesty for the huge undocumented population. Shortly thereafter, an unprecedented meeting of business and labor union officials was convened in Washington DC to work out common positions on immigration matters. Among those groups present were the Essential Workers Immigration Coalition which, despite its name, is a business association committed to greater access to medium and low-skilled foreign workers; and several unions including the Service Employees International Union (SEIU), the United Farm Workers, the Hotel Employees and Restaurant Employees International Union and the Union of Needletrades, Textiles and Industrial Employees. These latter two federations are currently merged as UNITE (see Watts, 2002: 145). At the moment, it appears the union movement is quite open to embracing low-skilled immigrant workers.

On the question of the H-1B and L-1 programs, organized labor takes a much more traditional position. In March 2004, the Executive Council of the AFL-CIO said that such programs "are in effect transfer pipelines that enable foreign professionals to gain knowledge and come here and then take them [sic], along with American jobs, when they return home" (AFL-CIO, 2004). The Federation's Department for Professional Employees lobbied Congress against increases in H-1B ceilings throughout the last decade. The Federation's position is that employers should be prevented from laying-off U.S. workers and replacing them with H-1B workers and should be required to recruit and train U.S. workers to fill jobs (Smith, 1998).

The American labor movement is decentralized, and individual professional and trade union associations representing high-tech labor have taken the lead in opposing H-1B expansion. The most active include the Institute of Electrical and Electronics Engineers (IEEE), Washington Alliance of Technology Workers (Washtech) and the American Engineering Association (AEA). Washtech was founded in 1998 by Microsoft contract employees and is affiliated with the Communication Workers of America. The AEA dates from 1978 and describes itself on its website as a non-profit professional association committed to the protection of high-wage American technology jobs. H-1B workers themselves are marginal to public debates about the program. However, the Immigrant Support Network is a loosely coordinated group representing H-1B workers that seeks to secure bargaining power, human rights and more direct avenues to legal permanent residence (Konrad, 2001).

The chief organization devoted to reforming American immigration policy in a restrictive direction is the Federation for American Immigration Reform (FAIR). FAIR engages in active lobbying of Congress and its representatives are fixtures in the media commenting on immigration matters. FAIR has been extremely active in contesting the validity of claims of a shortage of high tech workers and in resisting raising the cap on H-lBs (see www.fairus.org). The Center for Immigration Studies, a Washington DC research center linked to FAIR, is the source of considerable research and commentary, mostly overtly critical, of expansive immigration policies (Vaughan, 2003).

Political Parties and Skilled Migration Politics

The explanation for the substantial opposition encountered by proponents of the expansion of employment-based visas, particularly the H-1Bs, is to be found not so much in the lobbying activities of these associations critical of immigration, but in the restrictive impulses of many Republican members of the Congress. The Republican sweep of 1994 brought into office a host of ideologically conservative lawmakers. Many favored more open immigration policies as part of their general pro-business, open markets ideology but others advocated tighter control of the borders and greater protection of American jobs (Rae, 1998). The election of George W. Bush accentuated Republican division on immigration as evidenced by the unexpected torrent of intra-party criticism unleashed by his early 2001 expansionist proposals (Edsall, 2001).

The leader of the restrictive wing of the Republican Party in Congress was Tom Tancredo (R-CO), a three-term lawmaker who was reportedly told by Bush adviser Karl Rove "do not darken the door of the White House" due to his challenge to the president on immigration and other issues (*Denver Post*, October 20, 2004). Tancredo founded the seventy-two-member Congressional Immigration Reform Caucus as well as Team America, a fund-raising vehicle dedicated to sending to Congress persons committed to "defending our borders" (www.campaigncontribution.com).

Although the Republicans in the House and Senate were split over immigration, key votes on immigration matters from 1995 to the present have, nonetheless, followed party lines. Gimpel and Edwards argue the chief characteristic of Congressional decision-making on immigration in the 1990s was increasing partisanship: "immigration policy has grown both increasingly controversial and partisan. The

Congress that sat between January 1995 and January 1997 was one of the most partisan in history. Predictably, most of the floor votes on immigration policy show strong lines of party cleavage even after other variables are taken into account" (Gimpel and Edwards, 1999: 285).

Conclusion

The politics of skilled migration has intensified in the last two decades amid growing concern over the quality and quantity of scientific and engineering talent being produced by the American educational system and the burgeoning significance of a global competition for talent. This chapter has considered some of the key developments in this regard, starting with the 1990 Immigration Act and following a series of legislative battles over the importation of highly skilled non-immigrant workers. What conclusions about the modes of skilled immigration politics does this narrative support?

While there is significant overlap between the general or broad politics of immigration policy and the specific politics of skilled migration, the issues are to a considerable extent handled separately and the disaggregation of the immigration policy process seems likely to continue if not accelerate. The overlap is evident in the importance of key lawmakers and certain broadly focused immigration lobby groups involved in almost all immigration questions. But it is also clear that, even given the logrolling that was necessary to build the left-right coalition in 1990 and to hold it together thereafter, some coalition members have narrowly construed interests. Associations representing high-tech firms are not likely to expend political capital on refugee issues, for example; nor do they evince much interest in undocumented farm workers. Political convenience may suggest occasional alliances behind a more comprehensive immigration agenda but they are otherwise likely to keep their attention on issues closer to home. The trend toward the disaggregation of immigration policy making has been evident at least since SCIRP issued its findings in 1981 and IRCA passed in 1986 but the watershed event may have been the splitting of the Simpson bill in 1998. By separating the discussion of legal and illegal immigration policy, this tactic allowed restriction-minded legislators to support tough measures at the border and to later vote to open the tap for H-1Bs. The emergence of security as a key element in immigration policy since the attacks of September 2001 increases the tendency to separate consideration of border controls and undocumented immigration from other issues.

Although employment-based immigrant and non-immigrant visas raise many of the same issues, it is apparent immigrant visas are less controversial and less salient to key interest groups and the public. It has been fourteen years since the employment preference of IMMACT was last altered. In the same period, the H-1B program has been more or less continually in play in the Congress. This is not because employment-based immigrant visas are more contentious than temporary visas for work; the employment preference of IMMACT is integrated into the overall preference system and is, consequently, more difficult to change. The only way the employment category could be altered is as part of a general overhaul of the immigration act. Moreover, any change in the numbers of work visas has immediate implications for family-based immigrant visas and activates the large and powerful family lobby. Raising the number of employment-based visas may imply a trade-off with the family category. In 1990, this was finessed, to the frustration of the bill's initiators, by increasing the size of both the employment and the family categories. Because temporary work visas do not compete with family migration, the left-right coalition was able to sustain itself throughout the H-1B conflict. Although their main interests did not always converge, business interests and the family lobby did not have mutually exclusive goals.

Critics of the H-1B program, on the other hand, emerge from radically different camps. Exclusionist groups (FAIR, for example) oppose current levels of permanent immigration and oppose the H-1B program, in part, because they believe it leads to permanent immigration. Disaffected American workers in the technology sector oppose the H-1B program because it is responsible, in their view, for their economic troubles. Various demographers and academics critique the H-1B program because they question the validity of claims of a skilled worker shortage. Humanitarian and immigrant rights groups complain the H-1B program leads to the exploitation of temporary workers. This diverse set of groups has little in common. They do not all rank H-1B reform at the top of their concerns, often disagree vehemently on what should be done and do not have common views on other immigration issues.

Work-based programs have clients, and these clients have gotten what they wanted on the whole, but this has not always produced client politics. Evidence that client groups have been largely successful in their main battles includes: (1) increasing the employment-based preference category in IMMACT; (2) persuading Congress to raise the H-1B ceiling twice since 1998; (3) defeating the imposition of most of the proposed protections for American workers affected by the recruitment of H-1Bs; and (4) preventing discussion of more extensive rights for H-1B holders from reaching the public arena. The client mode seems a relatively good fit for employment-based immigrant visas, although our reservations with respect to our initial hypothesis for this program seem to be borne out by the ambiguity of the evidence from our case study. The linkage between the employment preference and the family preference pushes the politics of employment-based immigrant visas toward the client mode but their potential redistributive consequences for native workers elicit the attention of organizations representing those likely to bear those costs.

Too much opposition developed around H-1Bs to justify fitting the politics of temporary skilled non-immigrant visas into the client category, where it certainly belonged when the H visa category was invented in 1952 and, in 1990, when the H-1B was hived off. These programs seem increasingly to be perceived by most actors as redistributive and, hence, produce a robust form of interest group politics. Organizations on both sides clearly identified themselves as winners and losers, depending on the outcomes adopted by Congress. Those groups advocating expanded recruitment of temporary workers won the day but those on the losing side were loud and made themselves heard. The outcome in Congress was often in doubt and, on both occasions when the H-1B caps were lifted, the change was temporary. The losers lacked strong allies apart from the trade union federations, which were not well-established in high-tech industries and feared alienating their newest and fastest growing constituency among undocumented immigrants. Unemployed technology workers proved difficult to organize; angry web sites were a good way to let off steam but had little political payoff. Democrats in Congress were more sympathetic to the plight of native workers than Republicans but they lost control of both chambers of Congress and the White House in the period under review. Given their weak organizational base, the anti-H-1B groups relied on entrepreneurs to organize the losers–FAIR, targeted campaigns to defeat immigration liberals and politicians like Tom Tancredo and Lamar Smith.

In sum, temporary skilled migration programs evoked significant strands of client, interest group and entrepreneurial politics, in different combinations. The resulting amalgam might best be labeled 'asymmetrical interest group politics' given the disproportionate influence of the pro-immigration forces. There were entrenched interests on both sides but the expansionists enjoyed major advantages. They were significantly aided by the booming high-tech economy of the late-1990s, but appear to have survived even the devastating technology recession since 2000. When the technology sector recovers, claims of skills shortages will be more plausible than ever and a more straightforward client politics may reassert itself.

Notes

1. The five categories were (1) priority workers including individuals with extraordinary ability, outstanding professors and researchers and certain multinational executives and managers (40,000); (2) immigrants with advanced degrees or exceptional ability (40,000); (3) professionals and skilled and unskilled workers (40,000, only 10,000 of whom may be unskilled); (4) special immigrants (10,000), and (5) investor immigrants (10,000). See Papademetriou and Yale-Loehr (1996).

2. The Immigration and Nationality Act of 1952 created the H-1 visa for a variety of professionals, from nursing to entertainment. Generally speaking, the H-1 visa, which had no cap, provided few protections for American workers against foreign competition and this was a key element in motivating Congress to reorganize the temporary visa programs in 1990.

3. The cap pertains only to new visas issued annually. Since recipients can stay up to six years if their visa is renewed, the actual number of H-1B workers in the country at anytime is far greater. The 65,000 cap is also a floor below which U.S. policy may not go in accordance with negotiations under the General Agreement on Trade in Services to which the U.S. became a signatory in 1994. Unlike the cap on employment-based visas in the permanent immigration program, the 65,000 cap does not apply to the families of the H-1B visa holders, whose numbers are not limited.

4. According to its website, GUIRR is an organization that "provides a platform for leaders in science and technology from government, academia and business to discuss and take action on scientific matters of national importance. These include issues facing partnerships between government, universities and industry, the academic research enterprise, training of the scientific workforce and the effects of globalization on U.S. research." It was created in 1984 and is sponsored by the National Academies.

5. ABLI is now known as Compete America (www.competeAmerican.org), according to whose website it is an organization of over 200 corporations, universities, research institutions and trade associations.

6. High-tech firms were generous in donating to electoral campaigns. Computer and Internet companies gave $8.8 million in political action committees, soft money and individual contributions during the 1995 to 1996 election cycle and $38 million in 2000 (Center for Responsive Politics, 2002).

6

Interests and Institutions in Skilled Migration: Comparing Flows in the IT and Nursing Sectors in the U.S.

Jeannette Money and Dana Zartner Falstrom

Most of the recent literature in the United States on skilled migration focuses on "high tech" workers in the information technology sector. Yet, at the same time, to the extent labor shortages existed in the information technology sector, similar shortages were visible for other highly skilled workers such as registered nurses. This chapter examines the disparate outcomes of skilled migration policy in the United States involving different economic sectors. Labor market demands are not automatically translated into immigration flows. Rather, we argue, geographically concentrated political support for, and opposition to, immigration is filtered through national political institutions to produce the actual flows of migrants. Thus, there is nothing particularly distinctive about skilled migration politically.

Support for skilled migrants is driven, as for other types of voluntary economic migration, by the inability of domestic employers to attract a sufficient supply of domestic labor. Opposition to skilled migrants is generally less than for other types of migrants because skilled migrants generate less competition with the host country residents over social services and issues of societal identity. Therefore, when support is geographically concentrated in swing constituencies, it is likely that states will facilitate skilled migratory flows. The thesis is supported by a comparison of policies adopted by the United States for registered nurses (RNs) and information technology (IT) workers in the 1990s.

The argument and evidence are presented in seven sections. In the first section, we pose the empirical puzzle by presenting evidence of labor shortages for two types of skilled workers that generated different policy responses. In section two, the similarities of sectoral labor market conditions are elaborated, ensuring the comparison is an appropriate one. In section three, we review proposed theories of migration politics and extend these theories to include a spatial component, a detailed specification of interests, a time component, and an institutional element. In the fourth section, skilled migration is examined in light of these interests and a research hypothesis generated. Section five applies this theoretical framework to the high technology industry in the United States in the late 1990s. Section six applies the framework to the nursing profession in the United States during the same time frame. We conclude in section seven.

The Empirical Puzzle

During the late 1990s, there were frequent reports of "skills shortages" in the United States as well as in other advanced market-economy countries (Iredale, 2001: 20). In the United States, the period of the 1990s was a period of economic growth; the economy flourished, pushed in significant part by the rapidly growing "high tech" sector,[1] and unemployment fell to record low rates across many industries. Skilled workers of all types were in demand but complaints about the absence of an adequate labor force to meet demand was especially vociferous for high tech workers in information technology and for registered nurses. These two professions are similar on a number of dimensions.

a.   Despite changes in legislation during our time period (1990s), these two groups remained under the same umbrella non-immigrant category, the H category, designed for skilled workers and other select temporary workers coming to the United States.

b.   Visas for both groups require the foreign worker to meet minimal job requirements/levels of skill.

c.   Both sectors (nurses and high-tech specialty workers) reported employee shortages during the period from 1990 to 2000.

d.   Both classifications have provisions in place designed to protect U.S. workers from foreigners filling vacant positions at a lower salary.

e.   Both sectors saw Congressional action in passing legislation throughout this time period.

f.   There was international competition for both information technology professionals and nurses (Iredale, 2001: 19).

Despite these similarities, however, the H-1B worker program received favorable Congressional action in the form of a larger quota and other terms and conditions during the 1990s, while the H-1A nurses experienced the opposite—tighter restrictions and quotas and eventually the end of the H-1A program and its replacement four years later with a much more restrictive program. Table 6.1 presents the different flows of high tech workers and RNs that reflect these policy choices, rather than underlying labor market demands. In 2001, for example, 384,191 H-1B workers were admitted to the United States, approximately 70 percent of which were high tech workers, while during the same year (US INS 2001b), only 627 registered nurses were admitted (US INS, 2001a). In 2001, only twenty-nine registered nurses were admitted under the new H-1C program. Thus the empirical puzzle focuses on the similar labor market shortages met with dissimilar policy responses.

Sectoral Similarities

The comparison of registered nurses and information technology workers is appropriate only if conditions affecting the supply and demand for highly skilled workers in the two sectors are similar. The evidence presented above, and elaborated below, suggests that the demand for skilled workers in the two sectors was vociferous.

Table 6.1
Entry of High Tech Workers and Registered Nurses

YEAR	H-1B WORKERS ADMITTED TO THE US	H-1A NURSES ADMITTED TO THE US
1989	89,864	
1990	100,446	Admissions began in Oct.
1991	144,467	2,130
1992	110,223	7,176
1993	92,795	6,506
1994	105,899	6,105
1995	117,574	6,512
1996	144,458	2,046
1997	240,947	551
1998	302,326	534
1999	355,605	565
2000	384,191	627

Source: US INS 2001c

The actual "shortage" of skilled workers in either sector is a matter of active debate. Freeman and Hill (this volume) cite reports from reputable institutions, Rand Corporation and the National Research Council, denying the existence of shortages of highly skilled workers in engineering and information technology while other researchers reported significant shortages. Statistics for nursing reveal a similar picture. The 1996 National Survey of Registered Nurses reported a total registered nurse population of 2,558,874, of which only 59 percent were employed full time as nurses. Of the remainder, 23.6 percent were employed part-time (twenty hours or less); 1.4 percent were seeking nursing employment, 4.3 percent were employed in non-nursing occupations, and 11.6 percent were not actively seeking employment. The registered nurse labor force could be expanded by 29 percent if all those not employed full-time became employed full-time—this in light of a reported 6 percent shortage in nurses (Unites States Department of Health and Human Services, 2003). Moreover, the nursing "shortage" experienced during the late 1990s and early 2000s was, in fact, filled to a large extent by older nurses (above the age of fifty) returning to the workforce, enticed by a significant increase in nursing wages. Two-thirds of the 100,000 increase in hospital employment of RNs from 2001 to 2002 was filled by this group of RNs; the remaining one-third was filled by foreign-born nurses (Buerhaus et al., 2003). So the debate over shortages and the need for immigrant workers is a political one: labor market shortages exist under the prevailing labor market conditions.

The supply position of the two industries was also similar. Batalova and Lowell (this volume) indicate the difficulty in clearly defining "highly skilled" workers, but a common characteristic is the higher levels of human capital reflected in the education and work experience of the skilled migrant. The human capital component suggests a potential supply problem in both the local labor market—time is required to produce a larger supply of individuals with the appropriate human capital—as well as the international labor market, which requires a supply of labor with the appropriate human capital.

From the perspective of the international labor market, an international labor supply responds to national labor market demands—in much the same way that the demand for illicit drugs creates a supply. The incentives provided by salary differentials between developed and developing countries (and to a lesser extent by differences in salary and the salary package mix among developed countries) create a supply of skilled professionals (Iredale, 2001).[2] This process is facilitated by the "internationalization" of professions: a "convergence towards international standards and procedures away from nationally defined standards and national forms of regulation," a process that may also be described as "westernization" or "Americanization," given that standards converge on those of advanced market-economy countries (Iredale, 2001: 21). Although Iredale acknowledges differences among professions and states that "IT professions and industry are relatively free of national or professional controls while the medical and nursing professions are relatively nation and profession bound," she also acknowledges "nursing is also becoming a more universal occupation."

Individuals invest in developing a set of internationally recognized skills to take advantage of these salary differentials, either through private or public education channels. Some governments of developing countries even see these individuals as promoting development goals and facilitate skilled migration. The Philippines is well known for a government strategy of educating nurses to developed country standards as a means of enlarging the pool of remittances received from expatriate labor, pulling even those trained as doctors into the nursing emigration loop (Brush et al., 2004). Other developing countries and Soviet successor states are beginning to follow the Philippines' example (Aiken et al., 2004).

The matching of national labor market demands with an international labor supply has been facilitated by the growth of intermediaries. Agencies have sprung up to handle professional migration placement—a now lucrative market (see Brush et al., 2004 for nurses). Informal migrant networks also develop to facilitate the flow of skilled migrants. And multinational corporations serve as intermediaries by creating internal labor markets that are not bounded by national borders (Lavenex, this volume). They hire in multiple national locations and then transfer employees across national boundaries, all within the same corporation.

The human capital requirements for skilled migration thus do not constrain the provision of skilled migrants and appropriate intermediaries have responded to market opportunities in both information technology and health services. For this reason, the differences in policy outcomes cannot be attributed to either domestic or international labor market conditions. Hence, we turn our focus to the political dynamics of immigration policy.

The Politics of Immigration Control

Much of the literature addresses the determinants of flows from the perspective of individual migrants and the firms that employ migrants, leaving aside the policy choices of states that govern those flows or, at best, placing these factors in the equation as a cost to migrants and employers. This research begins with issues of labor market supply and demand (Iredale, 2001); Massey et al., (1987) and others focus on migrant networks and the process of linking initial migration to subsequent migration. Yet other analysts focus on the micro components supporting international labor flows: the nature of careers, the role of intra-company labor markets and the lubrication provided by recruitment and relocation agencies (Salt, 1997). All of these theories may be useful for understanding the social and economic processes that affect migration flows, but they do not address the political process governing migration policies. Therefore we need to focus directly on theories of migration policy.

There are three alternative approaches to analyzing the politics of immigration policy, that can be viewed as either competing or complementary: human rights (Hollifield, 1992a), international factors (Rosenblum, 2003, Rudolph, 2003), and domestic politics (Freeman, 1995; Money, 1997, 1999). Because skilled migration generates few human rights issues or international responses, I focus on the approach developed by Freeman (1995) and extended and elaborated by Freeman and Hill in this volume. Freeman develops a typology of immigration politics determined by the distribution of costs and benefits. Where policy benefits are concentrated and costs are diffuse, the political arena should be characterized by "client politics," lobbying by groups that want to receive the concentrated benefits; groups that experience diffuse costs find it too costly to organize an opposition. Where both benefits and costs are concentrated, groups on both sides of the issue mobilize, creating "interest group politics." With diffuse benefits and concentrated costs, a political entrepreneur is needed to overcome problems of collective action, hence the rise of "entrepreneurial politics." Finally, where both benefits and costs are diffuse, "majoritarian politics" arise.

This framework provides a useful starting point for analyzing the politics of immigration control. However, it can be extended by specifying the characteristics of costs and benefits emanating from migration flows. Once the components are clarified, it becomes obvious the political dynamics of immigration control change over time, as the costs and benefits do not remain static. Moreover, Freeman and Hill, even in the updated version, do not systematically incorporate the role of political institutions. Political systems include both political institutions and the spatial distribution of interests. Once these elements are taken into account, it becomes possible to develop specific hypotheses about the politics of skilled migration. The proposed theory is compatible with the Freeman framework but enhances it by incorporating additional explanatory variables and by providing predictions of policy outcomes in addition to political behavior.

The Geographic Concentration of Migrants

Although it is usual to think about national markets for goods and services as well as national labor markets, in fact, labor markets are, to some extent, local. Witness recent unemployment figures for the U.S. states, ranging from 3 percent (Hawaii, 3 percent; New Hampshire, 3.3 percent; Virginia, 3.3 percent) to more than double that rate (Alaska, 7.3 percent; Michigan, 7.3 percent; and Washington DC, 9.0 percent) (United States Bureau of Labor Statistics, 2005a). One reason for the continuation of local labor markets within a nationally integrated market is the presence of geographically clustered industries (Krugman, 1991). This may be easiest to think about when the industries are based on natural resources—mining and agriculture come to mind as do industries that rely heavily on raw materials, such as the steel industry. However, the same principle holds true for many manufacturing industries because of the benefits of agglomeration. The initial location of an industry can be quite accidental; but once the innovative firms become established in a particular area, the benefits of agglomeration tend to attract new firms entering that market to the same location. As a result, the demand for specific types of labor is also geographically clustered. This is a characteristic of the high technology industry in the United States that is concentrated geographically. In 1997 figures, California, alone, produces 18 percent of national high-tech output; Texas ranks second with 7.8 percent. California, Texas, New York, Illinois, and Massachusetts are the highest high-tech employment states accounting for more than 40 percent of high tech employment (Weinstein and Clower, 2000: 32; table 6.2).

The geographic concentration is reinforced by workers' social networks. In the absence of international migration, national labor markets facilitate the migration of domestic workers from one location to another, as new industries take root and increase their demand for labor. However, because of social networks, moving generates high costs. Workers are less willing to leave their extended families, friends, schools, etc. So the costs of attracting domestic workers is high and reflected primarily in wage differentials as, within a national labor market, non-wage amenities tend to be more uniform (work practices; worker benefits; unemployment benefits; educational quality; social insurance, etc.). So-called "non-tradables," such as real estate, can create differentials as well; moving from a location with low real estate costs to a location with high real estate costs is more costly in terms of wages offered than vice versa. And government provided safety nets allow unemployed workers to avoid moving to obtain employment. Workers' social networks, as well as these other factors, thus create, or reinforce a certain degree of localism in labor markets that may be absent in goods and capital markets.

If employers are unwilling or unable to provide a wage differential sufficient to either attract non-labor market participants in the local vicinity or labor market participants from elsewhere in the nation, they are faced with an unmet demand. In order to meet that demand, employers turn to workers with a lower reservation wage—workers from outside the nation. Thus, even in industries that are not geographically concentrated, such as nursing, the demand for labor tends to be geographically concentrated even within a nation.

As a result, the demand for migrants is geographically concentrated, even in the presence of well-integrated national labor markets. White (1993) and King (1993) provide empirical reports of the geographic concentration of migrants generated by this local demand. Massey and others (1987) explore the migrant networks that reinforce the geographic concentration of immigrants in the wake of this initially localized demand. This localized demand and geographic concentration of immigrants is critical to understanding the political process.

The Distribution of Benefits from Immigration

Presumably benefits from voluntary migration accrue to the migrant—otherwise the immigrant would not choose to migrate. However, those benefits are not germane to the politics of migration in the host country because that migrant cannot participate in the political process. Therefore, the distribution of benefits that are politically important must be benefits that accrue to domestic political actors.

Although the empirical evidence presents a somewhat mixed picture, economic theory suggests employers are the primary domestic political actors that benefit from migration (Borjas, 1994; Simon, 1989). The most significant benefits are associated with an expanded and more flexible labor supply. An expanded labor supply allows employers to alleviate production bottlenecks created by a shortage of labor and to moderate wages and benefits. A migrant labor supply is more flexible than the domestic labor supply (Piore, 1979). Foreign workers can be hired on a temporary basis to work swing shifts or overtime, allowing employers to respond to fluctuations in product demand and to take advantage of round-the-clock production facilities.

However, employers have a number of strategies other than the import of labor to minimize production costs, including the export of capital to cheap labor or the reorganization of the production process to reduce the demand for expensive labor resources. So benefits from migration are concentrated for employers but vary by the degree of labor scarcity as well as the flexibility of the labor force and the flexibility of the production process. Hence the concentration of benefits varies over time and by industry, leading Iredale (2001) to suggest that migration should be classified by profession or industry. Benefits are most concentrated when labor is scarce and in industries with inflexible labor forces and inflexible production processes.

Freeman and Hill (this volume) point out concentrated benefits also accrue to migrant families interested in family reunification and, among others, to immigration attorneys whose livelihood depends on an immigrant clientele. As a result, these groups may enter the political process, although it is unlikely that there would be differential rates of political activity on these issues between nurses and information technology workers. There are a number of diffuse benefits from migration, such as lower costs of particular products and lower inflation rates. But the diffuse nature of benefits means it is unlikely that these beneficiaries will find it cost effective to organize in support of migration.

The Distribution of Costs of Migration

Because immigrants are geographically concentrated, conditions in local communities that host immigrants trigger opposition to immigration through the level of host/immigrant competition (Olzak, 1992). The competition contains at least three dimensions: labor market competition, competition over state resources, and competition over societal identity.

Labor market competition is not uniform but rises in economic recession because host country workers become willing to take less remunerative employment. Competition over the state provision of private goods (welfare payments, etc.) is a function of the access of immigrants to state based resources and the characteristics of migrants. Migrants without families generate fewer demands than migrants with families; high paid migrants pay more in taxes than services received, whereas low paid migrants pay less in taxes than services received (Martin and Midgley, 1994; Simon, 1989; Smith and Edmonston, 1997). Competition for state supplied public goods (roads, sewerage, schools, etc.) is a function of the size of the immigrant stream, as public goods can become crowded at least in the short-term.

Conflict over societal identity is a much more amorphous concept that is difficult to explore empirically, even though many researchers believe this is an important component of the level of opposition to immigration (Waever, 1993). Some indicators of the potential for conflict over societal identity are the number of immigrants, the distinctiveness of the immigrant population, and the level of immigrant incorporation. Although there are reasonable estimates of the first indicator, the number of immigrants, the two other indicators are difficult to operationalize, especially since the immigrant community, in turn, shapes the contours of the host community as well as adopting some elements of the host society. Societal indicators may include the number and size of anti-immigrant organizations and publicly voiced claims making and protests against the immigrant population (Koopmans and Statham, 2000).

In sum, opposition to immigration is driven by competition between the host and the immigrant communities. The first dimension, labor market competition, is triggered by economic recession. The second dimension, competition over state resources, is triggered by the characteristics of migrants and the rate of growth of the immigrant community, as well as the level of access immigrants have to publicly provided goods. The third dimension, conflict over societal identity, may well exist but is difficult to analyze empirically.

The argument is conjunctural; that is the level of support for immigration may not be directly related to the level of opposition to immigration. Opposition could be high while support is low, for example, under conditions of high unemployment; or opposition could be high while support is also high, for example, under conditions of low unemployment but with large immigrant inflows that triggered competition over state supplied public and private goods as well as tensions related to societal identity.

Transforming Local Interests into National Policy

Local demands will be addressed at the national level if a majority of the national constituencies favor the same policy. But, because support for, and opposition to, immigration are concentrated spatially, this scenario does not occur frequently. The question is how these parochial interests are transformed into national policy that requires a political majority. One important mechanism for turning local interests into a national policy is "logrolling," whereby a coalition is formed by trading favors: one legislator votes for another legislator's local pet project in order to receive that legislator's vote for his own local pet project. But immigration policy does not provide tradeoffs of this type for non-immigration constituencies. Hence there needs to be an alternative mechanism for aggregating support for policies that affect only a few constituencies. James (2000) argues that the construction of national coalitions is possible by incorporating the local interests in swing constituencies into national party platforms. Political parties then serve as the mechanism for creating a majority vote for essentially local policies.

From this perspective, local preferences are not translated on a one-to-one basis to the national political agenda. Both the size and the safety of the constituencies factor into the political calculus of national leaders when evaluating the level of electoral competition. The influence of local constituencies on national electoral outcomes depends, in part, on the size of the constituency seeking to add immigration issues to the national political agenda. In the United States, for example, states vary in the electoral support they can offer the presidential coalition in accordance with the number of their electoral college votes. Large states, such as California, are politically important because a victory there may swing the national presidential election to the winning party. The influence of local constituencies also depends on the "safety" of the constituencies. If the constituency cannot convincingly threaten defection to the opposing party, its policy preferences are less important to the national coalition.

National political institutions are crucial to understanding the transformation of immigration from a local to a national political issue; institutional characteristics define the significance of local support for, and opposition to, immigration in building national political coalitions. Presidential systems will reflect a different dynamic than parliamentary systems; proportional representation systems will reflect a different dynamic than single-member constituency systems. But the common thread running through all nations is the need for politicians to build a national electoral majority.

Predictions for Skilled Migration Policy

On the demand side, labor market needs drive employer lobbying to loosen the barriers to labor migration, just like any other labor market flow. Lobbying organizations are likely to be industry specific and carry names that connote a national organization. But underneath the national veneer, because labor market needs are geographically specific, we should see support from firms that are *spatially concentrated*.

Opposition to skilled migration however, should be smaller than the opposition that develops to unskilled/semi-skilled migration. There are two reasons for the diminished nature of political opposition. First, highly skilled migrants earn, on average, higher wages and are therefore more likely to provide a net contribution to the provision of social services rather than being net recipients of social services (Smith and Edmonston, 1997). The average high-tech wage in the U.S. in 1997 was $53,145, versus $30,053 for the average private sector wage (Weinstein and Clower, 2000: 34, table 8). High-skill migrants are more likely to have employer supplied health care; to pay substantial taxes; and to own property and pay property taxes that contribute to the provision of local services such as education. They are also likely to come in smaller numbers than unskilled labor, as they work in capital, rather than labor-intensive industries.

Second, highly skilled migrants are less likely to generate conflict over societal identity. Based on their earnings, they may avoid problems associated with integration into the host society faced by unskilled or semi-skilled workers. Almost of necessity, highly skilled migrants will be fluent in the language of the host country or will rapidly become fluent. These language skills will allow the migrants to learn the social cues that permit them to interact more easily within the host society. More importantly, they can afford to hire services that allow them to retain a considerable amount of autonomy within the host society, reducing contact that may generate conflict with the host society over cultural or identity issues.

This distribution of costs and benefits, combined with institutional structures, allow us to hypothesize that when unemployment is low, employers will petition for freer access to immigrants and opposition will be limited. Local governments and publics, in the communities where highly skilled migrants are located, are unlikely to organize, limiting any opposition to labor market competitors. Placing this distribution of interests within U.S. political institutions, it suggests that support for skilled immigration in presidential swing constituencies is crucial for a positive policy outcome. Thus employers will be able to extract a more permissive migration environment only if they are located in swing constituencies. Much is made of the Congressional activity on immigration issues. But most of that activity does not produce legislation, and the legislation that produces majorities in both houses still needs the signature of the president. Hence, the president is a crucial player in putting some immigration issues on the agenda and ensuring their successful fruition.

The theory presented here does not make a distinction between the temporary versus permanent nature of the immigration flow. We argue that this distinction is overdrawn in the literature and not particularly important empirically. In the United States, Lowell (2001a) presents evidence that "the number of permanent visas processed has continued to decline markedly since 1995 due to processing backlogs at the involved U.S. agencies, which diverts employer and foreign worker demand from the permanent to the temporary visa." But temporary migration is an avenue to permanent migration. Piore (1979) points to the permanence of temporary migration. Lavenex (this volume) also notes the length of stay for "temporary" skilled migration has been defined as ranging from three months to five years, completely obliterating the significance between "temporary" and "permanent" categories of skilled migrants. Empirically, Glaessel-Brown (1998: 326) reports that for nursing, "permanent jobs are being filled by a succession of temporary workers who tend to stay and adjust status if given the opportunity." In 1985, for example, "45 percent of visiting and temporary foreign health professionals adjusted to permanent status in 1985" (Glaessel-Brown, 1998: 326). This discussion suggests that there is likely to be little difference in the politics of "temporary" and "permanent" skilled migration; rather, immigrants choose the channel that most easily allows them to enter.

We now turn to the two economic sectors, information technology and nursing, to evaluate this hypothesis.

The High Technology Sector

History of Admissions to the United States

The H-1B non-immigrant category for specialty workers was first enacted by Congress in conjunction with the Immigration and Nationality Act of 1952 (Pub. L. No. 82-414, 66 Stat. 163, codified as amended at 8 USC §§1101 et seq.; see Kurzban, 2000). Significant amendments were made to the H visa procedures with the Immigration Act of 1990 (Immigration Act of 1990, Pub. L. No. 101-649, 104 Stat 4978). Up until the mid-1990s, the number of H-1B workers allowed into the United States every year was capped at 65,000, but until 1997 the cap was never reached and the INS never counted the number of petitions filed (Kurzban, 2000).

Ultimately, Congress increased the number of new H-1Bs allowed to enter the United States to 115,000 in FY 1999, 115,000 in FY 2000, and 107,000 in FY 2001. These provisions were part of the American Competitiveness and Workforce Improvement Act of 1998 (Pub. L. No. 105-277, Title IV, 112 Stat. 2681, and its implementing regulations, 65 Fed. Reg. 80110-80239, Dec. 20 2000). These increases, however, proved to be insufficient, so in October 2000, just prior to the 2000 presidential election, Congressed passed the American Competitiveness in the Twenty-first Century Act that enlarged and extended the quotas: 195,000 for FY 2001, 195,000 for FY 2002, and 195,000 for FY 2003 (Pub. L. No. 106-313). This series of legislation also created other beneficial provisions, such as removing from the numerical limitations those H-1B workers employed by institutions of higher education, those working in a nonprofit research organization, or those working for a governmental research organization. These regulations also instituted a new fee of $1,000 for all new H-1B applications. This money was intended to fund scholarship and training programs for U.S. workers. Educational institutions and nonprofits are also exempt from this fee. Throughout the fiscal year, at least up until 2001, the cap continued to be reached just prior to the end of the fiscal year.

We argue that this recent migration policy response is due to organized support for higher levels of skilled migration located in swing constituencies.

Labor Market Shortages and Employer Demands

In the last decade of the twentieth century, the information technology sector emerged as a leading sector in the U.S. and other advanced industrial countries, spurring economic growth and increased productivity in the economy as a whole. Established companies in information technology, such as Oracle, Cisco, Microsoft, IBM, and Sun Microsystems, scrambled to find enough employees to fill their vacant positions and, at the same time, had to fight for scarce workers with the continuously emerging dot-com start-ups. In 2000, the OECD reported the information technology sector faced "a shortage of around 850,000 qualified people in the United States" (OECD, 2001).

In order to fill this growing need for workers, U.S. companies began to hire skilled foreign workers to fill their many high-tech positions, bringing thousands from countries around the globe, but particularly from the technology centers of India and China. For example, in 1994 the percentage of foreign labor in the U.S. workforce numbered 9.8 percent. By 1999 that figure had increased to 11.7 percent (OECD, 2001). This increase was largely due to migration involving highly qualified workers (H-1Bs) which rose sharply between 1990 and 2000, assisted by "better employment prospects and the easing of entry conditions," due to new legislation in the U.S. (OECD, 2001). According to the Immigration and Naturalization Service,[3] approximately 70 percent of the total H-1B petitions were for computer-related and engineering occupations (US INS, 2001c).

Geographic Location of Labor Market Shortages

Table 6.2 illustrates the geographic concentration of labor market shortages as well as the position of the industry politically. The top ten states experienced rapid employment growth in information technology, averaging 16 percent from 1990 to 1997 (only two states experienced a small decline). These states also attracted the largest proportion of temporary immigrant workers, with nine of these states in the top ten choices of temporary workers.

Analysis of Political Incentives

With the boom in the high technology sectors during the 1990s, companies began to hire many more H-1B workers than ever before. In 1997, for the first time, the INS began counting the number of H-1Bs and the cap was reached prior to the end of the fiscal year.

Table 6.2
Geographic Distribution of Labor Market Shortages – Late 1990s

	High Tech Employment by State 1997	Percent Change in Employment 1990/ 1997	Top 10 States of intended residence for temporary workers- 1996	Number of Top 50 Leading Employers of H-1Bs	Top 10 States of Intended Residence for Temporary workers (as percent of state population- 1996)	Swing States in 1996 Presidential Election (Clinton v. Dole)
California	1 (784,151)	+9 %	2 (69,222)	21	4	X
Texas	2 (375,933)	+37%	4 (29,791)	1	10	X
New York	3 (320,410)	-9 %	1 (75,740)	6		
Illinois	4 (207,201)	+14%	8 (16,308)	1	9	X
Massachu-setts	5 (205,091)	-7 %	6 (19,023)	1	2	
Florida	6 (193,559)	14 %	3 (38,121)		1	X
New Jersey	7 (179,528)	5 %	5 (25,396)	4	3	X
Pennsylva-nia	8 (159,952)	13 %				
Virginia	9 (154,712)	27 %	10 (13,220)		8	X
Georgia	10(132,524)	54 %	9 (15,325)			

Sources: For columns 1 and 2, Weinstein and Clower, 2000: 31, Table 5; for columns 3 and 5, U.S. INS 1996; for column 4, U.S. INS 1999-2000; for swing states, see Shaw, 1999.

In response to this, the high tech sector, in conjunction with pro-immigration lobby groups and business interests, lobbied Congress to increase the number of H-1Bs allowed into the United States every year. Freeman and Hill (this chapter) enumerate the many groups involved. These groups were well placed to exert pressure as six of the ten states where the high tech sector is concentrated were swing states in the 1996 presidential election (see table 3.2). And, although the lobbying organizations are endowed with "national" titles, the membership in the organizations is highly geographically concentrated, reflecting the geographic concentration of the industry itself. For example, over half (56 percent) of the membership of the Semiconductor Industry Association is based in California, and 80 percent of the membership is based in the top ten states listed in table 6.2 (see http://www.sia_online.org).

Responding to the pressure generated by the high tech lobby, Congress increased the number of new H-1Bs allowed to enter the U.S., as described above. The hypothesis for the high tech sector is thus supported by the evidence. Freeman and Hill predict "modes of politics," rather than outcomes, but also note the success of the group. Thus our account is congruent with the Freeman and Hill description, although this account focuses on the geographic concentration of the interest associations and their political significance for the presidential coalition.

Registered Nurses

History of Admissions to the United States

The U.S. has regularly imported nurses to ease its nurse shortages and nurses trained abroad now represent around 5 percent of the total U.S. nursing workforce. This flow has been dominated by nurses from the Philippines, representing approximately 75 percent of foreign nurses until the mid-1980s; the flow has since expanded to include substantial numbers from Canada, the U.K., India, Korea, and Nigeria (Brush et al., 2004). All U.S. nurses must pass the National Council Licensure Examination (NCLEX-RN) to practice as registered nurses (RNs). Concern about the quality of foreign nurses led the Division of Nursing (United States Public Health Service) to commission a study of foreign nurses. This resulted in the creation, in 1977, of the Commission on Graduates of Foreign Nursing Schools which administers a pre-immigration competency examination of foreign nurses' clinical knowledge and English proficiency (United States Public Health Service, 1997). To take the exam, foreign applicants must demonstrate their education meets U.S. standards (Aiken et al., 2004).

The vast majority of nurses are not eligible for an H-1B visa because most nursing jobs do not require a bachelor's degree or equivalent, which is a requirement for the H-1B. Most general nursing positions can be filled by someone with an associate's degree in nursing or a nursing diploma. Some nursing positions, such as an anesthesiology nurse or nursing manager, may require a bachelor's degree and, if so, they may be eligible for an H-1B. But, for most positions in the nursing profession, the requirements for H-1B are not met (United States Government Department of Labor, 2005).

Due to the severity of the nursing shortage in the late 1980s, and the forecasted continuation of this shortage for the 1990s, Congress, in 1989, passed the Immigration Nursing Relief Act of 1989 (INRA). This, in conjunction with IMMACT90, established the H-1A category for professional nurses. The 1994 North American Free Trade Agreement (NAFTA) also has a category for nurses, but Canada is facing its own nursing shortage and the requirements for Mexican nurses are more stringent so few have taken advantage of the program (an explanation of the differing requirements can be found at: U.S. INS 1999). The H-1A visa category, however, admitted a limited number of nurses to the United States; and expired at the end of its mandated period on September 1, 1995 for new nurse admissions. The program was extended in October 1996, (Pub. L. No. 104-302, 110 Stat. 3657) but only for those nurses already in the United States as H-1A nurses who had not yet completed their five-year period and needed extensions. Moreover, this extension was valid only until September 30, 1997. After that, no further action was taken on the H-1A program. Therefore, for a four-year period from September 1995 to November 1999, there was no visa program available for nurses to enter the U.S. During this period of time, there was disagreement among groups as to whether the nursing shortage was continuing or not. But underserved areas remained underserved and, as the figures above indicate, the Bureau of Labor Statistics continues to see vacant positions into the future.

On November 12, 1999, President Clinton signed into law the Nursing Relief for Disadvantaged Areas Act (NRDAA) (Pub. L. No. 106-95, 113 Stat. 1312 November 12, 1999). This created a new non-immigrant category for nurses, the H-1C, which became effective on September 21, 2000. The criteria for hiring H-1C nurses are very stringent. It is a program for foreign-born registered nurses to work up to three years in certain hospitals that serve "Health Professional Shortage Areas" (HPSAs). The program only applies to hospitals, and does not apply to clinics, registries, home health care agencies, or skilled nursing facilities. The hospitals must also be designated by the Department of Health and Human Services as HPSAs as of March 30, 1997 (rather than thereafter), have a minimum of 190 acute care beds (thus eliminating all small- and medium-sized hospitals from participating), have a minimum of 35 percent of the patients covered by Medicare, and a minimum of 28 percent of the patients covered by Medicaid. With these criteria, only fourteen hospitals have been designated for the H-1C program, listed in table 6.3.

Table 6.3
H-1C Designated Hospitals

1. Beverly Hospital, Montebello, California
2. Doctors Medical Center, Modesto, California
3. Fairview Park Hospital, Dublin, Georgia
4. St. Bernard Hospital, Chicago, Illinois
5. Mercy Medical Center, Baltimore, Maryland
6. Lutheran Medical Center, St. Louis, Missouri
7. Elizabeth General Medical Center, Elizabeth, New Jersey
8. Peninsula Hospital Medical Center, Far Rockaway, New York
9. Southeastern Regional Medical Center, Lumberton, North Carolina
10. McAllen Medical Center, McAllen, Texas
11. Mercy Regional Medical Center, Laredo, Texas
12. Southwest General Hospital, San Antonio, Texas
13. Beaumont Regional Medical Center, Beaumont, Texas
14. Valley Baptist Medical Center, Harlingen, Texas

By many criteria, the H-1C program is unusual. Not only is the coverage very restrictive, but even where allowed (in the fourteen hospitals listed above), the program limited the number of visas per year to 500. The program also limited the number of nurses who may petition in any one state. States with populations of nine million or more in the 1990 census were eligible for up to fifty nurses per year, and states with populations of less than nine million were eligible for twenty-five nurses per year. This meant the five hospitals in Texas had to share the 50-nurse allocation for that state, which equaled ten nurses per hospital.

Moreover, when these hospitals began submitting the attestations required under the immigration laws to become eligible to hire foreign nurses, they ran into more difficulty. As of March 2001, nine of the fourteen hospitals on the list had submitted attestations. The Department of Labor approved only four of these, denied one, and left four under review as of May 21, 2001. Of the four under review, the DOL had indicated intention to deny three of them, even though they were on the list of fourteen eligible facilities. The DOL's comment was "they do not meet the other requirements of the H-1C law" (ImmSpec.com, 2001).

Finally, the designation of the HPSA, as defined by the immigration law, drastically undercuts the actual number of HPSAs in the U.S. A search of the HPSA list provided by the U.S. Department of Health and Human Services revealed at least 385 designated shortage areas in forty-two states meeting the metropolitan and population requirements. It is likely the other eight states did not have HPSA areas in the search because, on the whole, the populations are not large enough: Idaho, Montana, Nebraska, North Dakota, South Dakota, Vermont, West Virginia, and Wyoming (U.S. Government, Department of Health and Human Services, 2005). These criteria (metro area and population group) were chosen because it is these areas that would seemingly be the most likely to benefit from foreign nurses, and might also meet the additional requirements of the immigration law (such as the requirement of 190 acute care beds and patients covered by Medicare or Medicaid). Yet, obviously, despite this huge need, the INS laws are such that only fourteen hospitals in only nine states meet the criteria.

Why, in light of similar labor market positions, did the health care industry fare so poorly in terms of its demands for foreign nurses? On many dimensions, this sector actually had advantages absent in the information technology sector. There were mechanisms for admitting foreign nurses to the U.S. labor market, an established flow of migrants from at least one country, the Philippines, and a network of immigration attorneys to facilitate that flow. Nonetheless, the health care industry came up empty handed because the labor market shortages were concentrated in states that were not politically important in terms of their ability to swing national electoral outcomes.

Labor Market Shortages

Coincident with the high tech worker shortage, the nursing sector was also experiencing a shortage of registered nurses to fill all the vacant positions. Much speculation existed (and still exists) on the nursing shortage but the general consensus is that long hours, low pay, and poor working conditions account for the decrease in available nurses, while the aging population—particularly the 78 million aging baby boomers—points towards a need for more nurses in the near future.

In fact, the Bureau of Labor Statistics predicts the number of nursing positions will increase 23 percent by 2008 (American Medical Association, 2001). The average hospital vacancy rate for nurses grew to 14.7 percent during the first quarter of 2000. Government projects indicated that by 2015, 114,000 full-time equivalent RN positions will be unfilled nationally. There is also a shortage of home health aids, physical therapists, medical assistants, radiological technicians, occupational therapists, epidemiologists, biostatisticians, and environmental health specialists, as well as a severe shortage of licensed pharmacists. The United States Department of Labor lists registered nurses as one of the top ten professions that will experience the largest job growth in the 2000 to 2010 period, with 2,194,000 new jobs expected (U.S. Bureau of Labor Statistics, 2005b). Furthermore, the Council of Medical Services reported in June 2001 that there is a "profound shortage of qualified registered nurses (RNs)" in the U.S. (American Medical Association, 2001). This picture is confirmed by the United States Department of Health and Human Services report (2003) entitled "Projected Supply, Demand, and Shortage of Registered Nurses: 2000–2002." The report indicates that in 2000, the supply of full-time employed registered nurses was estimated at 1.89 million whereas the demand was 2 million, a shortage of 110,000 nurses, or 6 percent of total demand. Based on trends and anticipated supply and demand, the shortage is expected to grow as follows: 12 percent in 2010, 20 percent in 2015 and 29 percent in 2020. Also in 2000, thirty states were estimated to have shortages. In 2020 it is estimated that forty-five states will have shortages. Those with no shortages include Kansas, Iowa, Hawaii, Vermont, and Kentucky.

Geographic Location of Labor Market Shortages

Table 4 illustrates the geographic concentration of labor market shortages. A survey, done by the same group at the Department of Health and Human Services (1996), tallied the number of counties within each state that currently have nursing shortages relative to the total number of counties, using data from the American Hospitals Association Annual Survey data base.

A second indicator of labor market shortages in the health professions is the Health Professionals Shortage Areas (HPSA) designation. According to the Nursing Relief for Disadvantaged Areas Act of 1999 (NRDAA) amending the Immigration and Nationality Act (found at 8 USC 1101(a)(15)(h)(i); 20 CFR 655), a geographic area will be designated as having a shortage of primary medical care professionals if the following three criteria are met:

a.   The area is a rational area for the delivery of primary medical care services.

b.   One of the following conditions prevails within the area: 1) The area has a population to full-time-equivalent primary care physician ratio of at least 3,500:1 or 2) The area has a population to full-time-equivalent primary care physician ratio of less than 3,500:1 but greater than 3,000:1 and has unusually high needs for primary care services or insufficient capacity of existing primary care providers.

c.   Primary medical care professionals in contiguous areas are over-utilized, excessively distant, or inaccessible to the population of the area under consideration.

These two indicators of nursing shortages are presented in table 6.4. The top ten states include New York, Montana, Kansas, Mississippi, Minnesota, Iowa, Massachusetts, Nevada, Nebraska, and Rhode Island. Many of these states also have significant numbers of HPSAs, but none was considered a swing state by the political analysts of the 1996 presidential election.

Analysis of Political Incentives

Although the nursing profession, unlike the high tech industry, is highly unionized, there is little if any political opposition to immigration of foreign nurses. The most important national nurses' organization is the Tri-Council whose members represent the most important national organizations representing the nursing profession: the American Association of Colleges of Nursing, the American Nurses Association, the American Organization of Nurse Executives,

Table 6.4
Geographic Distribution of Labor Market Shortages – Mid 1990s

	Percent of counties with nursing shortages	Number of HPSAs	Swing states in 1996 presidential election (Clinton v. Dole)
New York	63.9	13	
Montana	61.4	0	
Kansas	55.2	3	
Mississippi	51.8	3	
Minnesota	50.6	11	
Iowa	45.9	1	
Massachusetts	42.8	7	
Nevada	41.1	4	
Nebraska	40.2	0	
Rhode Island	40.0	4	

Sources: For columns 1 and 2, the numbers are based on Primary Medical Care needs in Metropolitan areas by population group, from US Dept. of Health and Human Services, 2005; for column 3, see Shaw, 1999.

and the National League for Nursing. The position papers of the Tri-Council focus on education, the work environment, increased public funding of nursing education, and the use of technology to "enhance capacity of a reduced nursing workforce" (Tri-Council, 2001). Immigration is simply not an issue. Moreover, surveys of registered nurses reveal a preference for working with foreign RNs as opposed to less skilled, but local, hospital aides (Aiken et al., 2004).

Many groups mobilized to support greater flows of foreign nurses. Congress heard testimony related to the nursing shortage from such advocates as immigration attorneys, the World Bank, state and national hospital associations, as well as from nursing unions such as the Service Employees International Union. According to an immigration specialty service that follows closely immigration legislation, "many advocated the easing of immigration restrictions for foreign nurses as a short-term approach," to resolve the nursing shortage. Moreover, "several of the witnesses from the health care field, while focusing more on the statistics describing the current shortage, echoed [the] suggestions [to ease immigration restrictions]" (ImmSpec.com., 2001).

However, these groups were ill placed to exert political pressure. None of the ten states with the most severe labor market shortages were swing states in the 1996 presidential election. In fact, with the exception of New York, foreign nurses are located in states without severe shortages. "In 1992, California and New York were home to nearly half of all foreign nurses in the U.S. By 2000 their share had declined to 38 percent, while the combined shares of the next most frequent locations—Florida, Illinois, Michigan, New Jersey, and Texas—rose to equal them" (Brush, et al., 2004). California, Texas, and New Jersey are "bottom ten" states in terms of nursing shortages.

Despite the lack of opposition and indifference to employers' lobbies, Congress passed legislation that failed to facilitate the immigration of foreign nurses. The odd structure of the program that was adopted may be due to the particularistic interests of House Immigration Subcommittee Chairman Lamar Smith (R-TX) who, according to AILA (2000), "despite his record as a vigorous opponent of 'guest workers,' was an outspoken supporter of the H-1C law." It is interesting to note that two of these hospitals listed are located in the congressional district and five in the home state of Congressman Smith (see table 6.3 above).

Our account differs substantially from the Freeman and Hill account that overlooks the demands for skilled migrants in the nursing sector altogether. If the expansionist coalition reported by Freeman and Hill was robust and permitted an effective alliance with the high tech sector, it is not clear why these forces would not be attached to the nursing sector as well. We are able to answer that question. The critical element missing from their analysis is the political power of the constituencies, measured in terms of political swing. The nursing profession, however, is distinctive in that the health care profession is not geographically concentrated, so the option of building a legislative majority is open, should the labor market projections of the Department of Labor of future widespread shortages come true.

Conclusion

When examining skilled migration in the United States, and more broadly in the global economy, the discussion has been dominated by a focus on the *actual* flows stemming from the political successes of specific sectors of the economy, rather than on a close examination of labor market conditions and shortages, and the differential ability of economic sectors to press their labor market demands at the national level. This focus has obscured the politics of skilled migration policy.

In this chapter, we have drawn on a theoretical framework based on the distribution of costs and benefits accruing from migration, and have specified those costs and benefits, as well as added spatial and institutional elements. In so doing, we are able to explain the disparate policies governing skilled migration in two economic sectors experiencing shortages of skilled labor. Researchers must remain sensitive to these variations. Flows are the results of government policies in light of underlying economic conditions. To overlook or under-theorize the politics of migration, whether skilled or unskilled, is to miss a large component of the picture. Moreover, in our view, skilled migration is not particularly distinctive from other types of voluntary flows of migration. Money (1999) has employed the same set of variables to explain the politics of previous flows of predominantly unskilled migrants in OECD countries.

Are there plausible alternative explanations for the disparate outcomes of these two economic sectors? At first glance, the differences in labor market organization, with nurses heavily unionized and high-tech workers unorganized, might have played an important role. Clearly, these factors were important in the development of professional standards for nursing and the institutional mechanism to ensure the maintenance of these standards in the 1970s. With those standards in place, however, the unions and professional organizations representing nurses have not opposed immigration actively, or even passively. It is possible there are more nuanced differences between the sectors that have affected the lobbying efforts or policy outcomes. Unlike the information technology sector, nursing is a female-dominated profession with a significant portion of employment in the public sector. Although medical technology has also been changing by leaps and bounds, the health care professions are not often cited as being a "leading sector" or associated with international competitiveness. Future research would carry the evaluation of the hypotheses presented here to a wider array of sectors and more fully evaluate alternative hypotheses.

Most of the research on the politics of immigration policy focuses on domestic politics with the implicit assumption that international factors are unimportant. This chapter also adopts this framework. The two works cited earlier focus on factors that are negligible for skilled workers. The preferences of the sending states (Rosenblum, 2003), and the international security environment (Rudolph, 2003). However, Lavenex (this chapter) points to an interesting institutional development in the international system, in terms of multilateral and bilateral agreements that incorporate provisions for skilled worker flows. She suggests that these institutional mechanisms may have the potential to govern the flow of skilled migrants, as distinctive from the (non-institutionalized) flow of unskilled migrants. These institutional developments may indeed constrain the domestically dominated politics of skilled migration in the future. However, we have some experience with a much more fully developed regime for non-voluntary migrants, refugees, and asylum-seekers. The 1951 Convention relating to the Status of Refugees is the key legal document in defining who is a refugee, their rights and the legal obligations of states. Although the U.S., and other advanced industrial states, adhere to this convention, these states have found numerous mechanisms, such as carrier penalties and third country passage, to deflect the flows of asylum-seekers (Guiraudon and Lahav, 2000). If this experience is any example, the new regimes being established are likely to have a nominal impact on the domestic politics of migration. In any event, domestic politics will remain a central component in understanding the policies states adopt relative to migration flows.

Notes

1.   For our purposes, high tech can be defined as manufacturing industries including computer and office equipment, communications equipment, electronic components and accessories, national security, defense and aeronautic components, navigation equipment, laboratory instruments, medical equipment and drug manufacturing. High-tech service industries include telephone communication services, computer programming, data processing and other computer related services, engineering and architectural services, and research, development and testing (Weinstein and Clower, 2000).

2.   This chapter focuses solely on host countries and avoids issues arising in the home countries of migrants. The home country perspective often views skilled migration as a "brain drain," raising issues of the ethics of developed nations, appropriating human capital from countries that desperately need the human capital and have often paid the costs of training; this is especially true of the literature on international nurse migration (Brush et al., 2004). However, Oded Stark (2004) has recently argued that the supply of human capital in developing countries increases in response to international labor market incentives and that some of that human capital remains in the developing country, actually leaving the country better off than before. From this perspective, the "brain drain" is not an issue; developing countries actually benefit from the international labor market incentive structure that causes their populations to develop larger amounts of human capital than would otherwise be the case.

3.   The Homeland Security Act of 2001 dismantled the Immigration and Naturalization Service, and moved its functions to the Department of Homeland Security. For the purposes of this paper, however, as the time frame we are discussing is pre-HSA, we will continue to use Immigration and Naturalization Service, and its acronym, INS.

Part Three

The Human Face of Global Mobility

7

Symbolic Analysts or Indentured Servants? Indian High-Tech Migrants in America's Information Economy

Paula Chakravartty

"Companies are still importing foreign computer programmers at the same time American computer programmers are out of work and thousands more lose their jobs each day. The H-1B visa program was supposed to provide "temporary" workers during times of increased hiring but failed to provide any adjustments for a downturn in the economy. If America wants to keep its high-tech advantage with the rest of the world, we must protect the futures of our American high-tech workers and the futures of our American students seeking advanced technical degrees. We must protect the vast amount of sensitive and personal computer data that foreigners should not have access to by eliminating the H-1B and L-1 visa programs."
                                     —Homepage of "Hire American Citizens"
                                          http://www.hireamericancitizens.org

"The British were drawn to India as a physical place; a repository of precious raw materials from which the natives might be parted, a locus of beauty and mystique. The new American attachment is not physical but conceptual—the lure of cheap, smart, pliable labor. Among Chennai's janitors and security guards, as well as its bankers, the need for discretion about that labor is understood. Even the ephemera of the United States offs-shoring debate becomes front-page news here, many of Chennai's young professionals now know the names John Kerry, Lou Dobbs, Benedict Arnold and Timothy Platt—the latter the proprietor of a U.S.-based website called "yourjobisgoingtoindia.com" which is as closely followed in Chennai as it is in Silicon Valley. Fascination with the American controversy is more bemused than fearful."
—Katherine Boo, *"The Best Job in Town: The Americanization of Chennai"*

The movement of skilled workers and jobs between Chennai and Silicon Valley or Bangalore and New Jersey, brings to our attention the importance of translocal networks and the resilience of nationalism as outcomes of global integration. As the above statements suggest, the industry-specific debate taking place in the U.S. since the late-1990s within the information technology (IT) sector over the temporary H-1B visa program—that employs a large proportion of computer programmers *from* India—has, in the last year, spilled over to encompass a much wider transnational public debate over the outsourcing of white collar jobs *to* India. In these debates, the "two sides" are usually made up of corporate proponents of liberalization who promise long-term positive outcomes for workers and consumers across national borders versus opponents who often cite the vulnerabilities or shortcomings of the workers from Asia—in this case India—as a threat to the standards, pay and ultimately employment opportunities for workers in North America—in this case the U.S. For instance, opponents of the H-1B program repeatedly argue Indian computer programmers who are on H-1B visas are "indentured servants" who are under-qualified, willing to work for lower wages and susceptible to exploitation because of their non-immigrant status (Matloff, 2004, 2003, 2002). While many of these critics attempt to distance themselves from "immigrant bashing" and vociferously support the migration of "deserving immigrants"—those who really are the "best and the brightest"—their arguments are invariably nationalist in spirit, pitting the rights of American citizens against the contamination of the very meaning of "white collar work" by Third World workers.

The H-1B is a nonimmigrant visa program that, in contrast to permanent employment-based immigration, allows employers to hire foreign workers with "specialized knowledge and skills" in engineering, mathematics, education, medicine and the like, on a temporary basis in a "specialty occupation." Their visa status is tied to their employers. If they lose their job, they are forced to leave the U.S. within a very short time. India is the country of origin for the majority of all H-1B workers. In 2001, for example, 49 percent of all H-1B petitions were from India, with China at second place with 8 percent (Matloff, 2003; Wassem, 2001). Moreover, Indian H-1B workers are concentrated in the information technology (IT) sector, with 92 percent of H-1B petitions from 2001 in "computer related or engineering occupations" (Hira, 2003a: 14). Although these are temporary visas, significant numbers of H-1B visa holders applied for, and successfully transitioned to, permanent or green card status in the late-1990s, helping to double the overall Indian population in the U.S. in the 1990s to approximately 2 million (Khadria, 2001).

In India, the American H-1B visa program was targeted by firms, educational institutions and temporary placement agencies, popularly referred to as "bodyshops," that functioned as transnational "temp" agencies placing mostly young, male, newly trained computer programmers from India in jobs in the U.S. for a three- to six-year period. Symbolically, Indian H-1B workers contribute to larger nationalist myths in India about the financial success and political influence of high-skilled Indian migrants to the U.S. Hindu nationalist organizations, like the former ruling Hindu nationalist party the Bharatiya Janata Party (BJP), emphasized a homogenous and privileged Indian immigrant community in the U.S., highlighting the role of globetrotting Indian symbolic analysts as catalysts of economic expansion in both the U.S. and India (Chakravartty, 2001b).

In the U.S., the sudden influx of young Indian workers in New Jersey, Silicon Valley and other high-tech centers, created tensions about the future of "good American jobs" and the rise of "electronic sweatshops" filled with "techno-slaves" willing to suffer exploitative conditions for dollars and the price of a green card. In the U.S., the H1-B issue has been politically controversial from its inception. A variety of domestic organizations, ranging from unions and white-collar associations to online anti-immigration organizations, have consistently argued that migrant high-tech workers serve to displace American workers by lowering wages and increasing contingent and, therefore insecure, conditions of work for American workers. These organizations have documented patterns of ageism and reverse-racism where foreign workers, represented as both unqualified and servile, replace "native" workers.

In the U.S., the visa program is rationalized as a response to the severe shortage of skilled workers in computer sciences and engineering, making the temporary visa program necessary (Yale-Loehr, 2003). This justification is vehemently denied by opponents of the program in the U.S., including labor unions and nativist groups who argue the program serves as a backdoor immigration policy lowering wages and job security for American workers (Matloff 2004, 2003). Since the events of September 11, 2001, opponents of the H-1B program have highlighted the threat these workers pose not just to wages and job security but to national security; mobilizing new momentum against both temporary visa programs like the H-1B and the intra-company transfer (L-1) programs and immigration more generally (Chakravartty, 2005).[1]

As the editors of this volume point out, theorists of global integration have paid insufficient attention to skilled labor flows, particularly when those flows are from Asia to North America. Nevertheless, in the past several years, there has been growing interest in studying immigration of highly skilled workers in the U.S. Much of this research has been quantitative and focused on the demographic role played by these workers in the U.S. labor market (Espenshade, 2001; Kuh, 2000). Other qualitative studies have examined the role of transnational ethnic entrepreneurial networks in facilitating migration (Saxenaian 2000, 1999) and the process of in-and-out migration from the sending nations (Khadria, 2002; Zhao et al.., 2000). Finally, recent policy-related research has focused on temporary migration and its impact on both U.S. (Hira, 2003a; Matloff, 2003; Rosenblum, 2001) and Indian IT sectors (Chanda, 2003; Hira, 2003b; Kapur, 2001).

What makes the case of the H-1B debate interesting is not just the fact these are "skilled" migrant workers—whereas the focus of research on migration to global cities has been on "unskilled" migrants from Asia (Sassen 1998)—but also the fact they are skilled Indian workers as opposed to either Asian entrepreneurs (Ong, 1999; Saxenian, 2000, 1999) or skilled Irish or Russian computer programmers (O'Riain). In other words, their class identification as skilled workers has to be weighed in relation to their configuration as racialized subjects whose "indentured servitude" is marked simultaneously by a colonial division of labor and the legacy of Orientalist discourse. Abdelmalek Sayad, a sociologist who wrote about Algerian migration to France, argued, emigration and immigration are intrinsically related and must be studied as a single object of analysis where "emigration-immigration is the direct child of the very colonization that generated underdevelopment..." (2004: 64-65).

In this, chapter I draw from the work of Sayad and others who have called for greater attention to both material and symbolic power, shifting the debate about migration beyond cost-benefit analyses (Bretell and Hollifield 2000; Smith 2001). Indian H-1B workers have faced the brunt of the opposition against what is clearly a flawed temporary visa program that privileges corporate flexibility at the cost of workers both "American" and immigrant. Taking this as a starting point, this chapter considers the experiences of Indian migrant workers as they make sense of their role in an asymmetrical global information economy. Central to my argument is that there are at least two identifiable trajectories Indian H-1B workers follow, reflecting distinct class and caste backgrounds that then shape their experiences in the U.S. and their sense of possibilities in terms of returning to India. These separate trajectories complicate the binary classification of these high-skilled workers as either "symbolic analysts" or "indentured servants" by proponents and opponents of the temporary visa program in India and the U.S. respectively.

Research Methods

Research for this chapter is based on interviews with Indian H1-B workers and analysis of online materials, media coverage and policy documents relevant to the H1-B policy debate in the U.S. and India between 1999 and 2004. The interview data were drawn from a larger qualitative research project conducted by me with the assistance of two research assistants, Angela Carr and Shannon Stoenbreck. The interviews were non-random and open-ended and were conducted by telephone with 121 H1-B workers of Indian origin who spoke to us between May and December 2002. These interviews were a result of an on-line survey of H1-B workers that was completed in May of 2002 as part of a collaborative project with economist Sundari Baru for the San Diego-based Center on Policy Initiatives. We advertised the survey on a dozen websites that target H1-B workers, and the response was overwhelming. We had over 3,000 respondents when we had estimated approximately 300. Out of these respondents, over 2,000 were of Indian origin. In the survey there was an option asking workers if they would volunteer for a follow-up telephone conversation, and we had over 500 workers willing to do so. With the assistance of my two research assistants, I was able to complete open-ended interviews with 200 H-1B workers, out of which 121 were of Indian origin.

The demographic characteristics of the 121 Indian workers we interviewed fit the general assumptions about young, male H-1B workers established in earlier studies (Lowell, 2001c). Eighty-four percent of the workers we spoke with were male, and 73 percent were under thirty-five years of age. Fewer than 2 percent were over the age of forty-five. Sixty-six percent were married and most had spouses on H-4 dependent visas where the spouse could not seek employment or education. Many respondents talked about their wives as professionally skilled, but frustrated, "housewives." We made an effort to speak to female H-1B workers and of the 16 percent of female H-1B workers in our sample, all were married and were hired by companies from within the U.S. as, in most cases, they had completed their degrees from U.S. universities. In terms of overall education, 60 percent of the workers we spoke with held undergraduate degrees from India, while less than 10 percent had postgraduate degrees from the U.S. Although our sample was not representative, the fact that the majority of H-1B visas are issued in India's southern provinces was reflected in our study sample. Fully two-thirds of our respondents came from four southern provinces: 26 percent from Andhra Pradesh, 12 percent from Tamil Nadu, 10 percent from Karnataka and another 19 percent from Maharastra. The remaining third of our sample came from a variety of mostly urban areas across India.

Most of the workers we spoke to were recruited in India on campuses or through offshore companies based in India. We chose to speak to a smaller number of workers whose visas were sponsored directly by the company, and it was not surprising these workers had a more positive experience overall. Our interest in the workers who had come through "bodyshops" stemmed from the general assumption they were more likely to face potentially exploitative situations. Our interviewees told us the management of the "bodyshops"—if not the ownership—was most often Indian or Indian-American with many experiencing recurring cases of mistreatment, false information about pay, hours of work, sudden relocation, a practice of putting workers between jobs "on the bench," and multiple examples of "bodyshops" illegally holding immigration documents to prevent workers from seeking alternate employment. Nevertheless, these kinds of negative experiences did not define the conditions faced by the majority of the workers we spoke to, for whom temporary migration had been a much more complex process. The workers we interviewed in 2002 had survived the initial downturn of the IT economy as well as the immediate backlash against South Asian and Arab immigrants following the attacks of September 11, 2001. (Das Gupta, 2004).

Over 60 percent of our interviewees had filed for, and were close to getting, green card approval. Even for the other 40 percent, the fact they were still in the U.S. and willing to talk to researchers by telephone highlights the limits of any study based on self-selection. We likely did not reach the most vulnerable workers whose employment and immigration status was the most tentative at the time of our interviews. Voluntary interview-based research of this kind is meant to gauge a wide range of perspectives, as opposed to offering a representative sample of opinions, and to provide insight into respondents' experiences by taking seriously their assumptions about the world (Lamont, 2002).

In considering the experiences of Indian H-1B workers in the U.S, this chapter addresses three of the principal themes of this volume. How do Indian H-1B workers see themselves in relation to the "brain drain/gain" argument? How do Indian H-1B workers negotiate between the promise of a transnational corporate lifestyle and their lowly status as racially marked contingent workers in the America's national information economy? And how do the experiences of Indian H-1B workers stack up against the assumption that high-skilled migrants are less likely than low-skilled migrants to face discrimination? In the concluding section I consider how the answers to these questions help us understand larger concerns about nationalism, skilled migration and global integration.

"Too Many Brains to Drain":
Indian Emigrants as American Immigrants

The fact that the majority of H-1B workers in IT-related fields have been of Indian origin (and the subsequent alarm about IT-related jobs moving to India) is partially explained by the Indian postcolonial state's investment in a relatively new development strategy emphasizing its comparative advantage in IT services and skilled, low-wage labor. In the last decade, the Indian state has encouraged Indian-based, as well as foreign firms, to hire Indian workers in areas like computer programming for both short- and long-term positions in Australia, East Asia, Europe and North America. Between 1950 and the mid-1970s, the majority of Indian emigrants were "skilled" professionals moving permanently to the U.K., U.S. and Canada. The emigration of highly skilled workers does not represent groups spread evenly across India. Migration rates of skilled Indians have been higher amongst specific religious minorities (Jews, Syrian Christians, Parsis and Sikhs) and higher caste Hindus because of the higher levels of education and income. Researchers have argued that Indian migration to Northern destinations is largely from the middle-class "which often carries with it a sense of entitlement stemming from the privileges that India's upper classes enjoy" (Kapur, 2003: 3).

By the mid-1980s, highly skilled migrants to the U.S., known officially as "non-resident Indians" (NRIs), began to shape political, economic and cultural norms "at home" in part due to decreasing costs for international travel and the expansion of new communications technologies.[2] Reversing the political concerns of the 1970s over "brain drain," attention in policy and political circles in India turned to the potential for the economic contribution through "brain gain" or technology transfer by NRIs in the 1980s and 1990s (Desai et al., 2001; Nayyar, 2002, 1994). Along with Mexico, India has seen some of the highest amounts of remitted income in the last few years. In the Indian case, remittances have been estimated at $10 billion in 2001 and $8 billion in 2003 (Federal Reserve Bank of Dallas, 2004; Ratha, 2003: 159). In addition to direct financial contributions, NRIs started playing an important social role in shaping domestic policy in this period. For example, successful emigrants who inevitably returned home for visits, brought with them consumer goods as gifts and stories of technological goods and services that their Indian urban middle-class relatives desired. The growing demand for Western quality consumer goods and services among the urban Indian middle-class in the 1980s is generally seen as one of the greatest impacts of these new non-resident Indian networks (Chakravartty, 2001b; Grewal, 1999).

In addition to fuelling Indian middle-class frustrations with central planning, the 1990s saw an explosion of Indian media attention to the return of successful Indian immigrants to jumpstart India's own high-tech development in IT-friendly global cities like Bangalore and Hyderabad. Davesh Kapur has argued that the success, and particularly the "confidence," of the Indian diaspora in Silicon Valley led to "reputational spillover effects" such that "Indian software programmer" became a kind of "brand name" indicating quality in the same way that "made in Japan" signals reliability in consumer products (2001). In turn, Kapur (2001) and others have argued that successful NRIs from the U.S. began to play a greater role in charity and development projects in areas like health and education (Khadria, 1999). Although a relatively small community in the overall U.S. population, immigrants of Indian origin make up a significant portion of professionals in terms of absolute numbers. Reflecting this trend, Indian median family income in the U.S. has been consistently 20-25 percent higher than the general population (Ong-Hing, 1998: 161). It is this particular fact of higher family income that has been the focus of academic and popular interest in the financial success of the Indian-American community, specifically in the technology sectors (Chakravartty, 2001a; Kapur, 2001; Saxenian, 1999).

Asian-American scholars have focused on the social and economic privilege of Indian immigrants in the US, examining how the Indian community negotiates its own racial position as a "model minority" in a racially hierarchical society (Koshy, 2001; Prashad, 2000). Recently, some researchers have argued that the influx of Indian H-1B workers in the IT industry complicates the assumption of privilege associated with high-skilled migrants from India (Chekuri and Muppidi, 2003; Mir et al., 2000). Ethnographic findings in this area show there has been a noticeable shift in the profile of Indian "skilled" migrants following the influx of H-1B workers in the IT industry. Whereas permanent migration of skilled Indian workers to the U.S. in the 1970s and 1980s would most often be associated with the graduates of India's prestigious Indian Institutes of Technology (IIT)—publicly funded but elite institutions with an overwhelmingly upper caste, upper-class student body looking for economic opportunities in the West—the profile of the "non-permanent" H-1B computer programmer generally followed a less exalted trajectory. In contrast to the entitled IIT-trained engineer who left India in the 1970s and 1980s, when opportunities were limited in a still centrally-planned economy, the H-1B worker is not necessarily from the upper castes, or from a family based in a metropolitan center in India like Delhi or Bombay. Their training is more likely from private colleges specializing in computer-programming and they are often willing to travel on a temporary visa to the U.S. to gain access to employment, on-the-job experience and social networks abroad they might not have access to in India's cut-throat liberalized high-tech economy.

Our interviewees repeatedly scoffed at our question about the costs of "brain drain," arguing a Bachelors degree is "not good enough" in India and competition is fierce compared to the U.S. Murthy, a thirty-two-year-old from a small town in Andhra Pradesh, stated pithily what the most common sentiment on this issue was: "...If you see India at present, there are fifty to sixty thousand engineering grads but hardly 1,000 jobs. Better options here, so why struggle there?" Vijay, a twenty-seven-year-old from Bombay said plainly "India has too many brains to drain... Many of the brightest boys are staying in India. They are the ones running the show. We come because we need the exposure." By "exposure," Vijay is speaking about more than financial opportunities which, unsurprisingly, was almost always the first answer to our question about their motivation to pursue H-1B-based employment. Almost as important as income was the issue of "exposure" to the "most advanced technologies," "professional experience" and "contacts." Vijay's comments reveal how many workers we spoke to understood their relative position as "skilled" workers in India's liberalizing and deeply stratified IT-based economy.

While it is true that India's IT sector has expanded rapidly, generating dramatic rates of revenue for both domestic and transnational firms, according to the National Association of Software and Service Companies (NASSCOM), the IT industry had "created employment opportunities" for some 700,000 workers in India as of 2002 to 2003 (http://www.nasscom.org). This number includes computer programmers and data entry and call center workers and clearly demonstrates a significant proportion of the approximately 80,000 annual graduates in engineering and computer sciences India produces have sufficient motivation to look abroad for employment. In this same period, out of these 80,000 graduates, only 17,000 held engineering degrees from the prestigious public universities, while the rest were granted a range of certifications, diplomas and degrees from private institutions (Patibandla and Peterson, 2002).

This division follows the Indian state's investment in higher-level public educational intuitions at the expense of basic public education so the wealthiest citizens send their children to expensive private schools followed by extremely competitive state-subsidized private universities (Drèze and Sen, 1997). In India's thriving IT economy, the nation's most privileged IT graduates, from upper caste, upper-class and metropolitan backgrounds, have more access to the best jobs in India as well as more mobility toward permanent resident status if they come to the U.S. on an H-1B visa. Among the workers we interviewed, those who had completed secondary degrees in India or, more importantly, in the U.S., often described themselves as from "good families" or identified themselves as part of India's "middle-class." A clear marker of class and often caste, many of our interviewees said their families were "well off," not in need of "help." This group of temporary skilled migrants more closely resembles the previous generations of permanent skilled migrants from India to the U.S. They emigrate from India with the most cultural capital, often complaining most vocally about the failings of the Indian state and corruption, and told us about "giving back" to their families in the form of gifts to their parents or donations to charities ranging from temples to schools and hospitals. Anuradha, a twenty-nine-year-old woman from Delhi with a Masters from the U.S. said she donates money "to an orphanage for blind kids" and explained:

> There are many differences between classes in India. The rich are very rich and the poor are very poor. If they can't afford anything, they go to free schools. But the middle-class—people like me—don't go to those schools…I want to give back to my parents for giving me a good education, so I have to take the opportunities here to buy them gifts.

Anuradha, like most of the female H1-B workers we interviewed, was much more educated than her male counterparts. This is consistent with findings by feminist economists who have shown women in skilled technology-related jobs are disproportionately overqualified (Mitter and Rowbotham, 1995; UNIFEM, 2000). In this case, the majority had masters degrees, often from the U.S., in contrast to their male counterparts who mostly had undergraduate degrees. The small number of female workers like Anuradha we interviewed, as well as more than half of the male workers we talked to, emigrated from families they themselves described as "middle-class," "fairly well off," and the like.

In contrast, Hitesh, a thirty-three-year-old from a small town in Gujarat, explained that coming to the U.S. on a temporary work visa was a function of class and, less explicitly, caste:

> I came from a very lower middle-class family. My father died and my mother is a teacher. She has four children, two sons and two daughters. We're all bright people but we don't have resources. I send them regular increments. In India there is no medical and dental coverage. You're responsible for your own so you have to keep money aside. It's a socialist country but our community is (pause)… We're lower-class, and that's another story.

Sending remittances to family members is only one aspect of the reversal of "brain drain" argument here because for workers like Hitesh, as well as Vijay, who stressed the importance of "exposure," there is also the cultural capital associated with jobs abroad and the potential new transnational networks of colleagues and employers who could serve as resources once the short-term contracts expire. Additionally, for workers like Hitesh and Vijay, access to jobs through the H-1B visa meant income in dollars but also access to the "confidence" associated with the thriving transnational Indian IT economy. The discussion of "brain drain" shows there are clear and recognized hierarchies within the singular category of highly skilled Indian IT worker and those who are less privileged understood their responsibility to the Indian state; in contrast to the most privileged Indian IT workers who are seen as the main beneficiaries of both former and current state policy. Krishan, a twenty-three-year-old from New Delhi argued that, if anything, the Indian government should impose a cap on the "IIT (Indian Institutive of Technology and IIM Indian Institute of Management) graduates he described as "the premier institutes with top-level guys....They should have to work in India for five years at least. We are the guys who need the jobs here."

The Thoroughly-Modern "Symbolic Analyst?" Adjusting to the H-1B Lifestyle

Krishnan's motivation in coming to the U.S. was simple: "The U.S. is (the) final destination. It's more advanced than any other country." He added: "everyone has at least one friend here so they know how things work." Krishan himself was the first person in his family to seek work in the U.S. but he had friends from college who were "already" in the U.S. and felt he had a clear sense of the "American lifestyle" from stories in college, his online research on the subject and from conversations with people who had worked abroad.

Our study found, in general, networks of friends, family and colleagues who were already in the U.S. mediated coming to the U.S.; and news and details of the American lifestyle were everywhere before the actual journey to the U.S. even began. Krishnan's casual observation about everyone having at least one friend rang true in this way but who these "friends" were seemed to make a significant difference in how the H-1B worker would "adjust" to both work and life in U.S.

Those H-1B workers who had the strongest pre-existing ties to the U.S. before they emigrated from India—whether in the form of close family relations "established" in the U.S., a post-graduate degree from the U.S. or via direct employment by a U.S.-based firm—had the smoothest transitions to their new jobs and, more importantly, to their new lives and lifestyles. For example, Raghu, a twenty-five-year-old from Madras, was hired on an H-1B visa by a software firm while he was completing his Masters in Engineering in the U.S. He had to move from Iowa to Virginia but found housing "on the internet" and his company paid him a signing bonus he used as a down payment on an apartment. Although he found transitioning to work life relatively smooth after having spent some time in the U.S. for his Masters, Raghu felt his company expected him to work "20 hours a week more" than his American colleagues. Unsure about his future in the U.S., Raghu, at the time we interviewed him, was looking at "job possibilities in India, where things look great."

Like Raghu, Piyush, a twenty-seven-year-old from an "upper middle-class family" in Madhya Pradesh, had a software diploma from India as well as an MBA from the U.S. He had found his job in Milwaukee through headhunters who had contacted him online in India where he had been working for an offshore software company. He chose work with an "American consulting company" he felt had treated him fairly. He acknowledged that when he "landed back in America" he had an advantage over other H-1B workers because he "understood how the system worked." Having finished post-graduate education in the U.S., Piyush had family who were "established" and while his company had applied for a green card for him, he felt he could just as easily relocate to India, where successful friends were living like "kings" with the money they were making in the IT sector.

The relative ease with which Raghu and Piyush talked about moving between the U.S. and India—following job possibilities allowing them to pursue the transnational corporate lifestyle of a well-paid symbolic analyst—was not the experience shared by most of the workers we spoke with. Instead, many workers spoke of "social isolation" Indian H-1B workers often experienced as both individuals and groups of workers; segregated both at their place of work and often where they lived. It was common practice for "bodyshops" to place workers for weeks, if not months, at a time in shared, often crowded, accommodations in hotels, apartments or dormitories provided by the agency, sometimes at a steep cost to the workers themselves.

Suresh, a thirty-year-old computer programmer from a small town in Andhra Pradesh, with an engineering degree and a technical diploma in computer software from India, describes a "tough time" in his first few months in St. Louis. His agency put him up in a hotel for a month and sent him to driving school, paying for both services without realizing they were deducted from his paycheck. Eventually, other more seasoned Indian H-1B workers from his agency helped Suresh lease an apartment and buy a car. Similarly, Chandra, a twenty-eight-year-old computer programmer from Hyderabad working in New Jersey explained, "There were problems initially because of my lack of credit. It's very bad. I had to convince everyone to give me housing. My friends helped." Chandra said he spent the first six months in the U.S. between a makeshift dormitory and his office, relying on company vans for transportation. With minimal access to credit, references and, in most cases, poor public transportation, coupled with no prior experience driving, these workers were easily segregated not just in their places of work—where H-1B workers were often separated from "permanent" American workers, but also in terms of the places where they would seek housing. Reliance on colleagues with more experience in the U.S., as well as reliance on networks based on caste, language and through temples, mosques and churches was very common, especially for those H-1B workers placed in IT centers with large or growing South Asian communities, such as the San Francisco Bay Area, Boston, New Jersey and Chicago.

The segregation of Indian H-1B workers, was seen by Krishnan, the twenty-three-year-old computer programmer from Delhi who worked in Indianapolis, as an impediment to his vision of life in America:

> I don't want to live in a place with lots of Indians. It's a secret, so don't tell them (laugh). I chose an apartment on the other side of the street so I can feel like I'm in the States instead of South India.

Reproducing a sense of ethnic distinction between "North Indians" like himself, and the majority of H-1B workers whom he argued were from the Southern states, Krishnan complained "they" spoke "their language" making it harder for him to "mix" with Americans. In this case, Krishnan felt himself to be a minority in a majority South Indian H-1B workforce, in a city without a wider South Asian community. Krishnan's "othering" of his South Indian colleagues gives him a sense of cultural competence in his desire to "mix" with Americans, although he quickly adds he wants to do so without losing his sense of "Indian family values."

Krishnan's frustrated desires highlight the obstacles to a neutral transnational corporate lifestyle and his emphasis at the end on "Indian family values" introduces the symbolic importance of family in the lives of many of these workers who described their experiences as "profoundly isolating." The "family values" discourse here has a conservative dimension, in the way it naturalizes power relations within the Indian or "Asian" family as discussed by feminist scholars (Ong, 2000; Visweswaran, 1997). Most of the H1-B workers we interviewed felt their strongest social ties were with members of their "same community," specifically language group and religious (implicitly caste) affiliation. This was particularly true for workers who were the first in their families to migrate and for those living in parts of the country with relatively large Indian populations. Workers like Chandra and Suresh thus maintained strong translocal networks as well as close contact with their families through regular telephone and email contact and visits "home." They spoke frequently about the limitations of the short time periods that restricted their parents' visits to the U.S.

In contrast to Krishnan, other workers admitted having had limited "social experience" with "American" colleagues. For many, "fitting in" to American culture meant engaging in discussions about sports they were not familiar with and participating in "outdoor activities" like "camping and rafting." Although some H-1B workers felt non-resident Indians (NRIs) could play a constructive role in "cultural coaching," for instance "showing us how to behave at parties or when you go dancing," many others told us they had returned to India shortly after arriving, in order to get married to young women who likely had their own reasons to pursue transnational arranged marriages.[3]

As a result, most of the male workers in our sample were married. Their wives often joined them within their first year in the U.S. In most cases, their wives were on "dependent" visas (H-4) and thus could not seek legal employment or pursue education without applying for a new visa status. Koneru, a twenty-six-year-old from a small town in Andhra Pradesh working as a software engineer in Mountainview, California explained his wife's "suffocating" situation in the following way, "As far as my wife goes... If given a chance she would like to work. She has a masters in computer science but she's at home." Koneru had been in the U.S. for two and a half years, having married only a year earlier in India. Hitesh, the Gujarati computer programmer, who had described himself as from a "lower middle-class family" in the last section, told us his wife was a doctor in India: "She has a Bachelors degree. She had the advantage of learning and education but she can't use it here. So she's a housewife."

In contrast to these stories about "wives at home," the female H-1B workers in our sample told us of domestic responsibilities and some complained about the lack of "good help" in the U.S. compared to India. In Anuradha's case, her husband, who had been on an H-1B visa previously, was on the dependent H-4 visa when we spoke with her, having lost his job recently. In the case of the "dependent" husband, however, Anuradha told us if he was unable to find work in the U.S., he would "look in Europe" and they would move. For reasons of patriarchal norms as opposed to skill, this was clearly not an option available for the skilled wives of H-1B workers above.

The role of the gendered translocal family in the lives of this group of temporary highly skilled migrants, as well as the importance of language-based and regional networks in mediating the "adjustment" process, demonstrates the limits to the flexible and mobile lives associated with high-skilled transnational migrants. The initial segregation and, in many cases, the longer-term social isolation experienced by many of the Indian H-1B workers we spoke with, clearly support arguments about how levels of skill or even higher relative income, fail to erase socio-cultural differences, and racial and ethnic hierarchies, in terms of the lived experience of Asian "skilled" migrants in contemporary American society (Ong, 1999).

Discrimination on the Job and Beyond: Rethinking the Politics of "High-tech Servitude"

The segregation and sense of social isolation experienced by Indian H-1B workers cannot be separated from the discrimination workers faced both on and off the jobsite. Opponents of the H-1B visa program argue that H-1B workers are "indentured servants" who are legally prevented from demanding higher wages because of their precarious immigration status. However, these very same opponents, of what is certainly a flawed immigration policy, are conspicuously silent about questions of racial discrimination towards this group of foreign, mainly minority, workers. To be sure, as foreign temporary workers, Indian IT workers on H-1B visas are relatively more vulnerable to abuses on the worksite but their status as "skilled" workers does not preclude everyday exposure to both overt and subtle forms of racial discrimination as well as renewed xenophobic and nativist sentiments.

In terms of experiences on the job, most of the workers we interviewed who came through "bodyshops" felt that they were expected
to work for longer hours and for less money than "natives." Akshay,
a twenty-five-year-old software engineer from New Delhi working
in San Jose stated:

> "It's not as free of a market. Maybe not deliberately, but companies take them (H-1Bs)
> for granted, even clients....It's expected, I'd say 20 percent more...sometimes projects
> require overtime. The pay is lower, $20,000 at my level, because we are less mobile.
> They take advantage of the situation. Pay increases are not that often.

Hitesh told us he feels there is "discrimination in vacation" where
time off is precious and more of a privilege for H-1Bs then their
"native counterparts."

Anuradha, the twenty-nine-year-old computer programmer who
felt she had more options as someone with an MBA from the U.S.,
describes her situation in the following way:

> Although personally, I've had no problems, there are restrictions on H-1B holders. We
> have to work more. Everyone leaves around 3:30 or 4:00, working 7 to 8-hour days,
> but H-1Bs stay for 10 to 11 hours. The pay is less. I'd say it's 15 to 20 percent less. We
> don't get paid overtime. Natives don't care how much work they do. Professional
> respect is less than it is for a U.S. native of the same caliber.

In general, our interviewees spoke with greater ease about work-
based discriminatory practices having to do with wages and overtime, and were more circumspect in how they described prejudicial
treatment by "American" colleagues or neighbors. Mohan, a thirty-
one-year-old from a small town in Andhra Pradesh, working in a
small town in New Hampshire said of his co-workers: "We're viewed
as a technical resource....They look at me different because I'm not
aware of the slang and local culture." Later on, he goes on to say
he's living in a place with few immigrants:

> "Some of them have never seen an immigrant before. Professionally we're in lower
> positions because of our ethnic background. You get promotions faster if you're Ameri-
> can. Culturally, I don't know how to approach a manager for raises or promotions. I
> have to learn every process by myself."

In the same way, Rama, a twenty-nine-year-old software architect
also from Andhra Pradesh and working in Kalamazoo, Michigan,
said first he did not want to "complain" about co-workers, that it
was often a lack of understanding of culture not malice that explained
seemingly racist behavior: "I always feel like a second-rate citizen
(laugh), that's obvious. Insecurity, that's the greatest drawback. I
never feel free." Many of the workers we spoke to observed that

their clients' co-workers were unlikely to "mingle" and "tend to look down on" us despite "our technical abilities."

These potentially minor incidences of everyday discrimination, mostly brushed off by our interviewees as "misunderstandings," were contrasted with stories of "friends" who had suffered more significant forms of exclusion and humiliation. Many of these stories were in response to our question about their experiences after the attacks of September 11, 2001. This question elicited stories by workers like Chandra, the twenty-eight-year-old from Hyderabad, who told us:

> A couple friends of mine had a problem shopping. They have dark complexion(s). They went to the [store] and people mistook them for Middle Eastern guys. They started yelling at him while he was with his wife and family. He just left quietly.

Others told us of anxious moments when traveling. Several male workers, worried about harassment at airports, said they prefer to take the train as opposed to flying when they have had to change job assignments.

Santanu, a thirty-five-year-old software consultant from Ranchi, Bihar, had heard of friends in Chicago who had been "pushed off a bus" by an "angry American mob." Krishan, eager to make American friends in Indianapolis and careful not to associate with the "other Indians," told us:

> A friend of mine was at restaurant and people were looking at them, him and his family. He was a family guy, you know, there with his kids. This is the first time I've heard someone felt a difference, but me, never.

In most cases, our interviewees felt conflicted about the racism they had witnessed, especially since many of the workers we spoke to were not likely to see themselves as "victims" of any social order. Several of the more privileged H-1B workers in our sample deployed the discourse of the Asian as "model minority." These workers were clear to distinguish themselves as qualified and therefore deserving immigrants in comparison to the "illegals" who "should be deported."

In contrast, the majority of our respondents told us of how they had survived the harsh realities of the downturn in the IT economy and had experienced a backlash against immigrants "like us" they hoped would recede in time. Most knew of stories of "guys having to leave their homes overnight" because they had lost their jobs. As one worker told us, "it isn't easy to sell everything—your car, your condo—and pack up and move back with no warning." In the period we conducted the interviews—the second half of 2002—more workers were looking at the real possibility of returning to India, despite the fact over half of those we had talked to had filed for green cards. For many of these workers, racial discrimination experienced on the jobsite was coupled with overt forms of American nationalism and nativism in the post-9/11 political environment where questions of national security became more directly connected to concerns about skilled immigration and would eventually be linked to the movement of white collar jobs abroad.

The Indian Computer Programmer and Global Stratification

> *"H-1Bks will do exactly what you tell them to do and will not complain or question why. Aside from cheap labor, this might be another reason companies love H-1Bs. It does not matter how bad the design is or how badly the requested code fits in with the rest of the system. They will just do it and not question it. A good programmer will point out the flaw and offer suggestions for a better fit within the system....It turns out there is quite an illegal industry in India with links to American-Indian companies ("bodyshops") that deceive U.S. companies in order to funnel fraudulent, unqualified H-1B applicants with doctored resumes, imaginary degrees and refresher course diplomas, from fly-by-night Indian trade schools, into $50,000 H-1B computer jobs in the United States that pay only $3,000 a year in India (for which they would not qualify either)."*
> *—Richard Armstrong, "H-1B Myth: The Best and Brightest"*

Our research shows that the violation of established workers' rights in a variety of forms takes place especially when there is a "bodyshop" agency placing workers in client offices. These workers are expected to work long hours of overtime with no extra pay and have been trapped in unfair contracts with the agency holding the workers' immigration papers as a way to manage potential complaints. Between 1999 and 2001, there was a spate of legal cases filed by H-1B workers against specific firms like Microsoft over violation of legal rights. Testimony about exploitative conditions has been a common feature of Non-Resident Indian e-mail discussion boards as well as both NRI and Indian media.

The above quote from the organization "Hire American Citizens" aptly illustrates how the potential for exploitation of Indian H-1B workers by IT firms has been strategically used by opponents of immigration in general, and the H-1B program in particular, to make the case foreign workers pose a threat to American workers and national security, contaminating the very meaning of "good American jobs." In northern countries, high rates of migration and the unprecedented linkages that today's immigrants have with their "home" communities, challenge previous notions of assimilation and racial politics in receiving nations (Ong, 1999; Portes and Rumbaut, 2001).

Opponents of the H-1B visa program tend to conflate the experiences of the most vulnerable group of workers, those who work for "bodyshops" and have the fewest pre-existing networks when they come to the US, with the experiences of *all* Indian H-1B workers. Moreover, the potential vulnerability of these workers—the propensity for servitude—is taken for granted, reinforcing Orientalist imagery that resonates in the language of "techno-slaves" and "high-tech servants." Today, a variety of Indo-American watchdog groups and organizations like the South Asian Journalists Association (SAJA) and http://blameindiawatch.blogspot.com take issue with similar kinds of arguments about the "outsourcing" of white-collar work to India. [4]

Beyond the issue of agency, the preceding discussion shows that there is a recognized internal hierarchy within the category of "highly skilled" Indian worker that reproduces biases in educational access based on caste and class, among other factors. In other words, the workers we interviewed had a complex understanding of the stakes of temporary work in a foreign country, where access to higher relative pay was only one of the draws that made the risk of non-permanent migration acceptable. The "brain drain/gain" debate falsely assumes education itself is a neutral category (Iredale, 2001), such that everyone with a Bachelors degree in engineering or computer sciences from India might have similar kinds of access to jobs abroad or investment opportunities at "home." In fact, the relatively less privileged H-1B workers we spoke to generally felt they could not compete for the very best jobs in India. In the same way they were less likely to enter the U.S. as permanent migrants when compared to their counterparts from elite Indian institutions. For these workers, on-the-job experience in transnational firms, and access to new networks of translocal employers and colleagues, were important regardless of whether they ended up in the U.S. or in India precisely because it improved their chances in what they understood as a segmented transnational employment market.

Although many workers sought social networks through transnational employment opportunities, these job market-based networks were built primarily around social ties based on ethnicity, language and caste, often in response to exclusionary practices both on the job-site and in terms of housing. Further undermining assumptions about a neutral transnational corporate lifestyle, the vast majority of the workers we interviewed—once again, especially the less privileged—emphasized translocal gendered family ties, whether in terms of regular contact and visits with parents and extended family or through the common practice of arranged marriages with women from "home." Most significantly, the less privileged H-1B workers recognized their relatively limited access to upward career mobility and mobility across borders on their own terms, surely the defining features of a transnational corporate lifestyle.

Finally, my brief consideration of discrimination on and off the job experienced by my respondents shows that Indian temporary high-skilled workers in the U.S. are forced to negotiate new racial hierarchies amongst fellow immigrants as well as "Americans." In dealing with discrimination against South Asians as a racialized group, the workers we spoke with deployed translocal class and caste privilege to varying degrees of success depending on their sense of entitlement as both emigrants and immigrants. For example, the more privileged workers were more likely to make distinctions between themselves as "skilled" and, therefore, deserving immigrants as opposed to "illegals." South Asians have historically been resistant to identifying themselves as racial minorities in the U.S., preferring instead to self-identify as ethnic minorities (Prashad, 2000). Susan Koshy (1998: 105) has argued this is true for many other groups of post-1965 immigrants, who "negotiate the U.S. multicultural terrain by circumventing a confrontation with race, stressing instead ethnicity and class positions." The downturn in the IT economy and the anti-immigrant sentiment, targeted especially toward South Asian men in the period we conducted interviews, made it more difficult to avoid at least implicitly discussing racial discrimination in the form of the unpredictability of everyday life for the less privileged H-1B workers with whom spoke.

The ambivalent, if not negative, experiences of the workers we interviewed does not fit the Indian nationalist myth of universally affluent Indian "symbolic analysts" as exemplars of Indian success in the global economy. The separate trajectories towards temporary highly skilled work in the U.S. reflect India's stratified information economy and reinforce the resilience of caste and class hierarchies despite global integration. At the same time, the shortcomings of temporary work for the less privileged H-1B workers does not cancel out the potential benefits, including, but not limited to, higher relative salaries and the potential for permanent immigrant status in the U.S. For these workers, access to transnational networks, and the symbolic capital associated with transnational employment, made the risks associated with temporary work abroad acceptable. American opponents of the H-1B visa program who insist these are "indentured servants," too often rely on xenophobic and populist strategies to scapegoat immigrants in response to national policies that favor the interests of firms over workers, both American and Indian.

Acknowledgements

Research for this study was conducted with the assistance of Angela Carr and Shannon Stoenbreck, students from UC San Diego in 2002. The University of California Institute of Labor and Employment (ILE) and the San Diego Civic Collaborative provided funding for this project. I benefited greatly from thoughtful comments on this paper from Gianpaolo Baiocchi and Stephanie Luce, as well as the editors of this volume.

Notes

1. To get a better sense of the political sentiment against the H-1B visa effort, see the "h1b.info" website which provides an exhaustive list of organizations mobilizing against the temporary visa program: http://www.h1b.info/bookmarks.php.

2. The category of Non-Resident Indian (NRI) was created by the Indian government in 1975 to introduce a financial facility to allow persons of Indian origin in the U.S. and the U.K. to open and maintain foreign currency non-resident accounts in U.S. dollars or British pounds sterling. For India, the incentive was hard currency in a period of economic transition, while for NRIs, their balances and interest were securely repatriable in a period of global financial history that saw the beginning of the flexible exchange rate. For more, see Nayyar (1994).

3. For more discussion about the politics and practice of transnational arranged marriages, a topic closely associated with recent "skilled" male migration from India to the U.S., see the work of Priya Shah (2004) and Inderpal Grewal (1999).

4. The current backlash to the " outsourcing" of computer programming and call center work to India by a range or organizations and individuals in the U.S., demonstrates this logic that essentializes a "third world" workforce as servile and then uses these stereotypes to blame foreign workers for American economic woes. A recent and pernicious example of this can be seen in the case of a popular talk radio program where hosts called and verbally abused Indian call center workers for public amusement. See the article by Arun Venugopalan (2005).

8

Students without Borders?
Migratory Decision-Making among
International Graduate Students in the U.S.

Katalin Szelényi

In the summer of 2003, Liang,[1] a Chinese graduate student in electrical engineering, traveled over 400 miles for a reunion with his college classmates. Such gatherings are far from unusual—every year millions of people around the world undertake the journey to reunite with former schoolmates. Yet Liang's reunion had a strikingly uncommon characteristic. It took place thousands of miles from his homeland, on the west coast of the U.S. At the time of our conversation, close to three-quarters of Liang's undergraduate class resided in the U.S., mostly as graduate students or as young professionals, just a year or two after obtaining a graduate degree.

At first glance, Liang may seem to be a typical participant in China's "brain drain" to the developed world. As a graduate of one of the best Chinese universities—where his education received substantial financial support from the government—his decision to obtain a doctoral degree in the U.S. may prompt him to never return permanently to China, potentially preventing him from contributing his expertise in his homeland. Yet as I listened to Liang, it became increasingly clear his future may be much less deterministic than this first impression suggests. Although Liang had spent close to nine years in the U.S., his personal and professional plans continued to be strongly influenced by his relationship to China. Describing the strength of his ties with family and friends, the enduring force of traditional Chinese community values in his life, and his recognition of growing economic opportunities in China, Liang explained:

I might, for example, get a couple of years of experience here after I graduate and then probably either move back completely [to China], or start a company that has something to do with China.

Are Liang's views about his own migration options unique? How do students make their decisions to engage in international graduate study and what considerations shape their post-graduate migratory intentions—including aspirations to return to their home countries, remain in the U.S. or relocate to a third country? In what ways, if any, do students' conceptions of national borders and the possibility of migration across those borders change in the course of attaining their graduate degrees abroad? And, ultimately, what implications do international students' intentions and plans suggest for scholarly efforts to better understand the international mobility of highly skilled populations, as well as policy efforts to lessen the extent of the potential loss of human capital in students' countries of origin? Questions such as these take center stage in this chapter, reporting on a qualitative interview study with twenty-six international graduate students at a public Research I university in the U.S.[2] In doing so, the study offers a micro-level analysis of decision-making at various points of graduate study, presenting the views and experiences of students from three distinct parts of the world: Brazil, China, and Italy.

Stepping into the Limelight:
The New Discourse on Student Migration

Perhaps never before has the issue of international student mobility attracted as much policy attention and debate as in the years following the turn of the millennium. The aftermath of the September 11, 2001 terrorist attacks brought intense scrutiny and reevaluation of the foreign student program in the U.S. Arguably, the events of September 11 transformed the discussion surrounding international education from largely celebratory to a mixture of hostile and defensive. In earlier years, many observers applauded the ability of the U.S. to maintain its preeminent standing in hosting students from abroad (Desruisseaux, 1999). By contrast, the climate today is characterized by arguments for the overriding importance of security concerns and even the possible economic loss arising from the education of foreign students (Borjas, 2002). These views are opposed by those defending the continuing relevance of international education in contributing to international understanding and economic and scientific development (McMurtrie, 2001; Zakaria, 2004).

International student mobility, however, is not only significant from the perspective of educational, economic and security concerns. Foreign students also play a distinct, and increasingly recognized role in international migration systems. In particular, student migrations, especially at the graduate level, form an integral part of the cross-border mobility of the highly skilled; a population defined most commonly as individuals holding a college or university degree (Lowell, Findlay, and Stewart, 2004). While arguments for including students studying abroad in analyses of international migration have been made with growing frequency in recent years (Baláž and Williams, 2004; King, 2002; Kritz and Caces, 1992; Li, Findlay, Jowett, and Skeldon, 1996; Salt, 1997), our understanding of the short- and long-term migratory intentions and behaviors of students engaging in educational endeavors outside the confines of their home countries remains limited.

Yet the importance of closely examining international student mobility in higher education, particularly as part of migration systems, is underscored by the sheer numbers of individuals involved. In just the top ten countries of destination, including the U.S., the U.K., Germany, France, Australia, Japan, the Russian Federation, Spain, Canada, and Belgium, the number of foreign students in 2001/ 2002 exceeded 1.5 million (UNESCO, 2004). In the 2003/2004 academic year, the latest year for which enrollment data are available, 572,509 international students attended institutions of higher education in the U.S. alone. This figure represents a 2.4 percent decline from the previous year, the first decrease reported by U.S. colleges and universities in the past thirty-two years (Bollag, 2004). Close to 49 percent of all foreign students were enrolled at the graduate level (Institute of International Education, 2004). The top three countries of origin were all in the Asian continent: India, China, and the Republic of Korea together contributed close to 200,000 international students. The fourth and fifth source countries for foreign students in the U.S. were Japan (40,835) and Canada (27,017).

Other arguments for considering international student mobility as part of regular migratory systems stress "flows of foreign students follow the same channels as do those of other migrants from their country of origin," particularly because of the importance the roles "geographic proximity, colonial ties, or cultural affinity, especially language" (Kritz and Caces, 1992: 233) play in student migration, which are strikingly similar to some of the main attributes of migratory flows in a more general sense. Notably, receiving countries tend to host students from specific regions of the world, as seen in the considerable representation of European students in countries of the European Union (UNESCO, 2004). The impact of past colonial connections is reflected, for example, in the attractiveness of the U.K. to students from Hong Kong. And lastly, illustrating the importance of familiarity with the language spoken in the host society, "English-speaking students favor the U.S., the U.K., and Canada; and French-speaking students tend to study in France, Belgium or Canada" (Kritz and Caces, 1992: 233).

Exceptions to these patterns undoubtedly exist. The U.S., attracting the majority of its foreign student population from the Asian continent rather than the geographically closer regions of Latin America, is a useful example here (Kritz and Caces, 1992). In addition, the dominance of English-speaking countries as host societies is a remarkable feature of student migration, reaching beyond the questions of familiarity with the language spoken in the receiving country. The preeminent place that English, as lingua franca, has come to occupy among the languages of the world has strengthened the draw of the "anglo-saxon" countries as a preferred venue of international education.

Studies of foreign student mobility add a unique perspective to the field of international migration. In particular, the migratory experiences of foreign graduate students to the U.S., the focus of this chapter, are significant in furthering our practical and theoretical understanding of highly skilled migration. International graduate students enter the country on student visas and, therefore, are not considered immigrants. However, while international students' immigration status remains temporary in most cases, their sojourns in a foreign country are far from temporary, as they normally spend more than just a few months abroad. Their entry to the Unites States is to a large extent unlimited in a legal sense (i.e., there are no quotas regulating the entry of students into the country), although following the terrorist attacks students have been subjected to security measures in the visa application process that have hindered some students' ability to move freely between their home countries and the U.S. (Bollag, 2004; Field, 2004). During the past year, however, in order to make the arrival of international students and scholars in the U.S. a less difficult process, the visa review system was again reformulated by lessening the role of the Federal Bureau of Investigation, appointing several new consular officers, and introducing an electronic system to handle the security clearance associated with Visa Mantis (Field, 2004). In addition, foreign students are often directly recruited by higher educational institutions. This recruitment process is best understood in the context of a generally liberal policy climate for highly skilled immigrants. This has been marked, for example, by legislation such as the "The American Competitiveness in the Twenty-First Century Act of 2000," considerably raising the limit on the granting of H1-B visas (Cornelius and Espenshade, 2001).

A further important aspect of the migratory patterns of graduate students relates to the conceptualization of graduate school attendance as an intermediate period between temporary and long-term migration: when individuals are in the position to make their migration decisions from a direct, prolonged and also legal standpoint while still remaining in temporary contact with the receiving country. Simply, during the course of several years, foreign students are engaged in a pseudo-migratory or pre-migratory environment, where they live and work (many foreign graduate students are employed as research or teaching assistants in their departments) in the setting they will possibly select for long-term settlement. While international students are most often outsiders in a legal sense, they are also insiders because of their day-to-day interactions with the cultural, economic, and educational aspects of the receiving state. This aspect of graduate education provides exciting opportunities for research since it allows for a direct examination of the decision-making process while in the potentially transformatory environment of the host country It also allows us to explore the impact of the students' initial intentions regarding the role of their U.S. graduate education experiences in their lives.

The Migration of Brains: Drain, Gain, or Circulation?

Graduate students' decisions regarding return to their home countries—remaining in the host society or relocating to a third country—are closely related to the issues of brain migration or more specifically: "brain drain," "brain gain," and/or "brain circulation." Some other often-cited concepts involving the movement of the highly skilled include "brain exchange," "brain waste," and "brain strain" (Lowell and Findlay, 2001; Lowell, Findlay, and Stewart, 2004). Together, these are some of the key questions underlying the study of highly skilled migration (Finn, 2003; Glaser, 1978; Johnson and

Regets, 1998; Salt, 1997). In fact, it is in this context the mobility of foreign students has been studied most frequently (Bratsberg, 1995; Das, 1969; Glaser, 1978; Huang, 1988; Johnson and Regets, 1998). Prior to relating these concepts to the specific case of international student migration, a brief discussion of the literature on skilled migration is in order.

The literature on international highly skilled migration has undergone significant changes since the 1960s, the time of the early literature on this form of cross-border labor mobility. In particular, conceptualizations of the extent and impact of high-skilled migration have progressed through several debates. On one side of these arguments are largely pessimistic notions of cross-border human capital transfers, with some countries—mainly those in the industrialized world—benefiting, and others—primarily developing countries of emigration, suffering significant losses in economic and educational development, as a result of the departure of their educated populations (Bhagwati and Dellalfar, 1973; Bhagwati and Hamada, 1974; Carrington and Detragiache, 1998; Haque and Kim, 1995). The concepts of "brain drain" versus "brain gain" thus refer to the permanent or long-term migration of highly skilled individuals from the perspective of sending, as opposed to receiving, countries. As Lowell and Findlay (2001) explain, "A 'brain drain' can occur if emigration of tertiary educated persons for permanent or long stays abroad reaches significant levels and is not offset by the "feedback" effects of remittances, technology transfer, investments, or trade. 'Brain drain' reduces economic growth through loss return on investment in education and depletion of the source country's human capital assets" (p. 7). While the actual extent of the "brain drain" remains unknown due to data limitations, some indications exist that a number of countries lose a substantial proportion of their highly skilled residents. The migration of persons with tertiary education from some of these countries, for example small nations in Africa, the Caribbean, and Central America, exceeds 30 percent of the highly educated population (Carrington and Detragiache, 1999). The term "brain gain," by contrast, depicts the educational and economic gains made by the countries that host highly skilled immigrants for extended periods or, in many cases, permanently.

More optimistic accounts questioning the primarily adverse effects of highly skilled migration date from as early as the 1960s (Grubel and Scott, 1966). Such conclusions also characterize recent economic analyses, arguing that a "beneficial," or "optimal," "brain drain" can exist where the promise of employment in a foreign country raises the sending countries populations' affinity for educational pursuits in their home countries, regardless of whether initial plans to emigrate materialize (Beine, Docquier, and Rapoport, 2001; Mountford, 1997; Stark, 2004; Stark, Helmenstein, and Prskawetz, 1997). These forces, then, lead to educational and economic development in that "when human capital accumulation is endogenous, and when successful emigration is not a certainty, the interaction between human capital accumulation decisions, growth and income distribution can lead to the result that a 'brain drain,' either temporary or permanent, may increase, (in) the long-run, income level and income equality in a small open economy, and, in certain circumstances, may even be preferable to a non-selective 'general' emigration" (Mountford, 1997: 302-303). Other recent research has shifted the emphasis from "brain drain" to "brain circulation," or return migration that "re-supplies the highly educated population in the sending country and, to the degree that returned migrants are more productive, boosts source country productivity" (Lowell and Findlay, 2001: 8). Yet other conceptualizations stress the importance of considering highly skilled migrants as part of scientific diasporas, through which émigrés often continue to contribute to their home countries, even when their stays abroad have become permanent forms of settlement (Meyer, 2001). The discourse on highly skilled migration, through the representation of several competing arguments, has thus evolved into a maturing field within the study of migration systems. However, many areas of this form of migration remain little studied. One such area concerns the international mobility of students.

Movement for Brain Training:
Students in International Migration

International student migrants occupy a distinct position in conceptions of brain migration. Indeed, "students are the only group who migrate primarily in order to enhance their human capital and, ostensibly, for fixed time periods. This can be termed 'brain training,' in contrast to other forms of 'brain distribution'" (Baláž and Williams, 2004: 218). Scholars of migration have sporadically recognized the importance of studying the migratory patterns of students in the specific context of brain migration and several attempts have been made to estimate the extent to which students participate in the processes of "brain drain," "brain gain," or "brain circulation." Much of this research is based on students' intentions to return to their home countries upon graduation.

In one of the earliest studies of student migration to the U.S., Das (1969) found "a very small proportion of the African and Latin American students wish to remain here permanently. This is true for the less developed and developed countries. It is the Asian students, specifically students from the developed countries, who plan to stay in this country" (p. 130). It is important to note however, there are changes in students' patterns of staying in the U.S. over time from the same country. Das' conclusion, therefore, is only applicable for the specific time period—the late 1960s—included in these analyses. For example, while Das indicates African students were not likely to plan to stay in the U.S., later analyses show considerable stay-rates for students from Egypt, South Africa, and other African countries (Finn, 2003). Based on the considerable variations in students' intentions to return, Das concluded 'the phenomenon of 'brain drain' or 'brain interchange,' or 'brain exchange' varies from country to country, region to region, continent to continent, and less developed to developed countries" (p. 153).

Varying intentions to return, or stay, in the U.S. by country of origin have been confirmed by later analyses as well (Finn, 2003; Glaser, 1978; Johnson and Regets, 1998). In a relatively recent study of foreign-born science and engineering graduate students earning doctoral degrees between 1988 and 1996, 63 percent of all students had plans to remain in the U.S., while an additional 39 percent had firm plans to stay, indicating they had received firm offers to engage in postdoctoral research, gain employment, or pursue R&D teaching, or other activities in the U.S. (Johnson and Regets, 1998). The national variation in the latter category is notable. While 47.9 percent of Chinese and 54.7 percent of Indian students indicated firm plans, only 22.6 percent of South Korean and 27.5 percent of Taiwanese students did so.

Other research measuring the extent of foreign doctorate recipients' stay rates relies on students' income tax records, defining a person as a "stayer" if s/he paid U.S. taxes on earnings of at least $5,000 at given time periods following graduation (Finn, 2003). Of foreign-born doctoral graduates in the science and engineering fields receiving degrees in 1999, 71 percent were in the U.S. in 2001. With regards to long-term stay rates, of all students receiving their doctorates in 1991, 58 percent were in the U.S. in 2001. Interestingly, however, just around the same percentage of these doctorate recipients were in the U.S. just two years after graduation, specifically in 1993. In fact, the year-to-year stay rate of the class of 1991 hovered around 58 percent in each of the years between 1993 and 2001. These findings led Finn to conclude "there is a certain amount of churning going on with respect to past classes of foreign graduates of U.S. universities. Some leave after staying here for a while, and these are largely replaced by others who return to the U.S. after living abroad for a while" (p. 5).

Examining the determinants of foreign students' non-return to their home countries, analyses have relied on Immigration and Naturalization Service data reflecting adjustment from non-immigrant to immigrant status of foreign students and, in one case, professionals, including students, as a sub-population. Exploring macro-level predictors of non-return to home countries, assumed largely as a sign of "brain drain" in the U.S. and the source countries, one such economic study shows U.S. immigration policy has a significant effect on students' and professionals' rates of adjustment to immigrant visas, with differential impacts based on specific countries of origin (Agarwal and Winkler, 1985). Another analysis, restricted entirely to foreign students arriving in the U.S. from twenty-five countries in the 1960s and 1970s, suggests that "income differentials do not play a predominant role in determining student 'brain drain.' Professional opportunities are, at least, as important as purely pecuniary comparisons in emigration decisions. In addition, political and social considerations play no less significant roles than economic variables in motivating the stay of foreign students" (Huang, 1988: 240). These findings were confirmed by Bratsberg's (1995) extended analysis of students from sixty-nine source countries arguing "students tend to return to rich and close countries and to countries that value their investments in education highly" (p. 381).

While macro-scale economic analyses offers much insight into the determinants of brain migration by foreign students, undoubtedly, too, there are a myriad of micro-level factors involved in students' decision to remain in the U.S. or return to their home country. However, the literature on these facets of decision-making is limited at best, and much remains to be learned about students' initial intentions to migrate and the impact of the "study abroad" experience on decisions related to future migrations and settlement. While two studies begin to offer a more human-centric approach to student migrations at the undergraduate level (King and Ruiz-Gelices, 2003; Li et al, 1996), and one study considers the factors that influence graduate students' and professionals' views about returning to China from the U.S. (Zweig, 1997), these analyses are presented in a quantitative manner. Yet, decision-making, *is* a highly qualitative process, in which student migrants simultaneously consider a multitude of factors and evaluate the interconnections among cognitive and affective motivations and aspirations. And while aspirations and intentions are by no means a direct reflection of actual migratory behavior, they are, beyond a doubt, an important indication of the ways in which students assess their migration options. They weigh their aspirations, abilities, national and transnational connections, as well as the opportunity structures they perceive in their home countries, the U.S., and other potential countries of destination. With these considerations in mind, the study discussed in this chapter reaches beyond statistical enumerations of students' non-return and economic analyses usually offered to explain student migrations. By exploring the multiple facets of migratory decision-making among international graduate students in the U.S., it brings forth new understandings of the relationship between international students' migratory intentions and the processes of "brain drain," "brain gain" and "brain circulation."

Methodology

The twenty-six international—Brazilian, Chinese and Italian—graduate students participating in this study were enrolled at a large public Research I university on the west coast of the U.S. (Western University) during the 2003-2004 academic year.[3] Invited through email announcements sent by the university's Registrar's Office, all students participated in a one- to two-hour semi-structured interview and received a $25 incentive for their participation. The study's design relied on the qualitative guidelines presented by Maxwell (1996). The students in the sample represented a variety of disciplinary affiliations across the physical sciences, engineering, humanities, social sciences, and the professional schools. The specific disciplines included anthropology, applied linguistics, business, economics, education, chemistry, civil engineering, electrical engineering, environmental science, epidemiology, film, information studies, linguistics, materials science, political science, and social welfare. In addition, the majority of the eleven female and fifteen male students were enrolled in Ph.D. programs, while some were in the U.S. to obtain a masters or professional degree.

Importantly, the interview questions related to making migratory decisions were part of a more extensive protocol probing issues of identity, transnationalism, and globalization. While specific questions were designed to address students' intentions and decisions regarding migration, it is important to note the participants engaged in lengthy discussions of their stays in the U.S. and their relationship to their home countries, relating many of their experiences to their personal, professional, and migratory plans. All interviews were tape recorded and transcribed verbatim. The interview transcripts were then coded for themes related to students' intentions regarding their decisions to come to the U.S. and their post-graduate plans.

The choice of the three source countries, Brazil, China (People's Republic), and Italy, was driven by several considerations, the most important being the goal of representing several major world regions. However, because of the low attendance of students from countries in Africa, the Middle East, and Australia at Western University, we limited our recruitment to countries in Asia, Europe, and Latin America. Our decision to focus on one specific country of origin in each of the three regions, rather than inviting international students from a variety of nationalities, was based on the importance we assigned to examining students' experiences in particular national contexts. Another key consideration in selecting the three nationalities related to the considerable number of Brazilian, Chinese, and Italian graduate students attending Western University. The representation of Chinese students was substantial, at several hundred, while the enrollment of Brazilian and Italian students was around thirty-five each. By focusing on these countries, then, we were able to assure anonymity to our participants.

Brazil, China, and Italy offer three diverse contexts for the study of graduate students' migratory decision-making. Beyond the immediately apparent variation in the economic backgrounds of the countries—with Italy representing the industrialized end of the spectrum in contrast to the developing economies of Brazil and China— notable national differences exist in the ways in which the extent and impact of highly skilled emigration are conceived. Concerns about "brain drain" in China have been prominent for the past several decades. The migration of students for graduate study has been at the forefront of these concerns. While since 1978, China has supported international education by sending students abroad on government-supported programs, efforts to encourage the return of Chinese students have also been undertaken with increasing frequency. These diverse efforts include both incentives in promises to provide better professional, housing and educational opportunities to returned scholars and their families (Biao, 2003), along with more creative strategies—such as the public humiliation of publicizing, in the mass media, the current or former foreign students' contractual letters emphasizing their "obligations to return and repay the country, the people and the Party for benefits and opportunities received" and "obligations to the motherland, the nation-state or the cultural tradition" (Broaded, 1993: 296). Importantly, China is the second leading place of origin of foreign students in the U.S. In the 2003-2004 academic year, 61,765 Chinese students were in the U.S. with 82.2 percent of that total studying at the graduate level. Chinese students also appear to be the most likely, of all nationalities, to stay in the U.S. upon graduation (Finn, 2003).

Brazil presents an entirely different picture in terms of the international migration of its student population. While representing the thirteenth leading country of origin among all foreign students in the U.S., the number of students from Brazil is substantially smaller than from China, at 7,799 in 2003-2004. In addition, Brazilian students are among the most likely to return to their home country after obtaining their advanced degrees. Of students receiving their Ph.D. degrees in 1996, only 25 percent were still in the U.S. in 2001 (Finn, 2003). However, in recent years, some concerns of a "brain drain" from Brazil began to attract the attention of the scholarly community and policy makers, with a considerable proportion of student scientist population leaving Brazil to complete their academic training. According to a recent study, between 1993 and 1999, 966 scientists emigrated, with 60 percent moving to the U.S. or Canada. While Brazil's loss of scientific talent is lower than in some other countries, such as Thailand and Argentina, some concern surrounds the high levels of financial losses—estimated at around $100 million just for the 966 scientists—associated with the emigration of the highly skilled (Guimarães, 2002).

Italy presents a further variation. The number of Italian students in the U.S. is relatively low; 1,995 Italian citizens attended institutions of higher education in the U.S. in 2003-2004. Of this number, 60.3 percent were graduate students. The stay rate of Italian students is slightly higher than that of Brazilian students and substantially lower than in the case of students from China. Of students who received their Ph.D.s in 1996, 39 percent were in the U.S. in 2001 (Finn, 2003). Despite the high level of industrialization characterizing Italy's economy, the concept of the "brain drain" is far from irrelevant. In fact, according to a recent estimate, Italy lost increasing percentages of its highly educated citizens during the 1990s. In addition, while the overall percentage of college-educated Italians going abroad since 1996 hovers around 3 to 5 percent, some indication exists that large proportions of student émigrés are graduates from the best Italian universities (Becker, Ichino, and Peri, 2003). To a large extent, emigration is facilitated by the structure of Italian academia. Some of these problems relate to the complicated system of academic appointments in which the relatively few academic positions might take up to a decade to achieve for Ph.D. graduates, and also in which research receives low levels of funding from the government (Pelizon, 2002).

Reasons to Migrate: Initial Plans and Post-graduate Intentions

One of the primary functions of graduate education is that of conferring to students high levels of professional preparation. Undoubtedly, the successful completion of a masters, professional, or doctoral degree prepares students to assume key positions in society through the acquisition of both professional expertise and responsibility in specific fields of study. The decision to seek a graduate degree abroad, however, reaches beyond simple aspirations to high levels of professional preparation. After all, the international graduate students participating in this study might have chosen to stay within the borders of their home countries and spare themselves the effort of taking difficult admissions exams in a foreign language, gathering information about educational institutions thousands of miles away, or adjusting to a foreign environment for periods of several years. Graduate education in a foreign country thus appears to considerably complicate the process of attaining a graduate degree. Yet U.S. higher education presented a distinct attraction to the twenty-six international graduate students, in both the more immediate sense of furthering their educations as well as in relation to their long-term personal, professional and migratory plans.

By virtue of their enrollment in various graduate programs at Western University, the students in this study managed to overcome potential problems and uncertainties surrounding their participation in graduate education abroad. However, the ways in which they conceived of their future professional roles and potential countries of residence, showed variation that was most significantly characterized by the degree of dilemma students expressed regarding their plans for their futures. The majority of these graduate students mentioned at least some uncertainty as they spoke of their future professional and migratory plans. In fact, several students indicated they preferred not to actively think about their futures since those decisions did not appear immediately relevant. However, it was clear that, in one form or another, all students had spent time considering their plans after graduation. Several students expressed interest in seeking out further short-term professional development opportunities in the U.S. immediately after graduation, referring to this option as a direct continuation of their graduate education. Thirteen of the twenty-six students—six Brazilian, four Chinese, and three Italian— were largely undecided about their future countries of residence. At the center of their dilemmas lay three main options that included settling in the U.S., returning to their home countries or moving on to live in an as yet unidentified third foreign state or a variety of countries. This latter option was well reflected in Gustavo's comments:

> I see myself living here, in Europe and in Brazil. I don't see myself living in only one place for the rest of my life. Maybe Africa. If I had the opportunity, I would move anywhere.

The remaining thirteen students—six Chinese, four Italian, and three Brazilian—expressed only slight dilemmas. Eight of these students wanted to return to their home countries while five preferred to stay in the U.S. While it is not the intention of the analysis presented here to draw definitive conclusions related to differences across the three nationalities represented by the students, it is, none the less, interesting to consider the link national differentiation plays in terms of country-of-origin differences.

The students' decision to come to the U.S,. and their post-graduation aspirations, appeared to be shaped in highly similar contexts characterized by a diversity of factors falling within the larger categories of the following: 1) the international context surrounding students' daily life and education; 2) social ties; 3) the influence of states and state institutions; and 4) the role of personal and professional interests and aspirations. These factors, in turn, took on different forms and significance depending on whether they exerted their influence prior to coming to the U.S., or in the course of graduate study. Because of the similarity of these contexts, the following sections discuss these factors in shaping both students' initial intentions and their plans after graduation.

Decision-Making in an International Context: Access to Information Across National Borders

Graduate students' decisions to seek international educational opportunities, as well as their future professional and migratory plans, were shaped by a diversity of factors related to the highly international context of their personal, societal, and educational experiences. Perhaps most importantly, the majority of students highlighted how globalization—through the connectivity of countries and cultures and the increased ease of obtaining information about foreign countries—played a major role in facilitating their ability to undertake international graduate study. As Fabio, a Brazilian political science student, explained:

> Personally, I should be happy with globalization and really it's good for me. I managed to access a lot of information about the U.S. I made a much more informed decision than my father did twenty years ago because there is just so much information around and so many people had gone back and forth.

Information about the general educational system was crucial in allowing students to make comparisons between the opportunities available in their home countries and the international educational experience. Students often emphasized the superior quality of graduate education in the U.S., especially with regards to research facilities, technology, and disciplinary expertise. In fact, the perceived excellence of U.S. higher education was the most often cited influence in the students' ultimate decision to study abroad. Ting described the popular Chinese reference to studying abroad as being "covered by the 'golden surface.' It means you're worth much more money and you will have better career opportunities in the future." Comparisons between national systems of graduate education were also prominent among the Italian students. In fact, some of these students had particularly damaging views of the structure of academia in Italy. As Gian Marco explained:

> Grad students in Italy, they become the secretaries of old professors. You know, they just run errands for professors. They don't have freedom in their research. It's just not real research like here, so I would never think about going to grad school in Italy.

While most students used specific web sites (those of educational institutions for example) to obtain information about the U.S., Chinese students were alone in discussing the importance of global internet networks in facilitating their ability to learn about educational opportunities abroad. Several students from China referred to Chinese internet groups established with the purpose of maintaining communication among Chinese nationals. This included those seeking to study abroad, current Chinese international students, and former students who had stayed in the U.S. or returned home. Beyond providing practical information and the opportunity to make contacts, these chat rooms are often sites for vivid debates on international graduate education, as well as the advantages and drawbacks of settling in the U.S. or returning to China upon graduation.

Information was also available to many students in formal academic settings. Several students described their exposure to western forms of curriculum and English language textbooks in their home countries. Often this experience was prevalent during the undergraduate years:

> As a senior, or even junior, I began to read literature and also studied textbooks and most of them are written in English and most of the research, (especially) most of the advanced research, is done here in the U.S. If you read the paper, journals, it is mostly written or developed by some American university.

Sandro discussed the graduate school options offered in his home country:

> There are a number of similar programs in Brazil and I saw that it is really similar. I mean they are the same books and discuss the same issues, but I wouldn't have the kind of international experience and that's an important part of the U.S. program.

Students' prior exposure to a westernized curriculum, and their awareness of western influence in graduate school, therefore, often facilitated the decision to undertake educational opportunities abroad.

If students indicated vast access to internationally situated information in their home countries, the availability of such information grew to even larger proportions once they were in the U.S. During international graduate study, the students came into intense contact with a wealth of information on the host society. Importantly, the students also tended to maintain high levels of contact with the events in their home societies through the media, the internet, and their relatives, friends, and acquaintances. Such high levels of engagement in the political life of their countries allowed students to make frequent comparisons between the U.S. and their home societies. Often these comparisons were mentioned in relation to the level of comfort they felt with their migratory options and their consequences in terms of their quality of life in both their personal and professional realms.

The interviews revealed important differences regarding students' perceptions of the living conditions and political climate in the U.S. and their home countries. Some Brazilian students expressed concern over the high level of violence at home:

> Maybe if we had good public safety, even if you have a good job, public safety is probably a huge concern, so … kidnappings and robberies are becoming more and more common, especially in the very big cities. So this may be another thing that motivates people to live in other places, especially in the U.S. and Europe. They are much safer.

Later in the interview, Luis related:

> In the near future, I will have kids, so I would have to consider a lot of things and again. Public safety is a huge concern in Brazil. I don't care about it right now, but when I have kids, I'll probably have to consider it. So I hope in the future, the situation is better in Brazil because my original plan is to go back there.

By contrast, the political system and current political conditions in the U.S. attracted the praise of some Chinese students. As Ting explained:

> I think the economy is the most important reason that holds students back from going back to China. The other one is political security. I know for myself and for a lot of people, our plan is to get a Green Card and then have some kind of international work. You can go back to China frequently but once something happens there, you can always come back to find asylum here.

Many Italian and Brazilian students, however, expressed considerable concern over the U.S. government, especially regarding its handling of the war in Iraq. In the words of Alessandra, an Italian student:

> With staying here, I definitely feel some discomfort, especially in the last few months when the war in Iraq started. I really found myself asking what I am doing here because the charges that the country was making were completely different from my ideas and my perspective. And at that point, Italy was actually unfortunately allying ideologically and politically with the U.S. But I felt also from the communication with my friends and my family that there was more a climate of dissent and there was resistance and there were rallies and it seemed to me that, at that point especially, I was really staying in this place that I don't belong to and I don't want to belong to.

Students often cited the greater availability of professional opportunities and research facilities in the U.S. International graduate students in the U.S. are exposed to cutting-edge research through their coursework and research assistantships, gain substantial knowledge and skills in their fields, and have access to state-of-the-art methodologies, technology, and data that may be unavailable in their countries of origin. The lesser availability of these opportunities in students' home countries was often mentioned as an inhibitor of return. On a related note, Fabio mentioned the high levels of comfort encountered in the U.S. as compared to Brazil as a factor complicating his decision:

> You see how much you have here and you start taking things for granted, such as you have a great library and you have greater access to people. People usually respond to emails. You see a lot of new things here and talk to a lot of different people and when you go back there, you see that things aren't as easy, the infrastructure and people are not as easily reachable.

It is important to note, however, Fabio was strongly contemplating his eventual return to Brazil, where he had already received an informal offer for a faculty position.

Among Chinese students, recognition of growing opportunities at home also prevailed. Liang, the student with plans to capitalize on this economic development by starting a business with connections in China and the U.S., was accompanied by several others who were also aware of macro-level changes in China. As Hou-En explained:

> I'm thinking about coming back because I believe that China is now in a transition phase and we do see a lot of future opportunity, in the next ten to twenty years. The national economy is growing at a very fascinating pace and the new business opportunities are very good.

Social Ties

Social ties, both informal and formal, played an important role in students' migratory behaviors. This influence was most readily noticeable in students' relationships with undergraduate and masters level professors and advisors trained abroad, friends and acquaintances, and family members. The support of faculty members for international graduate study was apparent in two main forms. First, they often emphasized the professional opportunities inherent in attaining a degree in the U.S. and pointed to the superior training their students would receive. Often their ideas about the opportunities of studying abroad were based on their own graduate school experience. And second, professors' social ties in the U.S. and more specifically, with U.S. universities, provided practical assistance to several students. A case in point is Luis, the Brazilian student, whose professor in his masters program not only introduced him to several faculty members from Western University, but also offered a personal recommendation to her former graduate advisor at the university: "I decided to attend this particular university because one of my professors was a student of the person I'm working for right now."

While professors' support for graduate study was general among the students, some noteworthy counterexamples also exist. Specifically, two Brazilian students spoke extensively about the conflicting views surrounding international graduate study in the Brazilian professional communities of economists and political scientists. These students described the attitudes toward studying abroad as highly divided between those favoring and those vehemently opposing such experiences. One side emphasizes the superior training opportunities students receive, while others argue "the things students learn here are just not applicable to our economy." Fabio, the student in political science, even indicated that his professor—who had also obtained a graduate degree in the U.S.—encouraged him to apply to universities abroad because of the isolation he felt in the Brazilian professional community. By sending his students abroad, his professor felt he could "create cohorts of people who can actually speak the same language" upon returning to Brazil. In addition, one Chinese student mentioned her professor's reluctance to support her decision to apply to a U.S. graduate program out of concern about the continuing loss of talent to western societies. These examples illustrate that while professors are overwhelmingly instrumental in encouraging their students to study abroad, in some cases faculty opinions in students' home countries are also likely to be characterized by some level of ambivalence regarding the value of international graduate study.

The importance of social ties in facilitating the decision to study abroad was not limited to the support of professors. The influence of family members, friends, and other acquaintances with prior international experience was also significant for several students in the study. Chinese students, for example, described the culture of their college years as significantly shaped by discussions of international graduate study. Upon entering their undergraduate institution, many of these students were immediately exposed to the stories of former students opting to earn their graduate degrees in foreign countries, especially the U.S., and soon discussions of study abroad opportunities became part of their everyday experience. As reflected in the words of a Chinese student: "A lot of my friends came here to study. You know, I just sort of joined my friends." It was not uncommon for Chinese students to indicate that up to 75 percent of their undergraduate class was studying for advanced degrees in the U.S. Several students emphasized the connection between the high quality of their undergraduate institutions and the high percentage of students coming to the U.S.:

> My undergraduate institution is probably one of the best schools in China, so a lot of them either came directly after graduating from undergrad or they got their graduate degree in China, then came over here to work or to pursue the Ph.D.

Importantly, this culture of studying abroad, apparent among Chinese students, was much less characteristic of the Brazilian and Italian students participating in the study. In fact, among Brazilian and Italian participants, the decision to pursue advanced degrees in the U.S., with few exceptions, was the result of a considerably more individualized decision.

The decision to study abroad was also rooted in the experiences of two students' family members. Liang's father was sent as a visiting scholar to the U.S. by the Chinese government in the 1980s: "So from him, I basically learned the educational system in the U.S. first hand. And also lifestyles and a lot of information regarding America." Fabio's father obtained his Ph.D. in Europe, returning to Brazil upon completion of his degree. The influence of this experience is apparent in Fabio's interpretation: "So since I lived in Scotland for four years, it was kind of a normal thing for me to go get a Ph.D. and maybe doing it abroad was familiar since a very young age."

Social ties also appear to play an important role in shaping the post-graduation plans of foreign graduate students. These influential ties exist at least in the forms of student-student, student-faculty, student-professional contact in the both sending and receiving countries, as well as personal relationships with family members and acquaintances at home and new relationships (including those with significant others) and friendships formed in the U.S. The professional ties students developed in the U.S. exposed them to further opportunities to migrate and their continuing relationships with faculty members in their home countries appeared to provide them with incentives to return.

However, the interviews revealed that relationships on a more personal level play just as important a role as professional ties in influencing students' decision to settle, migrate to other countries, or return home. Relationships with family members were among the most often cited reasons underlying students' decision-making processes and newly formed personal relationships in the U.S. were also a significant factor shaping the ways in which students conceived of their future professional opportunities and their decisions to migrate. Carla, a Brazilian student indicated, for example: "if I were not in this relationship [with a U.S. citizen], there would be a big chance I would be in Brazil right now finishing my thesis there."

The Influence of States and their Institutions

The role of various nation-states—in the case of this study, Brazil, China, Italy, and the U.S.—in students' past and planned migratory patterns manifested itself in a variety of ways. From the perspective of the U.S., immigration policies were prominent in facilitating or hindering migratory flows. This was perhaps best reflected in the ambivalence expressed by some students about the perceived openness of the U.S. to receiving students from abroad, as opposed to the policy measures implemented to more strongly monitor international student flows as a result of the events of September 11, 2001. Difficulties encountered when crossing international borders and obtaining and renewing student visas were often cited as inhibitors of the international graduate education experience, although obviously immigration restrictions did not prevent any of the interviewed students from coming to the U.S. The recognition of other direct state policies was apparent among Chinese students, many of whom were eagerly aware of the Chinese government's efforts to facilitate students' return upon completion of their degrees.

Besides the effect of actual policies, the actions of state institutions—such as international education agreements between public universities in sending and receiving countries—also held significant implications for the migration patterns of international graduate students. Italian students were the most likely to be influenced by this form of inter-state action through their frequent participation in educational exchange programs. Besides taking part in the Erasmus program in Europe (recently renamed as Socrates) several Italian students had the opportunity to spend a few months at Western University. As part of the Educational Exchange Program (EAP) between U.S. and Italian universities, these students made their decision to attain advanced degrees in direct contact with the educational environment of their graduate institutions. Through their experiences in EAP, Italian students were often studying and working with their future academic advisors and also gained first-hand experiences of living in the U.S. As many Italian students explained, these international educational experiences in other European countries and the U.S. culminated in their eventual decision to come to the U.S. by instilling in them a desire to seek further opportunities to study abroad.

In addition, financial support provided by national governments was prominent in the decision-making process of Brazilian students. Of the three nationalities represented in this study, only students from Brazil received financial assistance from their home governments. While almost all students considered funding an important issue when deciding to study in the U.S., the availability of state support was extremely important for some Brazilian students:

> The Ministry of Education in Brazil has a department that selects candidates, people that want to come to the U.S. or other countries…also Europe, but I believe that most people are coming to the U.S. So they select candidates and they provide us with a scholarship. So not only do they pay all the tuition but they also give some money for living expenses. And I think this plays an important role, at least in my case, and I think it's the case for the majority. People wouldn't be able to afford studying and living here. The cost of living is much higher than in Brazil.

While the program requires students return to Brazil upon graduation for at least a period of two years, these stipulations did not appear to prevent some students from considering staying in the U.S. In fact, one student described the state's ability to require his return as a "gray zone":

> The idea back in the Brazilian government is if you don't go back, they'll try to charge you for your money, but it's not clear if they can do that. … Because they can't charge back salaries and for some purposes, you could make a claim scholarships are salaries, so they could charge back your tuition but not the scholarship. But that's open-ended.

Carla, however, expressed an alternative perspective in explaining the role that Brazil played in her life:

> This agency funded my studies, like the country is making an investment in you and expecting some kind of return.…They want you to come back, period.

The migratory control function of the state is also apparent in a more subtle way. In order to better understand this sphere of state influence, it is useful to extend the discussion to educational and social policies instilling a certain level of patriotism in the students that may act to facilitate return. When responding to the question of what would motivate his return to his home country, Luis explained:

> Maybe…this pride of being Brazilian. I know we have a lot of problems and we have historical problems and economic problems. One reason may be the education that I had. We had civic courses.

For several students, patriotic sentiments were strengthened in the international environment. In the words of Ting:

> There's a very strong influence from the (Chinese) government that they want to instill the idea of nationalism in you, that you have to be proud of your country and we are the best ethnicity, like we are one of the best countries in the world.…I think in my generation we started to question it a lot, particularly these years; the economy developed so fast, we are open to different kinds of ideas from western countries.…But, on the other hand, I just have this sense we are very proud of our ethnicity, we want to maintain it. Particularly in a foreign environment, I feel particularly defensive about my national origin.

As reflected in these examples, the reach of state influence is quite prominent in terms of the development of national identity that, in turn, may influence eventual return migration or settlement.

Personal and Professional Aspirations: Curiosity, Opportunity and Responsibility

From an early age, attraction to international experiences and the drive to discover foreign countries and cultures compelled many of the students to seek education abroad opportunities. As Gemma, an Italian student explained:

> I lived in Germany for one year, with an exchange program, when I was in college. And then I lived in Ireland for a while. Every opportunity I had to live abroad, I took it.

As Gemma was describing her hometown, it became clear migration was not a common experience in the immediate environment where she was raised:

> I lived in a little town and it's really not common for people to go anywhere much.…It was not that I come from a place that is so awful that you want to run away. I mean it's a really nice place. It's just that I was really curious.

For some students, as in the case of Italians, these experiences began sometimes as early as high school, while for other nationalities—and this is generally relevant to both Brazilian and Chinese students—international study at the graduate level represented the first instance when students were able to satisfy their curiosity toward foreign countries through actual educational and living experiences.

Students' aspirations were also powerfully expressed in the professional realm, in terms of the importance they assigned to both their individual advancement and professional responsibility. Graduate school was looked upon as an important means to achieve a certain professional status, such as becoming faculty members, business executives, scientific researchers, film directors, or engineers, to mention just a few of the career options to which students aspired. Monetary considerations were also common. Undoubtedly, the students viewed graduate education in the U.S. as a pathway to higher incomes and more easily attainable career advancement. In this study, however, only two students defined their plans as overwhelmingly driven by the aim of individual advancement.

Beyond individual advancement, several students, prominently from Brazil and China, spoke at length of the social responsibility they felt toward their home countries. Social responsibility was often expressed as substantial concern toward the well-being of students' home countries and the emphasis they placed on their potential contributions to improve conditions as future leaders in their fields. As described by Wen-Hui:

> I think my biggest contribution will be after I get my Ph.D., when I go back home to work. I will bring new ideas. I think I will learn whatever I can learn from here and use it back home. I want to change the educational system in China.

Or as Gilberto put it:

> I love the country. I love the people. I love Brazil. Actually, I came here because maybe I will be helpful to my people, to help them in things like economic problems....I'm not here only with a personal goal in mind but also I have this idea of being helpful to my country.

These students defined their sphere of responsibility as belonging fully to their home countries and saw the international educational experience as a means to achieving that aim.

Social responsibility toward students' home countries, however, could not be directly linked to definite plans to return home. In fact, a number of students discussed their contributions to their societies through the experience of continued residence abroad, often by way of working for transnational organizations. As one Chinese student put it:

> "My biggest goal is probably working for the United Nations or some kind of international organization, to bring more advanced technology and ideas or ways of thinking to China. Basically, I think I'm learning things from here and I'm trying to bring them back to China, to my own native country."

In a similar vein, Carla, a student with highly uncertain plans about her future migratory paths explained:

> "From a professional point of view, the research I do is extremely focused on the Brazilian experience and I believe it will always be like this....Latin American people, and specifically people from Brazil, we sort of have a common research agenda which has a lot to do with economic problems faced by the Brazilian economy."

Students' perceptions of their sphere of professional responsibility were far from confined to the geographic spheres of their home countries. While some students clearly connected their contributions to eventual return, many others envisioned themselves as continuing to live in foreign states while consciously refusing to relinquish their national commitments.

Other students defined their contributions as situated in a regional or global sphere: "I wouldn't mind covering international issues, working in an international environment and promoting change on an international level, change in cultural programs or foreign policy." Most of these students were Italian, but two Brazilian and two Chinese students also expressed similar perspectives. Interestingly, migration decisions were more closely linked to this conception of professional responsibility, for few of these students wanted to definitely return to their home countries. Instead, they expressed considerable comfort with the idea of staying in the U.S. or moving on to live in other foreign countries.

Brain Migration Revisited

Migratory decision-making, in the context of graduate education abroad, is far from simple. In fact, in the lives of the twenty-six graduate students participating in this study, it took place at the confluence of a multitude of internal and external factors, including personal and professional aspirations, informal and formal social ties, access to information allowing students to weigh their options in an international context, and the subtle and not so subtle influence of the state and its institutions. To various degrees, graduate education in the U.S. harbored increased opportunities for individual advancement, the development of an expertise necessary for professional contributions, and the satisfaction of a curiosity toward exploring other cultures through intense immersion in U.S. society. In order to accomplish their goals, the students in this study made use of the increasingly international environment of educational opportunities and turned to a variety of resources such as internet chat groups, foreign-trained professors, or state-sponsored international education programs.

While the students presented a wide variety of experiences, intentions, and views, the transformational power of education abroad, within that diversity, was evident in redrawing students' conceptions of national boundaries and their own positions in relation to those boundaries. The students expressed a clear sense of national borders in their aspirations; the dilemma between returning to their home countries and staying within the geographical boundaries of the U.S., for example, was a major force shaping their plans for the future. However, students' position in relation to those borders became less defined. In particular, the education abroad experience appears to have emboldened some students to the possibility of continued existence away from their native lands. This is perhaps best reflected in the fact over half of the study's participants strongly considered a number of migratory options after graduation. Returning to students' home countries, thereby re-establishing more conventional conceptions of national borders, was only one of these options.

A fluid conception of national boundaries was also apparent in students' ideas about their professional contributions. Place of residence, and the geographic focus of professional activities, often had little in common in some students' minds. This was most readily apparent in the examples of students who saw themselves staying in the U.S. or working for an international organization, while at the same time continuing to use their research and other professional activities to address issues of importance to their home societies. This finding is especially significant in relation to common conceptualizations of the "brain drain," measured most often as the actual long-term absence of individuals (i.e., bodies with brains) from home countries (e.g., Carrington and Detragiache, 1998, 1999). To be sure, those students who will not return home are situating their physical selves away from their home countries; in this narrow sense, they are part of the "brain drain." However, a closer look at the aspirations of the students reveals their plans and notions of professional responsibility do not imply a contradiction between foreign residence and a strong focus on issues in their home countries. Nor do students keep their eyes closed to economic development at home. As exemplified by Liang, some student migrants are intent on capitalizing on domestic growth by engaging in transnational activities, thereby building cross-border partnerships. The loss of bodies, therefore, does not always imply the loss of brains as well. Instead, several students in this study—those whose professional focus remained on their homeland but who also considered the option of non-return—continued to commit their brains, and arguably their hearts, to their motherlands.

Yet other students saw their responsibility as more directly linked to an international sphere of existence. Evaluating these students' experiences, however, presents considerable challenge. What are the implications of students' choice to envision their contributions as belonging not to a specific country but more to a transnational context? While the sending countries of these students will count their loss as "brain drain," undoubtedly, other countries—and not necessarily the U.S.—would stand to benefit from their professional endeavors. A case in point is Chun-Hwa, a Chinese student whose field of specialization concerns the environment:

> I don't see any nation that can be developed without communicating with other countries in the world. And it's all about communication and cooperation among nations. I think the environment is really a world problem. It's not the U.S.' problem. It's not China's problem....You have to think of yourself as part of the world to be in good shape.

Arguably, in an increasingly global world, we cannot dismiss the importance of this sense of responsibility. In theorizing about highly skilled migrations the need has perhaps arisen to recognize the efforts of individuals like Chun-Hwa, who opt to reside outside of their home countries but, at the same time, concern themselves with issues of global relevance. Indeed, this emphasis on global, rather than just national responsibility, is also in line with the highly international context in which students form their initial migration decisions as well as their post-graduation plans.

Also important to note are the eight students who were strongly leaning toward returning to Brazil, China, or Italy upon graduation or after a few additional years of professional training in the U.S. The experiences of these students are clear examples of intended "brain circulation" (Johnson and Regets, 1998), where not only students' interests and aspirations are linked to their home countries, but we also see a reestablishment of an immediate spatial connection with the homeland. Some clear-cut examples of "brain drain," in its conventional conception, were present as well, as reflected by the students who preferred remaining in the U.S. without indicating plans to maintain professional contact with their home countries.

In their migratory intentions the students participating in this study represented several forms of brain migration. The most easily definable examples are those whose plans fell closely in line with "brain drain" (intending to stay in the U.S. with no professional contributions to home countries), or brain circulation (planning to return to home country). However, several students' aspirations defy straightforward categorization. Indeed, the experiences of the students who saw their future contributions as strongly connected to their home countries without linking those contributions to reestablishing residence in those countries, fall both within the concepts of "brain drain" and "brain circulation." In other words, the question of who gains and who loses becomes muddled and dependent on what we mean by the concept of citizen contributions. In this instance, while the home countries may lose the students' direct economic contributions (e.g., these students will not pay taxes at home), they will continue to receive the benefits of their educated citizenry through their professional endeavors. Even more difficult to categorize are the experiences of the students who envisioned themselves as living outside of their home countries and having the global as their sphere of responsibility. The professional activities of these students will have the potential to affect development in a number of countries. In this sense, their contributions may not be linked to one specific nation-state, and while it is clear that the home countries will experience "brain drain" (in terms of losing both economic and professional contributions), it becomes difficult to determine which country, or countries, will benefit from the gain. While the country of eventual settlement will reap the economic benefits of highly educated individuals residing and working within their borders, it may be impossible, or complicated at best, to situate the loss and gain of professional activities by individual nation-states.

Some policy implications also arise from this study. First and foremost, the students' experiences point to the importance of creating and maintaining diaspora networks that provide foreign-trained students with opportunities to maximize their intentions to remain engaged in the issues facing their home societies. It is rather obvious many of these students were eager to maintain not only personal but also professional connections with their countries. Diaspora networks or similar transnational professional associations provided valuable opportunities for facilitating their continued involvement. And second, the students in this study showed considerable awareness of migration-related policies, or lack thereof, in their home countries. Chinese students paid attention to government efforts to facilitate their return and Italians were aware of the absence of such efforts on the part of the Italian government:

> It doesn't seem like the Italian government is too concerned with this (the migration of the highly skilled) and that's too bad. I mean, I'm not going to make the self-serving claim they should try and do something to get us back into the country and do some good there, but in reality, they really should.

There are, in fact, many efforts under way at the level of the European Union to lure back highly educated Europeans residing abroad, especially in the U.S. However, the Italian students in this study did not appear to be aware of these Europe-wide undertakings. The importance of these policies is further underscored by the considerable degree of dilemma some students expressed in relation to their future plans. Governmental efforts to facilitate return, or continued engagement in domestic issues, coupled with non-governmental or professional social diaspora networks, might be the means to develop patterns of student migration that lessen the incidence of non-return or professional disengagement from issues of high importance in sending countries.

Notes

1. All student names mentioned in this chapter are pseudonyms.
2. The research discussed in this chapter is part of a larger study conducted in collaboration with Robert A. Rhoads, professor of higher education at the University of California, Los Angeles (UCLA). The study received financial support from UCLA's Academic Senate and the James D. Kline Fund for International Studies Award.
3. The original sample included thirty graduate students, ten from each country. However, by the time of the interviews, four of these students had secured immigrant visas to the U.S. These four students are not included in the present analyses.

9

Wired for Work: Highly Skilled Employment and Global Mobility in Mobile Telecommunications Multinationals

Ödül Bozkurt

"I was waiting for the tram, a little late for work you know. Cold, typical Helsinki day. I am in my work clothes; skirt, blazer, a little bit of make-up. There is this other young guy, I think Indian, a student or something probably, at the stop, too. This old Finnish guy arrived, he was kind of drunk—you know, you see that all the time around here—and first asked me, he says, 'Where are you from? Are you from Mexico?' I didn't answer and he turned to the Indian guy and shouted angrily now, 'Welcome to my country! Welcome to my country!' Yes, welcome indeed....You can get upset of course, but....He wasn't dangerous or anything. And he's had too much to drink and, well, they are not used to seeing these foreigners around."
—Sanam, thirty-one-years-old, Employee at Helsinki headquarters of Finnish multinational[1]

How did Sanam, from the Middle East, end up among the morning tram-stop crowd at the edge of Europe, in Finland? She is not married to a Finn, not a diplomat, not a refugee. Foreigners, especially those who are visibly identifiable, especially if they do not fit those categories, are still a rarity here. Surely, the little country that has given the world Linux and Nokia has vastly increased its reputation internationally in the information age, claiming almost a sort of mythical charm, often from afar, in high-tech circles. One might venture to guess that the fellow tram-rider in this anecdote may be among the still small, but increasing, number of foreign students in the engineering schools of Finland. Sanam, herself, is not a student either, though. She is an electronics engineer and moved to Helsinki about a year ago because this is where the headquarters of the multinational corporation she has been working for in the past four years is located.

211

The encounter is a reminder that Sanam has not arrived in the most cosmopolitan of cities, but one would certainly not think that, based on what one sees and hears while waiting in the lobby of the corporate tower where she works. Many of Sanam's co-workers in this facility do not look or sound like they were born and raised in Finland, though it is hard to tell if they are passing through town on a quick business visit, are staying on for some time or even settling down here indefinitely. One thing is for sure: this stream of passers-by does make it difficult to dismiss offhand the pictures and stories in the company brochure about a "truly global workforce" as nothing more than public relations. Indeed, the mental images that the term "workers on the move" conjures up have changed dramatically in the so-called age of globalization. As the editors of this volume note however, the geographical mobility of the highly skilled has so far received less attention than it deserves both theoretically and empirically.

The global circulation of labor does not take place, to the degree that it happens at all, in a friction-free, time and space-blind, impeccably "rational" labor market, as sociologists love to point out to economists. In much of the migration literature today, it is almost redundant to make the case that labor flows are informed by various forms of connections and networks that could, in purist economic theory, be regarded as imperfections (Boyd, 1989; Tilly, 1990; Gurak and Caces, 1993; Massey et al., 1993). A massive amount of scholarship has been devoted to the specific task of identifying the nature, power and resilience of the networks that give shape and form to contemporary migration; be these based predominantly on history, kinship, ethnicity or nationality. Highly skilled workers do not enter circuits of movement in a social vacuum; well-known cases like Silicon Valley attest to the possible significance ethnic/national/kinship ties can have on the flow of highly skilled labor (Alarcon, 1999; Saxenian, Motoyoma and Quan, 2002).

There is, however, a particular type of work organization inside which the movement of highly skilled workers might involve countries or cities where few, if any, of their co-nationals, or at least ones they are directly related to, may have set foot before; the multinational corporation. The spatial fragmentation of the production of goods and, increasingly also of services, in contemporary capitalism means these processes are less and less frequently contained in one geographical location. Multinational corporations are the organizational structures that are most adept at economic activity built around this principle. In essence, they are global networks whose functioning is predicated on the flow of resources inside these networks. An increasingly more valuable such resource is the multinationals' high-skilled workforces. As multinationals become leaner (and, according to many, meaner) by outsourcing more and more of the lower-value-added forms of economic activities to second or third parties, they also stand to become increasingly more concentrated direct employers of highly skilled workforces. At the same time, as multinationals take over domestic firms in a wide array of sectors and locations, they emerge as major employers around the world for workers with high levels of human and cultural capital. In other words, multinational corporations and highly skilled workers figure prominently on one another's vista in the employment relationship.

Multinationals might be said to "wire" the world for their own business purposes, connecting a number of nodes both literally and figuratively in the creation and expansion of their global networks. Such wiring, then, constitutes the infrastructure across which resources, including highly skilled workers, are likely to move or be moved. Strategic decisions drafted in corporate boardrooms about how, when and between which nodes to wire the world are translated into practical realities by actual workers, often setting them in motion, too. At the same time, highly skilled workers, who have already been set in motion around the globe in other ways, or, more importantly, who very specifically desire and pursue such motion, often turn to multinationals in their efforts to realize simultaneous geographical and professional ambitions. In investigating the global mobility of highly skilled workers, then, multinational corporations deserve a long and close look. The "anomalous" cases of those highly skilled foreigners like Sanam who now appear among the morning rush crowds on their way to the high-tech zones around places like Helsinki underscore a novel phenomenon. Though they are still rare, they are not as rare as they were ten years ago. What is the role multinational corporations play in making encounters with these foreigners, even in such places, possible and increasingly more common?

Multinational Corporations and the Mobility of the Highly Skilled

In management scholarship it is widely agreed that the core *raison d'tre* of the multinational corporation (henceforth MNC) as an organizational form is precisely the facilitation of flows of the factors of production through the inclusion of dispersed nodes of activity under one overarching network, thereby minimizing transaction costs over space (Porter, 1986; Ghoshal, 1987; Bartlett and Ghoshal, 1989). Much of the globalization literature also concurs on the centrality of mobility and flexibility and of, in turn, the way MNCs carry out business (Harvey, 1989, 2001; Sklair, 1995; Held et al., 1999; Friedman, 2000). Such agility over space, and around national regulation, is, in fact, what has made MNCs so crucial to the debates about the suggested enfeeblement of nation-states in the global economy today.

In terms of how MNCs "do globalization" by rendering the factors of production mobile, we know quite a lot about their command over capital but not nearly as much that over labor. In fact, MNCs are widely notorious (or famous, depending on one's position) for moving *towards* labor, rather than moving labor *about*, for cost, productivity, and efficiency purposes. The jobs that flexible arrangements, adopted by multinationals, help create and those they, concurrently, destroy, have been a hotly-debated topic in both scholarly and political conversations. Much of this attention has justifiably turned to the quality of working conditions MNCs offer to the low-skilled workforce they employ, mostly indirectly, around the world (among others, Barnet, 1995; McMichael, 1996; Klein, 2002; Bakan, 2004).

Highly skilled workers are usually only fuzzily sketched in on the fringes of this portrait and then, mostly in popular, rather than social science, media. Such depictions would have readers believe that the highly skilled employees of MNCs are "global souls" (Iyer 2000) who shuttle between meetings in equally sleek branch offices of their companies around the globe. Tirelessly mobile and effortlessly cosmopolitan, they embody the best that the "borderless world" (Ohmae, 1990) promises to be. Not only are they employed by MNCs, they are at the same time the most avid consumers of these companies' brand-name products and services. If anyone may have indeed gained the "freedom of extraterritoriality" (Bauman 1998: 28), that distinguishes the privileged of the contemporary era, it should be these people who are literally and figuratively "going places."

Given the emphasis on flows and networks in understanding transnational processes, especially as they relate to the movement of people in social science literature (Castells, 2000; Glick Schiller, Basch and Szanton, 1999; Sassen, 2000; Smith, 2001; Savage, Warde and Ward, 2003), it is interesting that the MNC-as-network has not been subject to much sociological analysis. In the "world cities" paradigm, there is detailed demonstration of how the central nodes of global financial flows are also homes to the headquarters of many multinationals, with special attention paid to the polarization of labor markets into a high-paying, high-skill and a low-paying, low-skill end in these urban spaces (Sassen, 2000; Massey, 1988). Despite the emphasis on the significance of the mobility of capital to the mobility of labor in this framework (Sassen, 1988), the *direct* role played by multinationals in human mobility remains an underexplored theme.

The massive management scholarship on knowledge transfer (Wernerfelt, 1984; Ghoshal and Bartlett, 1990; Gupta and Govindarajan, 2000) and expatriation (Edström and Galbraith, 1977; Dowling, Schuker and Welch, 1994; Selmer, 1995) inside the MNC does tell us a good deal about the circulation of human capital as conceived of, and intended by, corporations. These, however, retain a focus on issues of efficiency or productivity, as well as a largely prescriptive tone aimed at making the MNC a better-lubricated machine. Discussions of knowledge transfer are often disembodied in the sense that they do not, on the whole, make the connection between workers as real people and the knowledge they are expected to diffuse. Expatration and repatriation discussions do look at individuals, but with the important exception of Jon Beaverstock's work (Beaverstock, 2001a, 2001b, 2001c, 2005), which comes out of geography, workers are only of interest in their capacity as conduits. The bulk of this scholarship remains mired in a heavy dose of cultural essentialism on the one hand, and of practical psychologism, on the other. In general, these studies do not tell us very much about the variable modes of mobility as navigated and experienced by actual workers.

Here, then, I attempt to broaden our sociological understanding of the MNC and its role in human mobility around the world by focusing on the "middling transnationalism" (Conradson and Latham, 2005:229; Smith, 2005: 241-242) of its highly skilled employees, heeding Conradson and Latham's call to remain attentive to "everyday practices and geographical emplacement" (Conradson and Latham, 2005:227). In what different ways do highly skilled workers move inside the MNC? Does employment at multinational corporations help make migrants out of foreigners or only "traveling salesmen" (and women), whose "homes"—however often and for however long they are left behind—are not fundamentally reshuffled? How are employment at multinational corporations, various other forms of ties to specific locales, and the pursuit of geographical ambitions, related in the actual careers of high-skilled workers?

I address these questions by looking closely at the career trajectories of a group of highly skilled workers employed by two large MNCs in the mobile telecommunications sector. The cases of the foreign workers in the headquarters of these corporations in Helsinki and Stockholm claim a privileged place in this effort. The mobile telecommunications industry itself is one of the flagship sectors of the overall global economy today with respect to its sheer volume of business, its leading role in the creation of new technology, and the geographical reach of its markets. It is more serendipitous, rather than consequential, for the purposes of this chapter, that these MNCs are in the business of connecting people while they are mobile; yet the choice of this industry is emblematic of the world-wide global economy.

The Global Expansion of the Mobile
Telecommunications Multinationals

Mobile phones are ubiquitous today. It is hard to keep in mind how rapidly that happened. In 1995 there were about 50 million mobile phone subscribers in the world. In 2005 that number had reached 1.3 billion and, according to one top industry specialist, by 2010, it was expected to reach 2 billion (Valentine, 2004). In various estimations, 600,000 to 700,000 people are signing up for mobile subscriptions around the world every day. Judging by current trends, mobile phone subscriptions will have exceeded line subscriptions in 2005. Mobile phone penetration rates have increased exponentially, hovering now around 70 percent in Europe and reaching as high as 90 percent in Sweden and Finland. Importantly, expansion of mobile phone usage has not been an exclusively affluent-country affair. Although penetration rates are expectedly lower in poorer countries, mobile telecommunications technology is being adopted by them as well, often more rapidly than fixed lines. The sheer volume of business implied by even the most incremental increases of market penetration in China and India alone put the populous of developing countries at the heart of the mobile telecommunications industry's future. Certainly in terms of the markets it serves and the geographical reach of its products, this is a global sector.

The telecommunications industry used to be the quintessential service business functioning under the purview of nation-states with close links, in fact, to the military and defense industries. Recent developments—including the wave of deregulation that has swept over the world since the early 1990s, and the privatization of many national PTTs in otherwise quite different countries—have changed that. The liberalization of telecommunications coincided with the ascent of mobile technologies which, taken together, have radically altered the structure of the sector and its line-up of major players (Pehrsson, 1996).

Despite widespread deregulation, transnationalization tendencies in the operator segment of the sector have lagged behind those of privatization. For every operator with global, or at least regional, ambitions, such as TMobile or Vodaphone, there are several times as many national ones. By contrast, both the handheld device and the network infrastructure ends of the sector are dominated by multinational corporations, including the MNCs in my study. The Nordic region in general, and Finland, and Sweden in particular, have led the development, standardization, and commercial use of mobile telecommunications technologies. While the list of the world's top MNCs is dominated by American firms, the two giant Finland and Sweden-based MNCs have, in a way, created one significant sectoral niche that bucks this trend.

To be clear, that telecommunication technology is developed by only a few major companies and then sold to the rest of the world is, itself, not a new arrangement. In the age of line telephony, PTTs around the world purchased and used networks developed by Motorola, Ericsson, Siemens and the like. Yet, the claims that MNCs today have few, if any, special ties to headquarter countries are, at best, far-fetched (Mair, 1997); it is still the case that they are no longer merely domestic companies selling internationally. The telecommunications giants of the yesteryear were more strictly domestic in that their various functions, including manufacturing, were either exclusively, or much more densely concentrated, on their home turfs. Even when these companies had production plants in low labor-cost areas of the world in the past, these were in a limited number of locations. More importantly, before the liberalization of the

telecommunications industry, and especially the rise of mobile telephony, the presence of the MNCs away from their home countries
took the form mostly of dealing with overseas customers; typically
state-based economic enterprises for the sale, maintenance, and up-
grade of lines. This did not necessitate the setting up of permanent
offices in too many locations around the world. The proliferation of
branch offices in the sector came about as recently as the 1990s.
Thus, in addition to the reach of their markets, mobile telecommunications MNCs today are also global in the sense they physically
exist in their manufacturing plants, branch offices and even Research
and Development (R&D) facilities, across a much higher number of
geographic nodes around the world. Both MNCs discussed here have
offices and, hence, a permanent, material presence marked by the
same, globally recognized logo in over 100 countries.

Unlikely Destinations: Sweden and Finland

While the mobile telecommunications multinationals have, so to
speak, taken these Swedish and Finnish firms where they have never
been before, the headquarter countries themselves have been slower
to let in newcomers with high educational and professional cre-
dentials. Neither Sweden nor Finland is a popular migration destination for highly skilled workers or, for that matter, labor migrants
in general.

There are, admittedly, important differences between the experiences of the two countries' histories of immigration. Having sent as
much as one-fifth of its population to the New World around the
turn of the century, Sweden only began to receive sizeable numbers
of immigrants—around 10,000 per year—in the 1950s. This largely
unskilled labor migration reached its peak in the 1960s before it
dwindled. In the 1970s, immigrant arrivals were predominantly
through family reunification clauses, while starting in the early 1980s,
Swedish migration policy turned decisively towards the reception of
political refugees and asylum-seekers (Ekberg and Gustafsson, 1995;
Migrationsverket) Of the total of nearly 79,000 residence permits
issued by the Swedish Migration Board between 1994 and 2004,
slightly over 27,000 have been given for employment. Since the
early 1990s, close to one million of Sweden's population of nearly 9
million have been foreign-born (Statistika Centralbyrån 1997).
Among the roughly 1.8 million inhabitants of the larger Stockholm
region, 148,000 were foreign-born in 2003. Of these, those born in

Finland constituted the single largest group with about 20,000, followed by those born in Iraq (11,000), Iran (9,000), Turkey (6,000) Poland (6,000) Chile (5,000), Somalia (5,000), the former Yugoslavia (4,000) and Germany (4,000) (Utrednings-och-Statistik Kontoret, 2005) There is much talk today in the Swedish media and academia of a growing "multiethnic" or even a "doubly creolizing" (Hannerz, 1996) population, at least in Stockholm, albeit one with problems of segregation and discrimination (Frykman-Povrzanovic, 2001).

Finland is far less familiar with taking in outsiders. Itself traditionally an immigrant sending country, mostly to neighboring Sweden, Finland has only become a net receiver of migrants recently, since the early 1990s. The number of foreign-born in Finland has quadrupled in the 1990s though with a starting point of only about 25,000. With the country's total population being just over 5 million, this is still a very small number (Forsander, 2002, Joronen et al., 2002). Nevertheless, the introductory narratives of publications on population statistics often underline the "growing diversity" in Finland. As for much else, Helsinki is the hub for the immigration into the country; of the city's population of around 560,000, nearly 30,000 were foreign-born in 2003 (Helsinki City Urban Facts Office, 2004). Those born in Russia constitute the biggest group with about 5,500, followed closely by immigrants from the Baltic States, who number around 4,750. That there are over 4,000 residents of Helsinki who were born in Africa shows that although inflows are heavily tilted towards Finland's neighbors, they do originate elsewhere, largely due to refugee and asylum policies.

Sweden and Finland routinely rank at the very top of lists for all that is "good" in the world: quality of life, life expectancy, income equality, technology development, education, and much else in between. The Nordic countries, as a whole, have long represented the social-democratic model of strong welfare states (Esping-Andersen, 1990; Baldwin, 1990). Although there are obviously differences in the way they formulate public policy, against the backdrop of the world as a whole, both Sweden and Finland are clearly very generous in their universal welfare provision schemes that include the middle-class. At the same time, they have exceptionally competitive economies. The World Economic Forum ranked Finland first and Sweden third on its competitiveness report in 2004 with the U.S. squeezed in between.

Both countries have largely financed their generous welfare provision by doing business beyond their small domestic markets—again bearing in mind that Sweden's population is around 9 million while Finland's is around 5 million. They have both, therefore, long relied on international trade; the former mostly in steel, forestry and mining and the latter in pulp and paper products. Traditionally strong in engineering, both countries have become leaders in the development of new information technologies resulting especially in Finland's case, in being seen as a living example of the state-of-the-art information society (Castells and Himanen, 2002). These are places where, almost like social laboratories for futuristic technologies, the locals enthusiastically take to using the most cutting-edge gadgets. They have also become, mostly due to the successes of their MNCs, countries almost synonymous with the "mobile revolution" since the early 1980s. After all, the increasingly universal GSM technology followed on the example of the reginal NMT system that was developed and utilized in the Nordic region.

Both countries have literacy rates of 100 percent and have drawn upon their highly educated labor forces and, among these, especially the strong expertise in the technical and engineering fields, as valuable human assets. It is, therefore, probably not surprising that in both places, highly skilled workers constitute but a fraction of recent migrants. So far, they have not been needed all that badly. Against this backdrop, MNCs appear to be vanguards in importing the rare highly skilled foreigners, however small these still may be in sheer numbers. Stockholm and Helsinki, despite being important hubs in the Nordic region, the former more so than the latter, are not among major world cities in the sense of attracting long-term highly skilled settlers from outside. Although their image as futuristic, hyperconnected, tech-savvy places may pop up in academic treatises or in MNC public relations company brochures such as the one referred to by Sanam, touting "bright future, post-industrial, economies based on creative technologies," I promise you, Stockholm and Helsinki are places trend setters are either from or visit, but not often the places to which they move.

The headquarters of multinationals still retain the most important control functions (Massey, 1988; Sassen, 2000) and still are quintessential Rome of various—if not all—roads leading from the branch offices that cater to specific local markets around the globe. Both MNCs in this study have offices in over 100 countries around the world while their corporate functions, especially their R&D facilities, are locally clustered in the capital cities of their Nordic neighbors. Both MNCs were among the top ten employers, respectively in Sweden or Finland, though the weight of the Finnish MNC is considerably greater in the Finnish labor market than the Swedish MNC is in its home country. Because the number of workers in the MNCs fluctuated greatly following the boom and freeze of the mobile telecommunications market between the early 1990s and the early 2000s, exact numbers are difficult to specify. However, the payroll numbers of the two corporations were, at the time of research, merging around 23,000 in each headquarter country.

Following Real-life Career Tracks

Although I have placed the foreign workers employed at the headquarters at the center of this piece, the empirical material that informs my discussion comes from a larger research project. The project included a third mobile telecom MNC based in the U.S. and a third at a fieldsite in Istanbul, Turkey. In total, I carried out in-depth, face-to-face interviews with seventy-two MNC workers, quite evenly divided between Finland, Sweden and Turkey.[2] In Finland and Sweden, the bulk of the interviewees were employees of the MNC based there while in Turkey interviewees were quiet evenly divided among the branch offices of the three MNCs. Especially in the Turkish branch offices, which ranged in size from fifty to 200 employees, my interviewees included those high-up in the business hierarchy, including vice presidents and human resource managers. In general, however, my interviewees were highly skilled workers in middle-level ranks, with varying managerial duties and powers. Almost all of them worked in the network infrastructure, rather than mobile handset divisions, of the MNCs. There was a range in the primary functional divisions of their jobs, including research and development, marketing and sales, and more purely, engineering-based work which, itself, had numerous sub-categories.

All of the foreigners in the two headquarters, and the majority of the interviewees in the larger study were in the thirty to fourty age range. With few exceptions, particularly in Sweden, they belonged to the cohort of employees who entered their jobs in the mid-1990s. All interviewees had finished at least three but mostly four to five-year university degrees, and many had graduate degrees, including Ph.D.s. The vast majority of them had technical degrees, many of them electronics engineers or even telecommunications engineers, by training. There were a handful of workers with degrees in economics or management and even one interviewee in Helsinki who had a degree in philosophy. Women made up slightly more than a third of the interviewees.

I used several different initial entry points into the company networks in each site including official channels, engineering unions, prior acquaintances and, in one case, a list-serve for an "international club" of MNC workers. From these initial contacts, I found additional interviewees through directed snowball sampling. It was directed in the sense that despite the general tendency on the participants' part to refer me to an exceptionally well-traveled or a foreign colleague, I asked them to provide names for co-workers who may not be mobile at all. I also tried to pursue several functional strands within the organization such as R&D, marketing and sales or instruction so as to get a better-rounded picture of the range of motions and experiences. Twenty workers in the study were foreigners employed at the MNCs' in various functional divisions, twelve in Finland and eight in Sweden. Their countries of origin included Belgium, China, Germany, Finland, France, Hungary, India, Iran, Turkey, Sweden and Venezuela. Seven were women and thirteen were men. They ranged in age between their late twenties and late thirties. On the whole, the foreigners as a group had become settled enough to be migrants. This is, as I will discuss below, only one way that workers inside MNCs move, so in addressing these cases in greater detail I place them within the context of the larger research project.

Life-histories are an extremely useful tool in understanding both what people do while working for multinationals and what multinationals do with their workers. Although the average age of the workforce in the sector, because of its massive growth in the past decade, is skewed to the younger side, *all* of these foreign workers had worked for other employers prior to accepting a job with their current company. And of these workers, all of them had worked for another *type* of employer including academic institutions, government, companies, domestic firms in home countries, and domestic firms in Sweden or Finland. Their career histories therefore shed some light on the differences of working for/in a multinational as compared to other kinds of employers and the role these may play in bringing foreigners to unlikely destinations and/or keeping them there.

Global Dispatch: Moving to the Rhythm of Markets

When business is going well, there is much movement across the global network of mobile telecommunications MNCs. Among my seventy-two interviewees, only about one in ten had never traveled internationally for work. The movement of individual workers is closely tied to what transpires in the business markets so it is not surprising that this cohort, who mostly started their careers as the sector took off, were so likely to have gone overseas on the job. Mattias, whom I met in Stockholm, was a technical instructor in the late 1990s and remembers having counted to realize he had been "on the road" 140 days in 2000. Markku in Helsinki verified the mythical story that his MNC, at one point, chartered a weekly flight out of the city to a customer site in Southern Europe because it was cheaper to do so with the number of people they had working on a project.

When mobile telecommunications technology began its rapid expansion in the early 1990s and picked up still greater momentum in the middle of the decade, there was a flood of business for the MNCs as much of the world awaited being rewired. Governments around the globe, with the obvious concentrations in Europe, Asia and the Americas, issued their first operator licences through highly publicized competitive biddings, one after the other. If awarded a licence, the operator would proceed to purchase the network equipment from a vendor, like one of the two MNCs here, as well as the services involved in the installation and implementation of the network. Who gets the network systems up and running, and therefore makes conversations on one's mobile phone possible, remains largely invisible to the end-users. If the two MNCs in this study are globally recognized names today, it is mostly because they also manufacture mobile handsets but, in fact, bigger monies are often at stake in the infrastructure end of the business.

In this initial phase of the emergence (or, one could argue, creation) of brand new markets, basically from scratch, the geographical movement of workers from the MNCs' headquarters appears to have been pervasive. The first task at a given market location would typically have been the preparation of a contract bid to gain the "account," the business of a mobile operator. Because a contract requires exact specifications of technical details, it necessitates either constant, or very frequent, contact with the potential customer.

In many cases, a certain product or solution that is to go into the network has to be customized for the local market or according to what the mobile operator wishes to offer among its commercial services; which precipitates still greater customer contact. The preparation of a contract is an extensive affair organized as a major project. Even if specific parts of the project can then be delegated to workers who may be spatially dispersed, the need to be in close contact with the customer requires a permanent presence in the market unit at least by the core members of a contract team. This stage of courting the potential customer was narrated by many interviewees as having been "intense," involving eighty-hour weeks, sleepless nights at the office, and the like. An engineer from the Swedish MNC recalls the teams of three MNCs camping out at the same hotel in China while preparing bids on an account there and bumping into each other in the lobby during the days leading up to the customer's decision.

According to interviewees who worked on projects in the bidding phase in places as varied as China, Brazil and Moldova, to name just a few, contract preparation can last anytime between six months to a year and a half. Because the greater part of the world's markets adopted mobile technologies in the span of the same five to ten years, and also because in many markets there were multiple operators that were to build their own networks, the MNCs had to simultaneously set up shop quickly in a myriad of locations. In case of a successful bid, the actual "roll-out" begins. For the high-skilled workers, the "installation phase" involves everything from scoping out the appropriate spots across the operator's coverage area to place the base stations for transmission, to the supervision of their actual placement on these spots; an effort that may take them "climbing up rocky foothills," "driving around in cars on dusty roads for weeks," and sweet-talking their way into (and on top of) private buildings. The "implementation phase" involves getting the software running on the system that, in turn, is both preceded, and followed by, extensive testing. Throughout these efforts, contact remains close with the customer and tasks are carried out often in mixed teams of workers from both companies. After the system is handed over, contact is continued for maintenance, problem-solving and repair purposes. This is work that requires real people, in real time and space. Most of the time, for most of these tasks, the MNC has to dispatch workers to be on the ground, working hands-on and directly interfacing with customers.

Although the relationship with the customer continues in some form for as long as the equipment stays in use, the bulk of the network equipment vendors' business and profits is generated through the sales of the products and services involved in the roll-out phase of new infrastructure. Rounds of technological upgrades that build upon the existing network are, again, eagerly pursued as new business but these are, on the whole, not nearly as profitable as a cycle of infrastructure construction begun anew. It is only when customers adopt newer technology that is sufficiently different from the preexisting one that a brand new infrastructure needs to be put in place and that the stakes go up high again. This is why the expectations of the MNCs have been seriously thwarted since third generation mobile licenses were bought by operators for extremely high price-tags and yet commercially viable business plans, for their actual operation, have been so slow in coming.

That is also the reason, in many ways, during the time I conducted fieldwork, between the summer of 2001 and the winter of 2004, that interviewees almost invariably talked about how their life on the job had suddenly become static. The frenzied growth of the markets had subdued by 2000 and by 2001 there was very little new business on the horizon. As exuberant market outlooks got hastily recast and uncertainty about future sales and growth descended upon the golden sector of the global economy, the stock prices for many of the flagship MNCs either froze or fell drastically. As quarterly report after quarterly report revealed the need for a substantial reality check on expected earnings, executive boards became more vocal about the necessity for major restructuring. Big rounds of layoffs swept across the payrolls of most of the big players, including especially one of the MNCs discussed here. When there was work to be done around the world, moving people around was necessary, and when there was money to be made, there were the funds to pay for such movement. Once the sector went into a standstill, various forms of arrangements in which workers were moved around were the first on the chopping board of the corporations' long lists of cost-cutting measures.

The sequence in which markets unfold, as outlined above, also captures the overall direction and rhythm of most of the movement associated with highly skilled MNC jobs. The companies initially needed a mobile workforce or, rather, had to mobilize their current workforces, because they had to simultaneously accomplish two things. First, they had to carry out the tasks required by the various stages in market development as discussed above; and secondly, they had to build the local competencies in the market units hoping that business opportunities in these places would not be temporary. Until the latter could be achieved, the first was predicated on the allocation of resources from elsewhere in the MNCs' global network to the particular market unit in need.

For the immediate task of bidding for a contract, expertise was typically culled from the large and varied human resources of the headquarters. A contract bid is an extensive affair not only in terms of duration but also in terms of the variety of skills it requires. While some employees work on contract bids from beginning till the—variably bitter or happy—end, others come in to take care of specific tasks or to substitute a temporarily missing project team member. A project team is therefore made up of a combination of local workers and employees sent to the particular site for variable durations.

Building up local competence involved the hiring and training of large numbers of new workers around the world. Many of the MNCs' current country offices were set up in the 1990s to establish a more permanent sort of presence in chosen locations, especially if these markets were thought to be significant, even in the case that the first contract bids did not yield successful results. Organizational development of this sort necessitated the movement of individuals with sufficient leadership skills and, more importantly, managerial experience to the new markets. It is widely stated and known, especially in the Swedish MNC, that the top executives in market units are often from the headquarters. These managers, in addition to responsibilities associated with the immediate business in a local market, also need to undertake those having to do with the recruitment of locals and the consolidation of a solid skills base in the local unit. The goal is to get the unit to the point where it can stay afloat with, at most, intermittent support from either the headquarters or other centers of expertise. No matter how fast recruitment and training occur, getting a local office self-sufficient generally requires these dispatched managers to stay on the ground for considerable amounts of time, at least a year or, more often, two.

Global growth in the mobile telcommunications business, therefore, set large numbers of MNC workers on the road for different periods of time, to accomplish a variety of tasks in wide-ranging directions. The MNCs attempted to accomplish their stated goals by moving people about in a combination of short stays of up to six months, generally referred to as "business travel," and longer stays, anywhere from six months to two years, in the category of "overseas appointments," or, as they are more commonly referred to, "expatriate contracts." The career histories of many of the highly skilled workers in the sector today are checkered with a series of alternating moves of these kinds, the incredible momentum of the 1990s having filled up many resumes with interesting combinations of country names. On many occasions, business travel destinations morphed into "current addresses" which, then, changed again. These accounts show, like market expansion, the individual workers' geographical mobility can be frenzied, subdued, or be at a standstill.

Orbits Inside the MNC

The lists of city and country names plotting the career trajectories of workers reveal the difference the entry point makes for the orbit of one's movement inside the MNC. The personal histories of the workers at the headquarters almost invariably included travel, often multiple times, to the new markets as they emerged. In the earlier part of the 1990s trips to various European markets seemed to be common, while as the decade progressed the destinations became more varied, including markets farther away in Asia and North America. Given the goals such movement was intended to accomplish, as discussed above, it is not surprising that a pattern of ripples-from-the-center-to-the-nodes emerges from the individual histories taken together.

That is not to say, however, that the workers in the branch offices do not, or, during the boom of the sector, did not move. All of the workers of the Nordic MNCs I interviewed in the branch offices in Istanbul had been to the headquarters at some point, typically quite early in their tenure with their employer. It is important to note, though, even if workers from a local office move towards the "center" of the MNC, this center might not be the global headquarters. If there was a regional headquarters within greater proximity, this may be the most common destination of travel by those employed in the branch offices. Among the workers of the U.S.-based MNC's Istanbul office, for example, only one had traveled to the headquarters near Chicago, whereas almost all others had been to the regional headquarters in London.

Of course, not all the moves from local offices are even *up* the corporate geographical hierarchy. The larger, more established market units that had developed competencies earlier were expected to provide the expertise needed by the less established markets in their "vicinity." Many MNC workers in the Istanbul branch offices had extensively traveled to the less developed markets in places like Kazakhstan, Saudi Arabia or Romania; while both Venezuelan workers I interviewed in Stockholm talked about their multiple trips to and stays in various other Latin American countries after joining the MNC in the Caracas office. The different directions of the traffic between the headquarters and local offices correspond to differences in the reasons why travel would take place along each route. I have already detailed why workers from the headquarters would need to travel farther out across the MNCs' global network, but what brings employees in branch offices to those otherwise unlikely destinations in Stockholm and Helsinki?

In most cases, the first visit to the headquarters involved attendance in a training event with alternating sessions of classroom instruction and, if applicable, hands-on practice. Companies have largely standardized the training for specific technologies or skills and these are organized in modules offered at whatever specific location is calculated to involve least traveling by participants as a group. In recalling travel to the headquarters for training, workers talk about the considerable confinement of their time to the classroom and their interactions with the instructors and other course participants—usually a combination of others from various offices of the MNC and workers from customers. In town usually for two or three days, at most up to about a week, travelers for these occasions largely remain students/curiosity visitors with limited, if any, exposure to the workings of the company at the headquarters. In some other training arrangements participants get at least a rudimentary sense of the way work is carried out at the center, as when they are brought in to learn-by-doing, they take part in small projects or take on specific tasks in large ongoing projects. A good part of Jonas' job in Stockholm as a supervisor in a testing lab, for example, is the training of visiting workers from local offices around the world who come here to familiarize themselves with a particular technology during stays of about a month to six weeks.

In some other instances, travel to the headquarters involves reporting to, or consulting with, a higher-up who is in charge of a particular project in a given market unit. Although the on-site team has primary responsibility in the accomplishment of given tasks, they do have to report, in formal and informal ways, to a "responsible manager" at the headquarters. Some of these visits, in the accounts of the interviewees, appear to have been important in keeping faces attached to names and to help retain a stronger sense of the "reality" of the connection. Some others were more specific in goals and intentions, including reporting back of the demands of the potential and present customers, and assessments of whether the MNC would be able to deliver accordingly. Various accounts of going to the headquarters to "explain to them what (was) going on on site" communicate something of an ambassadorial spirit to these trips as they involved a sort of brokerage effort on the part of the local unit workers to negotiate a realistic solution between the headquarters and the current or potential customer in the market unit.

In general, then, when the workers from the headquarters go to the local markets, they typically do so as "experts"—to get things in gear, the business off the ground, and the branch office on track. When people from the nodes of the global network travel to the headquarters they usually do so for training and to get a level of exposure—though often strictly limited—to the larger company and to communicate the specific needs and ambitions of the market units. In this sense, travel between the headquarters and branches usually highlights the respective positions of MNC workers if not in command and decision-making, then, at least, in the knowledge hierarchy inside the global network.

The Benefits of Movement

Even if all the factors precipitating the movement of workers inside the MNC are at play in full-force simultaneously, the majority of the MNCs' workforces are, of course, "at home," rather than on the road, at any given point in time. Although movement on the job may sometimes become obligatory, generally the number of workers needed for dispatch is a fraction of the total number of workers in a given location. In other words, traveling on the job is often, at least to a degree, a matter of choice. Why would MNC workers want to move, either on "business travel" or "overseas appointments?"

Travel has its charms. Especially at the beginning of careers, when most workers did not have substantial family responsibilities, they were rather unanimously enthusiastic about an opportunity "to see different places and experience different cultures." Among high-skilled MNC workers from the branch offices in developing countries, even though many are from relatively privileged middle-class backgrounds, travel overseas, per se, was a novelty. Emre, from Turkey, commented that going overseas was "the stuff legends were made of" among his university crowd. For the generally well-traveled Northern Europeans, who may have gone vacationing in Spain with their families while growing up, or gone on rite-of-passage Inter-rail trips while in university, going to foreign countries is less likely to be a complete novelty. Yet, they, too, were active in seizing opportunities to travel on the job. In the case of short visits, part of the attraction is a chance to see places that are not "the most common destinations." As Andres said in Stockholm: "[You see the] main capitals in major countries, but you also see these smaller parts, small cities, different countries you would never go to on vacation." Interestingly, this notion the job might take one somewhere where one would otherwise not go, also came up frequently in the accounts of the workers from the branch offices. Çağlar sounded rather proud, recounting his first visit abroad ever, by stating: "You know, people go abroad first to France or England or such, I was going to Finland. I mean, who goes to Finland for their first time overseas?"

There are material benefits to business travel, the emphasis on which varied greatly among interviewees. In general, travel itself was not, by any stretch, a luxurious arrangement. Everyone, except the very top-level executives, traveled coach class and stayed in "good but not five-star hotels" or apartments rented by the MNC in country sites. There were occasional dinners with the management or workers of the local offices, but no lavish entertainment written off on the company account. The major material perk for travel seems to be the per diem travel allowance, estimated to be in the range of $50 to $75 a day in most travel destinations. The Nordic workers were especially quick to point out that this allowance was tax-free; many interviewees also emphasized that because they would be traveling to take care of what was usually an urgent task, they often did not get much time to spend money anyway. Coupled with the reimbursement of many personal expenses, the "extra cash" added up especially since, during boom times, so many workers were on business trips so often. Marja in Helsinki said particularly during the early years in her career, money from her travel allowance would almost match her salary.

Perhaps a still more beneficial outcome of traveling, one possibly with longer-term consequences, is the extension of one's professional network inside the MNC, especially globally. Because there are usually people traveling in from multiple locations to a particular site, the connections to be made during travel are not limited to those employed by the local unit. In the case of workers from various branch offices, this is also a frequent place to get to know others, typically in more supervisory roles, from the headquarters. Such contacts are crucial to one's inclusion in future project teams. Furthermore, connections first established during business trips can lead to subsequent offers for overseas appointments. An expatriate arrangement may well follow from repeated visits to the same locations, with each visit taking up to six weeks and involving close interaction with those in decision-making positions at a local office. Esra had traveled to Singapore twice already when that office suggested she come there on a two-year contract. Fredrik had traveled to South Korea back to back so many times that the local management there thought they should take him on as an expatriate so he could work with fewer interruptions.

Travel does seem to have somewhat diminishing returns however, if it involves only the repetition of the same or similar tasks and/or remains too strictly limited to the same destination or the same work partners. Many interviewees agreed after numerous experiences of "shuttling between base stations and customers' offices," "getting on those long flights to Asia," or "teaching the same things to the local staff over and over again," the excitement over travel for its own sake wears off rather quickly. Unless the professional capacity in which one is traveling, or the destinations, or both, change, travel can, and does, seem to lose much of its initial charm.

By far the more desirable, and desired, way to move on the MNC job ladder, both professionally and materially, is expatriation. Although, even in the most frenzied times, less than 3 percent of the MNC workers were on long term expatriate contracts, almost half of my interviewees had had such overseas appointments, some of them several times. In this arrangement, there was much greater emphasis on the "cultural experience" as opposed to the "place experience" so frequent in the travel accounts. The former is different in that it involves everything associated with functioning within a different working environment and "way of doing business" on the one hand, and, on the other, being an inhabitant of a foreign city or country.

These experiences are appreciated more on their own terms by some but they are also important because they fortify resumes. By definition, workers are sent out on overseas appointments if their specific skills or expertise are much needed at a particular site and, as such, the arrangement is a sort of official seal of recognition by the MNC. However, according to the interviewees, the acquisition of cultural dexterity and an enhancement of one's capacity to work in different settings with different customers and coworkers was just as significant for professional development. Vibeke, in Stockholm, voiced the common view on expatriate contracts in a somewhat cynical tone by saying "as long as one does not stay too long" these appointments are "flashy" and they "make it easier to go up the corporate ladder."

An overseas appointment is, of course, also the far more materially beneficial way to move inside the MNC. Although the specific conditions of the appointments vary considerably, expatriates typically receive generous salaries from their "temporary" employers and get to keep their home-country salaries too. Perhaps more importantly than keeping the salary of the home-base job was the fact the workers got to keep the job itself in the first place. "A *real* expatriate contract gives you the guarantee to have a job to come back to," said Markku, contrasting this with the newer (and fewer) arrangements offered to people in the cost-cutting era. Also, among the other fringe benefits workers on expatriate contracts enjoyed were: accommodations, often much more lavish than dwellings at home, a company vehicle and/or driver, children's attendance in international schools, and language classes for the employee and spouse.

There are, even in boom times, few instances of movement as expatriates *to* the headquarters to begin with. These typically involve, as Biörn, with twenty years of experience in the Swedish MNC, suggested, an effort to lure high-paid, top-level Anglo-American managers who need additional incentives to take their careers to these notoriously high-tax/suppressed-salary corporate labor markets. While this may generally be true, such must have been the extent of movement inside the MNC in the 1990s that three of the twenty foreign interviewees in Helsinki and Stockholm had, in fact, arrived there first as expatriates from the branch offices, especially those in the "periphery" of the global economy.

This closer inspection of the modes of movement on the MNC job shows that while high-skilled workers employed by these companies may be mobile and, in general, derive various benefits from their mobility, neither the "mobile condition," nor the benefits attached to that, are constant or continuous. MNCs take workers at the headquarters out to the world much more so than bringing them in to the headquarters. Yet, despite the unbalanced account sheet, that they were the locations for the headquarters of MNCs had resulted in Helsinki and Stockholm welcoming visitors who would otherwise most likely not ever had been there. Brief visits and the rare instances of relatively longer, but still temporary, stays aside, though, had MNCs in fact been instrumental in more permanent imports?

High Skilled Foreigners in the Stockholm and Helsinki Headquarters

Out of the twenty foreign workers I interviewed at the headquarters, four in Sweden and two in Finland had arrived there through their movement inside the MNCs' global networks. Praveen and Syed both came from the same branch office in India, two exceptional cases of workers from the branch offices arriving in Stockholm with expatriate packages. Tiscar had been hired in Venezuela, dispatched to Argentina on an overseas appointment where the working relationship with the Swedish workers not only led her to develop a great liking for and curiosity about Sweden, but also helped get a local contract at the headquarters. Luis, also from Venezuela, had been in Stockholm for five years and did not plan to return to Venezuela any time soon. Emre and Umur came to Helsinki from Turkey. Why would these highly skilled workers want to stay in these cities that are not "home" to many others with similar qualifications?

Materially, living and working in MNCs in Finland or Sweden on local contracts is far less advantageous than doing so on expatriate contracts. Praveen, Syed and Luis first arrived on lucrative overseas appointments. When the MNCs decided to do away with the expensive contracts, they were given a choice. They could either go back to their earlier jobs, which were in their home countries, or stay, but "go local." Praveen says that meant a nearly 50 percent reduction in his salary income; the same as for the other two coworkers. All three decided they would be materially better off if they stayed, defining "material" in wider terms than merely "financial," taking into consideration the overall quality of life. Praveen and Syed have children in school, and they both discussed the high-quality of education in Sweden as being important for their futures. Luis talked about the combustible political situation in his home country and how his concern with safety made Europe a sensible home. They agreed, as did other foreigners in Sweden and Finland alike, that the general orderliness and efficiency of life in and outside of work made living in these places a "comfortable" experience. A range of social services even middle-class workers can count on the generous welfare state to provide, from universal health care to public transportation to workers' protections, were also mentioned in support of this assessment.

The social democratic ideology permeating the organization of civic and worklife in the Nordic countries is certainly one, at its heart, about how material relations between the members of a society should be governed. These interviewees voiced a number of reservations about the "reality" of living under strongly social democratic regimes and discussed their personal conflicts with locally prevalent conceptions of work, leisure, competition, achievement and affluence. These comments were very often prefaced, however, with the expression of a strong preference to living and working in a "humane" country as opposed to what they portrayed to be the number one destination for those corporate workers in pursuit of "lots of money," "big cars" and "big homes:" the U.S. It is not wise to generalize from the views of so few but it's not completely unwarranted to suggest that socio-cultural notions governing the distribution of material resources in a given location also figure into the evaluations and calculations of migrants.

In terms of material and social/cultural considerations, in other words, many of the incentives to stay or leave are informed as much, if not more, by the *national context*. While the MNC might be instrumental in allowing foreigners their first step into unknown territory, long(er) term commitment decisions ultimately depend on the desirability of living in the larger local environment in which MNC nodes operate. This is truer still for workers who have families, as the well-being of other family-members are often even more directly influenced by the various kinds of resources nation-states make available to them in given settings. Expatriation contracts sustaining somewhat suspended lives in space in luxury-land are not tenable infinitely and if "overseas appointees" wish to stay somewhere they must do so as "locals." MNC employment is, therefore, able to bring in foreigners to the degree that life as a local is attractive to them at the headquarters.

Professionally, life *is* likely to be attractive at the headquarters. The headquarters is an attractive destination for MNC workers because the nature of the work experience is different at the organizational core. Here, in the interviewees' words, one is simply "closer to where it all gets done," where "decisions are made," and where "you can see how it all begins." Many who had worked in branch offices commented that the organizational depth is not comparable with the range of possibilities the headquarters offers. "You can only go up that far" in the branch offices and "there are not that many different kinds of things to do."

One of the most cherished advantages to being at the headquarters is that it is the best place to establish contacts and gather information about the various interactions across the MNCs' global network. To come around one full ironic circle, one of the ways in which such contacts and information make a difference in the career plans of employees is that they better equip them to find out about, and seize opportunities for, *movement* again. The headquarters are the single best-positioned launching pads for those seeking opportunities to move somewhere else that might meet their even more ideal company/country combination. It is not possible to generate definitive claims about the durability of the "settled" condition for those who had experienced first-hand how MNC-employment can enable one to move around the world. There were far too few cases at hand and, at the time of research, little opportunity to do anything but remain put, (and, if possible, employed) in the mobile telecommunications sector. Nevertheless, as the sector began to show signs of picking up at the tail end of the fieldwork, Luis, for example, moved on to another position in Spain. It is not unreasonable to think that once the sector kicks off into another round of "musical chairs," those who have gone through an intra-company move might attempt a subsequent one.

The foreigners MNCs bring in to Helsinki and Stockholm, therefore, may or may not be "keepers," to use the term by one interviewee. However, MNCs are also important in making encounters with highly skilled foreigners more possible and frequent in these contexts because, in addition to possibly pulling them in through their global networks, they also constitute a resort for those highly skilled workers who are looking for ways to *stay* and to do so without it having to be a professional sacrifice. Of the twenty foreign interviewees at the headquarters, twelve had initially arrived in Sweden and Finland for reasons and channels other than those internal to the MNCs. Eight were already living in these cities when they found and took the MNC jobs. Another four had decided, after earlier brief visits, that they wanted to move there more permanently and looked for a job that would allow them to realize that ambition. I consider a number of individual trajectories in detail here to understand the different ways in which MNC employment helps keep highly skilled workers in places like Stockholm or Helsinki.

One, albeit still uncommon, way to have arrived in Finland and Sweden for (future) highly skilled workers is as students. This was the case for six of my interviewees. Sweden and Finland are not even minor blimps on the global radar of foreign student flows. In Finland's largest institution of higher education, the University of Helsinki, out of over 37,000 registered students in 2003, there were only 1,266 guest students, only a fraction of which were conceivably there for the entire duration of their degree studies. In Swedish statistics at the national level, exchange students are grouped together with degree students but in 2003 there were a total of 5,509 new permits given to foreign students in the country altogether. Foreign students in these small countries are not only a small group in absolute terms but proportionally as well. However, among my interviewees, those who had initially come to Sweden and Finland to attend school did constitute a discernable sub-group. Starting off in India, Iran, Venezuela, Turkey and Hungary, these life/career histories reveal various commonalities.

After earning his Bachelors and Masters in electrical engineering, climbing up the work ladder to become the manager of a factory by his late 20s while also working as an instructor at the university, Tahsin says he looked at his life in Tehran and thought, "This is *all* I can do here. This is the limit. I *have* to go, I *have* to go, I have to *go*." To go abroad was an overriding desire and to go for a Ph.D. appears to have been both a means and an end. He estimates having written to over 500 technical schools "everywhere around the world" and sent just one letter to Finland: to a professor in Helsinki whose reference he found among the reference section of a technical book. He received a far more personal response than he had from anywhere else, one also containing a concrete offer for a research student with a contract and salary. It also seems Finland, as a destination, along with the "twist" it had taken for him to have an opportunity there, carried a considerable degree of exotic charm for Tahsin.

The "kismet" element is usually quite strong in the stories of those who ended up as students in Sweden or Finland, but Mert's story also covers the major "rational" reasons why the arrangement becomes possible for most foreigners. Mert turned to Nordic universities after his numerous attempts with American universities failed to return funding offers. When he found out that universities in Sweden and Finland did not charge tuition *and* you could work on a student visa, they emerged as an attractive possibility. The technical expertise in these countries, too, had put them on the map of potential destinations, as schools in Stockholm and Helsinki were famous for their research on magnetic fields, his area of specialization and interest. Mert figures he could not have gone to Germany, France or Italy, because there he would have had to not only learn but in fact study *in* the local language. In general, the reputations of Sweden and Finland in the technical fields (which are, in fact, not to a small degree, related to the two MNCs), not having to pay major tuition or fees for higher-education in these countries and the possibility to conduct studies in English, are the major reasons why overseas students are interested in coming here.

Some other foreign MNC workers had been more arrivals of the soul than arrivals of the mind. Vincent, from Belgium, had always found the school and work environment in his home country "stifling." He initially developed a liking for Finland and the "Finnish way of living" during anime film festivals he attended annually as a university student. Not only was he fascinated by the cutting-edge high-tech culture here but he just really "liked the people; straightforward, credible" and intensely admired "the combination of their art and math capabilities." He "knew this was the society he was looking for" so he set about looking for a job in Helsinki that would allow him to become part of it. Like Vincent, Scott in Stockholm was first motivated to move because he was attracted to a certain "way of living." He had been an exchange student in Sweden almost twenty years before this actual move and was always enamored of the place. Years later, when his job with his firm in California allowed him to travel in Europe with his wife, they realized that they liked it well enough in Sweden that they should look for ways to move there.

Still some other highly skilled workers end up developing a connection to Sweden or Finland through significant others. I met Esra, thirty-three-year-old electronics engineer from Turkey, in Helsinki.

Like many others in the study, she had entered the mobile telecommunications sector in the mid-1990s taking up a job with the leading mobile operator in Turkey whose major consultant was the national operator of Finland, a state enterprise only then turning private and selling its expertise overseas. Esra met her Finnish partner, who was in Istanbul with a consultant firm, during a project. Theirs is one of the many illustrations in the workers' career histories of how the global boom in mobile telecommunications brought about a whole series of unprecedented or, until then, rare working relationships between a whole range of organizations—and thereby people—around the world.

For Esra, Scott and Vincent, the location was the first part of the equation to fall into place. Their possibilities of moving to, and staying in, Sweden or Finland depended largely on their securing employment. For highly skilled workers already on solid career paths with favorable working conditions, finding not just *any* job, but occupationally satisfying ones, was the challenge. Those who had first arrived as students, too, were in a similar situation by the completion of their studies. While in school they had been on student visas, renewed annually and on the condition they return to their countries of origin upon graduation. In order to stay, they needed to find employment and of a quality not requiring a professional compromise. MNC employment provided the solution to the predicament of these foreigners. In what ways, though, does the MNC-as-employer make it possible, easier, or more comfortable for foreigners to stay in places not generally all that penetrable to them?

Life in Cosmopolitan Relief: Working at the Multinational Workplace

In formal interviews and informal chats with local and foreign workers alike, certain phrases came up repeatedly without prompting. References to how there were "people from all over the world" working in one's team or office building, how "this is a really international workplace," or how "things are really different here than they are outside," were almost universal. There is a tangible sense in which foreign highly skilled workers in the MNC headquarters see their work environments as far less parochial—a common complaint about general feelings about Sweden and Finland for most, though not all, interviewees—than their other everyday surroundings. As the previous discussion of highly skilled migration to Sweden and

Finland suggest, they may well have a point. In the workers' accounts, the MNC workplace emerges as life in cosmopolitan relief, not only differentiated from alternative workplaces but, in fact, disembedded to a certain extent from the surrounding environment at large. Of the various factors workers identify as the distinguishing features of the MNC workplace, the following are the most salient:

Language

By a large margin, the single most common and immediate answer to the question of why people found it preferable to work for a MNC was, , "language." *All* of the interviewees mentioned it as either the top, or one of the top, reasons that had in fact made it possible for them to get a job in the first place. For the outsiders coming in, being hired without the knowledge of the local languages was simply a necessity. For those who had been students, what had been the advantage had proven, in a sense, to be a disadvantage in preparing for the larger labor market, in that they had not been forced to become fluent in Swedish or Finnish. Neither Tahsin nor Mert had learned much Finnish by the time they received their graduate degrees. Likewise, Zahra, from Iran, had enjoyed making many foreign friends in her program, carried out in English, in Gothenburg, but that also meant she had only picked up conversational Swedish by the time she completed her Masters degree there.

Language mattered at several levels. In some cases, the inability to speak the local languages was a concrete obstacle to acquiring otherwise potentially desirable jobs because employers demanded that their workers be able to communicate in Swedish or Finnish. While Finnish is considerably harder than Swedish to master, even at the level of everyday proficiency for most foreigners, it also appeared, based on the interviewees' accounts, that more of the large employers in Sweden demanded competence in Swedish, and/or did so more officially. For Scott and Vincent, who lacked any knowledge of the local languages, several applications were stillborn on the language factor alone.

With some other employers, language was not an official requirement of the job and hence not as clearly a roadblock to getting hired. In both countries, the local populations in general, and the younger, highly skilled, technical workforces in particular, are known to speak English exceptionally well. Still, many MNC workers who initially looked into, or interviewed with, domestic firms noted that while people there were perfectly capable of speaking English, they did not seem as comfortable with it as locals working in MNCs. This observation was somewhat more common in Finland than in Sweden but was made in both countries. Furthermore, even if the foreign workers could "get their foot in the door" they voiced being self-conscious in settings where speaking English was more the exception than the rule and where others would have to make an effort to switch languages in order to include them in the ordinary business of the day. One interviewee said it felt as if one would be "professionally marginalized if everyone else had to constantly translate details to you."

What the *official* language of a company was also mattered because this meant much of the intra-company correspondence may or may not be readily comprehensible to foreign workers. The MNCs in the study had switched to English as their official language in the early/mid 1990s. As Seija, a Finn in the Swedish MNC pointed out, even if the immediate correspondent had put forth their inquiry in English, as long as the initial communication had been in Swedish, one was not able to follow the exact turns involved. She, herself, speaks Swedish but noted that because she thinks the e-mail she sends out "is likely to be passed on to someone else and on again to someone else, and on yet again to someone else…it makes much better sense to write it in English in the first place." Arnaud, who first arrived in Finland from France almost twenty years ago, making use of a clause allowing him to carry out his military service there, was one of the very first foreign workers in the Finnish MNC's headquarters. At the time, there used to be "so few foreigners in his building (he) knew all of them by name." Although he is a rare foreigner who is actually fluent in Finnish, he smiles when he reminisces about the impossibility of deciphering the company correspondence for his other foreign colleagues whereas, now, not only is the written communication in English, but so are "much of the conversations you overhear."

Global Reputation

If one of the things MNCs get out of being global organizations is a competence in managing multinational workforces, another is a global reputation. For the majority of the foreign workers in Finland and Sweden, the two MNCs were often the companies they had the greatest familiarity with even prior to moving to these countries, generating a level of implicit trust. Vincent applied for eleven jobs in Finland but chose the MNC because, he says, "a big move is always a plunge in the dark" and "if you're going to do it, you should go with the one you know best."

In a more minor way, the reputations also figured into the presentations of themselves and their professional stability to family and friends in their home countries. Hasan remarked that he was proud to be able to tell his parents: "*This* is the company I work for." Helsinki and Finland had, accordingly, been somewhat obscure for his parents, relatives, friends and colleagues in Turkey but the MNC itself is a "household brand: they all have the phones."

"Atmosphere"

Related, but not reducible, to the issue of language was the somewhat less tangible quality of the MNCs' "overall atmosphere" making them more comfortable homes for foreigners. In general, foreign workers, for different reasons, voiced their appreciation of the Swedish and Finnish "ways of doing business," often contrasting these with those of home countries as well as the United States and others. Nevertheless, both foreign *and* local workers identified a "diverse" workforce, being surrounded by people coming from and going to a whole range of places in the world, as one of the biggest attractions of working in the MNC. Some of the local workers who had been exchange students during their university years drew parallels between those experiences and their current work lives, underscoring the value they placed on both.

For the foreign workers, the "cosmopolitan atmosphere" of the MNC headquarters seems to have a still deeper meaning: Despite widespread statements about a fascination with, or an appreciation of, Sweden or Finland, the homogeneity of these national societies, especially across their middle-class, nevertheless often strains "outsiders" considerably. "Ethnic" migrants from the same home countries are either nonexistent or too few and, even when they exist, too different from their highly skilled "elite" compatriots in terms of class and habitus to provide full-fledged communities (Favell 2003). Hasan from Turkey said that while he did not "want to sound politically incorrect" there was too much cultural dissonance between his colleagues at the MNC and the "Kebap Turks," the Turkish migrants who across Europe are most visible in the small fast-food joints they own and run, and of whom a handful have also made it as far as Finland. Zahra attributed the greater affinity she feels for her engineer friends, of various nationalities, to the "shared predicament of being foreigners."

Accordingly, not only was the MNC as an organization more "culturally open" but, in being so, it was also a place for a greater concentration of foreigners and, hence, where being foreign was less marked and problematic. Completing the organizational openness and the presence of others sharing a similar status was the final element discussed by several interviewees, that their local colleagues here, too, "had a more global perspective."

Organizational Dexterity in Letting People Onboard

Specific practices enable and show the MNCs' organizational dexterity in making the workplace hospitable to foreign workers. Esra's career history highlights the advantage MNCs have over domestic firms in this respect. When her partner wanted to return to Finland after two and a half years in Turkey, he asked her to come along. Esra says she would "not have moved unless she had a job." Being a well-paid, fast-rising employee in an extremely dynamic and highly prestigious company, she would have been leaving much behind. She quickly found a job with the Finnish operator, which had previously been the state-owned and run telecommunications monopoly. Privatized in the early 1990s, the company was making efforts to become more globally active, though it never quite became a multinational like the MNC where Esra now works.

> (It) was a typical state company....Not as bad as a state company in Turkey but still less dynamic with everyone really set in their ways and everything was in Finnish. And I guess starting the first day they almost expected me to speak Finnish or something.

She felt that neither her department at a more formal level, nor her immediate colleagues, at a more informal level, were all that helpful and attributes this to a lack of experience with accommodating foreign colleagues. She constantly had the sense she was working inefficiently because she had not received guidance, despite the company's ambitions at the time to become an international player and "looking on foreign workers positively."

> There was probably no top-to-down flow. The top may have thought: "This will be good, to hire the foreigners" but to the people I worked with, this idea had not trickled down. They did not help, they did not hinder either, but it was as if I were just a Finnish person. Like you're just there, there is nothing extraordinary about you.

By contrast, the MNCs have more institutionalized forms of dealing with foreign arrivals. Henrik, a middle-level manager in the Human Resources Department of the Swedish MNC, worked in the special division devoted to handling "International Appointments," while Pia, in Helsinki, was a "Diversity Manager." Needless to say, the self-proclaimed tasks of organizational units should be taken with a grain of salt and the practical nature of their goals kept in mind. Nevertheless, their very existence points to, at the very least, an organizational recognition that the facilitation of worklife for non-mainstream workers merits a structured effort.

Informal practices that develop through experience can be even more crucial in feeling less anomalous at the workplace. The more a company deals with foreign workers, the more it is likely to have standardized ways of dealing with them and services to offer to them. The greater familiarity the local workforce has with the experience of working with foreign peers, the more likely they are to know how to get and keep people onboard.

Connectivity to the Global Network

The final way in which MNCs make staying in Stockholm or Helsinki not only possible, but also more comfortable for the foreign workers, has to do with the repeated theme of this chapter: they also help them move. MNCs were more appealing to the foreigners, as they were to many of the local workers, because, unlike, for example, a mobile operator, they promised travel. Esra recalls that after her interview at the MNC headquarters she was taken to the office where she would be working. There was nobody in the office. All the desks were obviously occupied but, at that time, empty. When she asked where everybody was, she was told all the engineers had been dispatched on a project somewhere in the world. "If you come here, it will be like that for you, too," her would-be manager commented. "I felt good about that," she says, "It felt nice I would have an opportunity to travel away from Finland to be honest." The prospects of travel, which all of the interviewees in the study had seen and enjoyed far more often during their initial years at the MNCs, have a special appeal for outsiders within the MNCs. They imply, at one and the same time, being embedded in a location, yet being freed from it to some extent. MNC employment gives these foreign workers some roots without tying them down.

Taken together, these distinguishing features of MNC employment, as identified and expressed by the foreign workers, describe a work life in cosmopolitan relief. This is a valuable, if rare, opportunity to offer highly skilled foreign workers, whose interests in staying in Helsinki or Stockholm are also largely curtailed by the perceived limitations of these cities.

Conclusion

If the sight of Sanam going to work in the morning in Helsinki is odd to the occasional town-dweller, it is less so to many others and much less so than it would have been ten years ago. It is important to keep in mind, in the overheated discussions over globalization, that many of the changes claimed to be afoot are gradual and relative. While much of the hype about the brave new globalized world is not fully merited, caution over the fanfare for its arrival need not mean brushing aside all claims that certain things may, indeed, be changing.

MNCs create workplaces that are wired, in various ways, past national borders to bigger and smaller nodes of a network across space. Admittedly, such networks densely overlap in certain parts of the world while largely bypassing others and are not fully, or authentically, "global" in the sense that they do not map out the world as we have come to know it in old-fashioned geography. Just how spatially inclusive the global network of a MNC is depends closely on the state of the sector and its markets at a given point in time. Likewise, the movement of workers inside the multinational infrastructure follows a rhythm largely dictated by markets. Such movement, after all, is not in itself a goal for the MNC as an organization but rather a means to put labor and skills to work where they are needed on the shortest notice and for the lowest possible cost. Corporate appreciation of international experience and exposure in individual careers is mostly because these are taken to indicate an acquired ease at moving about. An accumulated capacity to work and manage in diverse settings and with different workforces is, after all, the greatest insurance against possible friction in transit.

Due to the very nature of the relationship between the MNC headquarters and the local units in their global network, the flow of actual workers inside the MNC is heavily concentrated on the route from the center to the nodes. Nevertheless, hosting the headquarters of major MNCs has consequences not only for sending more locals out, more frequently, to a greater number of, and more varied, destinations around the world, but also for bringing, and keeping, highly skilled foreigners in. The case of the mobile telecommunications sector with two of its biggest players based in the homogeneous home turf of Finland and Sweden, underscore many of these points about how MNCs can be instrumental in lubricating the movement of highly skilled workers around the world, including to hitherto unlikely destinations. On the one hand, they establish links, not only figuratively but also quite literally, between points across space across which real-life itineraries then take shape. On the other hand, they create niches of employment that make working—and living—in otherwise quite inaccessible local contexts possible, or more rewarding.

While MNC employment may render highly skilled workers mobile to variable degrees and in variable ways, across variable routes and for variable durations, however, both the need, and the opportunities for, such mobility eventually depend on the overall direction, position and ambitions of the company in global markets. The fate of a sector or its particular MNCs, in turn, will significantly shape the nature of the work experience for their highly skilled workforces. Yet individual workers are not merely local leaves being blown around by global winds. A closer look at the MNC from the bottom-up, through the actual trajectories of real workers, with the accompanying multifaceted logics, justifications and assessments, reveals that the value of mobility and the desire for movement are highly contextual. Not more than a tiny fraction of even these purportedly most mobile of workers wish to play musical chairs *ad infinitum* and settling down with the MNC at a specific location involves, at least temporarily, "going local." The calculation is then one of whether or not being a "local," while working "in cosmopolitan relief," corresponds to a satisfactory combination of life in and outside of work. That calculation is one that inevitably has to take into consideration how, and to what extent, national policies and nation-states matter in giving shape and color to the overall life experience. While neither the MNCs nor the welfare states can really offer a fundamental solution to that one major source of foreigners' hesitation over staying in Stockholm or Helsinki—namely, the long dark winters—opportunities to travel on the job and labor laws with generous sick leave might help remove it.

Notes

1.   All names of individual persons have been changed here to protect anonymity.
2.   Having to do with issues of access, it did not prove feasible to conduct interviews in the United States.

10

London as Eurocity: French Free Movers in the Economic Capital of Europe

Adrian Favell

Think of London and the notion of "global city" quickly comes to mind. To nearly all observers it is unquestionably seen as the most international city in Europe—and possibly the world. For example, one of the key claims sustained by global city theorists— notably Loughborough University's well known *Globalization and World Cities* project (GaWC), and its tireless mining of data about service sector corporate city networks[1]—has been to show how London outstrips any other city on the European continent in its connections, spreading way out beyond the immediate local shadow of European integration (Taylor and Hoylor, 2000). There are also other well-noted aspects of this routinely cited global life of London. Its long history of immigration and asylum is second to none, something only deepened by the distinctively post-colonial multiculturalism that has developed in the post-war period (Favell, 2001). Moreover, in the liberal 1990s, it developed an extraordinarily open labor market for foreigners, with a remarkable degree of mostly undocumented immigration. London is also often seen as the acme of the polarized city, characterized by dominantly service-based industries at both top and bottom ends, driven by global industrial shifts in production and capital (Sassen, 2001).

London is certainly embedded in all kinds of global networks: transatlantic, far eastern, post-colonial and so on. But the emphasis of GaWC and others on the city as a virtual "space of flows" (Castells, 2000), and the almost exclusive focus on faceless data about corporate office networks in the work of economic gerephers, masks other key sociological aspects of the city, related to place and geographical propinquity. For London is also a Eurocity, of central importance to the regional economic and social system of Europe. Though this is well apparent in macro-level economic figures about trade and mobility within Europe (Fligstein and Merand, 2001), it is much less well documented at the micro level; at the level of individuals in their experiences, trajectories and transactions in and through the city. While politically Britain has, since the 1990s, drifted further out to sea, London has seen its own quiet European invasion, anchoring it firmly in the continent.

During this period, continental Europeans have moved to London in extraordinary numbers. The city has become a prime destination of European free movement of all nationalities, from across all of Europe (Dobson et al., 2001). One obvious Europeanizing story that will not be discussed here has been the enormous growth in migration from Eastern Europe, especially from Poland and the Balkans. Western European nationalities, meanwhile, are represented across the board, having benefited from European Union (EU) freedom of movement legislation. Among these new Londoners, perhaps the most striking story has been the relocation there of a new generation of talented and entrepreneurial young French people. London has, in other words, become a mecca for the young of Europe everywhere who have moved here in droves to learn the global language, and be part of the swinging, libertarian de facto capital of Europe.

In part, this new migration seems to confirm London's global centrality; it is the gateway for all Europeans to the global English language business, media and cultural worlds. But there is another side to being a regional hub of migration; it also embeds London profoundly in Europe and European social structures—despite the grating Euroskepticism of the nation around it. Relatively stable social systems of temporary and permanent migration to and from the continent make London a "Eurocity" every bit as Europeanized on this dimension as Amsterdam, Paris, Brussels, Munich, Barcelona or Vienna.

Here I offer a closer look at this essentially unknown, hitherto invisible, phenomena.[2] It portrays, at the micro level, the essentially human roots of London's understated regional embeddedness. I first give a brief overview of the phenomenon from the point of view of official and popular knowledge of the subject. I then present interviews telling the stories of five young women who have made London their home and pursued careers here. It goes through stages of their movement, settlement and integration (or not) in the city, what their personal experiences say about the free movement of a new generation of young Europeans, and what they say about London as a European international city. The paper reports on research for a forthcoming book, *Eurostars and Eurocities*, which is a study of free moving urban professionals residents in three cities, London, Amsterdam and Brussels (Favell, 2006; see also Favell, 2003). It also draw indirectly on my participation in the Framework V funded research network, PIONEUR, which has recently completed a survey of 5,000 European citizens resident in Britain, France, Germany, Spain and Italy.[3]

The Invisible Norman Invasion

What is remarkable is just how little London itself knows about the large numbers of Europeans in its midst. Ever present, yet quantitatively invisible, they are a crucial part of the city's dynamo, yet unregistered by the media and city government officials alike.

Most cities know something about their populations. The EU sponsored Urban Audit—an immense database of over 250 of the largest cities in Western Europe—has done wonders in compiling data on foreign populations in these cities.[4] However, Dutch project manager, Lewis Dijkstra, shrugs his shoulders and laughs when asked about data on the European population of London. The city didn't know. Trying to investigate the question myself, I found out little more. Very helpful and informative demographic officers in the mayor's office in London passed me around their colleagues for over an hour in search of somebody who might have a clue. Regional development officials, ethnic minority specialists all came up blank.

The mayor's office certainly talks the talk of Eurocities in all its official documentation (Mayor of London, 2002). Ken Livingstone is very pro-Europe and London is portrayed in dynamic European and regional terms which they rightfully do not see as negating any of its other many global aces but which, rather, only enhance its strategic economic importance. Fraternizing with colleagues from Stockholm, Paris or Madrid is, of course, another important way of emphasizing the shaky political autonomy of the city from national politics. Yet the most flesh-and-blood proof of this integration into European networks, beyond the more virtual flows of capital and the massive, ever-more European cross-border trade of London and

Britain, is the free movement of European citizens able to live, study and work in Britain. This is an opportunity they are taking up in large numbers. While the British press fumes about a handful of bedraggled asylum-seekers who manage to creep in through the Channel Tunnel, it casts a complete blind eye to the thousands of as-yet-unemployed young Europeans pouring into Britain on the Eurostar and cheap network airlines, with all their belongings in back-packs. The vast majority heading for London.

Getting a handle on numbers is not easy. Official census statistics are not going to be much use, given much of the migration is short-term and often not registered. The incoming Passenger Survey might give some indicators but these are projections based on tiny samples and only ask people about their intentions of staying long-term or not. The British Labor Force Survey is the most accurate source of official data, also given it counts by region (London and Southeast). But the numbers given by both this and the national consulates in question are likely to be below real figures. Anecdotal evidence I have accumulated suggests the clear majority of European residents in Britain never even thought of registering with their consulate, something that only becomes necessary if you need to obtain a new (European) passport without going home. Try running a random tele-phone survey, as we have done with PIONEUR, and you find prac-tically none of this target population has a landline telephone. Brit-ish police registration is remarkably porous and ineffective—unlike in other European countries, where it is a mandatory step before obtaining a social security number and being able to work. And as readers of British tabloid press know very well, it is indeed remark-ably easy to get registered with a general practitioner (GP) and get access to British national health service (for what that is worth—see below), without any other official documentation other than an ad-dress. On this level, it's all guesswork.

Faced with this official lacunae, the best thing to do is to talk to service providers (i.e., associations, organizations, magazines or websites for French expatriates in London) and employers. These are people who generally have a much more practical, hands-on commercial knowledge of these mobile populations in question; typi-cally because they want to sell something to them or get something from them. The consulate figures cite around 40,000 French in Lon-don, but the number discussed on service provider websites is more in the order of 200,000 French in London and the southeast. This leads on to the somewhat hyperbolic idea that London is now the fourth largest French city after Paris, Lyon and Marseilles. Whatever the actual numbers, this migration amounts to a new Norman invasion, not yet spotted by the Dunkirk spirited readers of the tabloids. Yet take a coffee on a train or a sandwich in an Islington bar and you will see them. They are the young folks handing out language school leaflets or wearing sandwich boards outside the Tottenham Court Road tube station. Hang out in a city pub or a café near the media offices off Oxford Street and you will hear many French (as well as Spanish, Italian, Danish and so on) accents speaking the EU's principal lingua franca, Euro-English. Working in pubs is no longer the exclusive province of Australians and New Zealanders on holiday visas (on these populations, see Conradson and Latham, 2005). And young Americans have been squeezed out by visa and work permit restrictions that favor European free movers over the so-called "special relationship" with the U.S.

One organization dedicated to promoting French relocation to Britain is *France libre d'entreprendre*.[5] Led by the vocal young French entrepreneurial exile, Olivier Cadic, it promotes the idea of Britain as a low-tax business environment for ambitious French people fed up with social security payments and a thirty-five-hour week. Many have offices clustered around the Eurostar train terminal in Ashford, Kent. With unemployment running at 12 percent in France in the early 1990s, versus 5 percent in Britain, the economic reasons for location became imperative for many. For a new generation of highly Europeanized, English-speaking, globally ambitious French professionals, England became an obvious option. Although ignored in Britain, the phenomenon received quite a bit of press in France. This is the consummate rational of the European free movement, entirely in accord with EU economic integration theory: mobility adjusts for economic differences between regions and will lead to economic dynamism, growth and creative transactions as well as soak up underutilized labor. The British economic "miracle" of the last few years has, in fact, in part been fueled by these European economic dynamics, building on Britain's strategic economic positioning and tax incentives (polite terms for "social dumping") and its ability to bleed "the best and the brightest" from its European neighbors. It is one of the hidden secrets of the so-called "British model" trumpeted by chancellor Gordon Brown over the supposedly high-tax "social" regimes of the continent.

I also talked with service sector employers, notably Pret (*Prêt-à-Manger*), a hugely successful London-based sandwich chain. This company actually has a recruitment policy tailored around these new EU free movement dynamics. They have capitalized on this talented and highly available workforce by targeting young Europeans as they arrive, and relying on social networks to pass back the word-of-opportunity to friends still at home. Pret's recruitment office is, in fact, found on platform two at Victoria Station, the historical gateway to Europe. Their personnel manager, herself a young Spanish women who had been in London for ten years or so, confirmed the scale of this commitment and the smartness with which the company has benefited from it. In fact, the recruitment office received 44,000 enquiries in the first quarter of 2003 with 251 job offers made. Ninety percent of the employees in shops are foreign, of which over a half are West European, with French the third largest group behind Italians and Spanish. All of the young West Europeans arrive ready and able to work, with no visa restrictions. Many are university educated but willing to take simple service sector work to be in London. Pret thus creams off some of the best educated middle-class youth from continental Europe—who are high in economic, human and social capital—but willing to work for small wages in return for congenial hours, a sympathetic corporate ambiance, and above all a great social life. Pret openly encourages socializing and networking between employees, organizing parties and publishing a magazine for them, as well as promising a structured career development plan without long-term ties. Again, this is rational European integration theory at work—which impacts the London economy in very direct ways.

Although impossible to get a complete overview of the working French population in such a huge and diverse city, I thus centered my inquiries on both the younger service sector population, and on London's information technology (IT), media and financial sectors which draw on some of Europe's most talented individuals. The sample of five interview subjects discussed here are part of a larger sample of twenty in-depth interviews I did with interviews and couples in London. This was supplemented by numerous secondary interviews with residents, employers, service providers, personnel consultants and city officials, ethnography of gentrifying neighborhoods, and collection of all available secondary data. The interviews selected here comprise four young French women and a fifth French *carte de séjour* (permanent residence) holder from Algeria, who was socialized exclusively in the French school system and spent her university years in Paris. Their themes and observations embody both the generalizable reality of European mobility as experienced by a growing numbers of young, essentially middle-class movers living in London, as well as their own personalized cases and perspectives. The long and winding interviews focused on their life history, migration choices, professional life, reflections on the city, social networks and, where appropriate, more practical details about housing, children, welfare, political participation and so on. The core of my work is dedicated to bringing alive the phenomenological worlds of these individuals and families. They are not technically representative except in the loosest sense of being a personalized portrait of an unknown London. Each micro life does, however, represent an embodiment of the broader macro trends theorized about by economic geographers and sociologists of mobility. It is, in other words, a way of putting a human face on generalizations that often miss the human story behind the theories, as well as grounding empirically some of the actual mechanisms that individually aggregate into broader social trends.

Life in the "Fourth" Biggest French City

Moving

Those missing from the official statistics are archetypically young, recent graduates eager to improve their English but who also see London as a privileged gateway to the wider world and bigger, better careers. The bottom line for such mobile young French, shared equally by the Italians and Spanish I met in all three cities, was they moved because of work frustration at home. These vocal, frustrated, mostly provincial French, did indeed "get on their bikes" as euro-economists would hope. Nicole,[6] a twenty-eight-year-old website builder from the north of France, on a modest income, summarizes this attitude:

> There was a big sense of frustration about the personal development thing. The Latin countries are absolutely not flexible on the work market, I can do anything I want there but it's not going to change my situation. You are just young, so your opinion doesn't count. They say you don't have any experience—even though you have!—and I was working crazy hours and being paid peanuts, no rewards. And still you live in Paris and it is very expensive....At the end of the day, I didn't study five or six years for that. I wanted to go abroad. Even if my experience in Paris had been nice, I think I already had it in mind going abroad.

This perspective is echoed by Valerie, a former broker in her early thirties, who at the time of the interview, was unemployed and interviewing again for work in London after a few months vacation travel (translated from French):

> The "Anglo-Saxon" mode of working is much more informal than in France, where its always "*Monsieur, voulez vous ...?*," whatever, you know, whilst here I can call my boss by his first name. It's more relaxed here, even if it always stays serious. I like this a lot. There is a hierarchy but it doesn't make itself felt…

I asked her if people expressed themselves here, because that is what others always say the English don't do openly.

> On the contrary, in France you don't give your opinion, you don't say what you think. When I came here, I found it difficult to say what I was thinking and they told me in the second job that I didn't talk enough. It was a team job, we had to share the stress. I wasn't used to expressing myself. My boss came to me one day, and said, "If you have any personal problems etc., you must come and talk to me about it." It's not like that in France. You don't talk personal stuff with your boss, and, in fact, they wouldn't want to know. It's just work and that's it, *basta*. There I'm just an employee, not a human being. That's how I felt. This is the reason I would have hard time returning to France because I'm used to this way of working now. I don't want to go backwards."

Valerie here offers some clues, perhaps, to the success of British capitalism: the interpersonal foundations of the "soft capitalism" in London and British firms abroad, written about by authors such as Nigel Thrift (1994) and Jon Beaverstock (2002), which in turn parallel the understanding of regional studies and urban economies in the U.S. offered by Michael Storper (1997) and Richard Florida (2002).

> I like the idea here of appraisals. In France, they didn't have anything like that. I worked [in Monaco] in a third-generation company founded by the grandfather, a family firm with no management method except hierarchy from the boss. There was no other stuff, no human resources and so on, to make the link between the managers and the workers.

Education is the crucial vector for young migration of this kind. The impact of the EU's student mobility program Erasmus (now Socrates) has been enormous. Nicole first got a taste for going abroad (to Wales, Aberystwyth) through Erasmus (King and Ruiz-Gelices, 2003). After this, the question was, where? Nicole summarizes it succinctly as, "the opportunities were in London." So despite not knowing anyone, having no connections and having thought first of other places like Amsterdam and Canada, she moved to London. Reasoning like the model rational migrant here, London *ceteris paribus* was the best destination.

As is well known, the British education system is also now servicing Europe with vocational and academic degrees, Masters, MBAs and so on. Europeans pay the same fees as British students and find university admissions officers sympathetic to their sometimes difficult-to-compare home country qualifications. In London they often find themselves outnumbering their British counterparts. Valerie completed a degree a couple of years back in IT and Finance at Westminster University:

> Well, I thought I'm going to college in Britain, I'm going to meet English people. No! It was strange. The first people I met were an Italian girl, a Russian, Czech, Spanish, another from Algeria....The English who were there were all Hindus, so among the *vrai vrai vrai* English there was only two *de souche anglaise* [of English roots]...

Some of these same young Europeans go on to people Ph.D. programs that might otherwise wither away due to the impossibility of recruiting British students. Ironically, now, many faculty departments find their best applicants from among Europeans applying to Britain's famously open university system; a rare model of free movement practice in Europe's often stiflingly immobile academic world.

Of course, London also offers many other quintessential urban attractions. Its cultural life is almost universally seen as youth oriented, avantgarde, and liberating. It offers Europe's most appealing and challenging rite of passage ("beyond *les 400 coups,*" as Valerie puts it) notably as a refuge from dull provinces, or overly protective family environments. It also offers the "outsider" freedom of not belonging yet feeling at home as a place of comfortable anonymity. These classic contours of the modern city, à la Simmel, are evoked by both Nicole and Valerie:

> Nicole: What I like in England, London, is it's definitely more open minded than France. Since I was a teenager, I had this feeling of frustration. It's not open minded in France, we are not encouraged to be so at home. On TV, in education, whatever, anybody who is trying to be open minded is looked at as someone eccentric. Stupid things like clothes. My French friends [when they visit] stare at people here, they have a more conservative style. They don't have a positive image of being eccentric. It could be fun, creative, but still it is something that means you are too different....The idea that it doesn't matter, who cares? It is more flexible...at work and in general.

> Valerie: What I like (here) is the *sentiment de liberté*. But whether it would be the same if I was born here...? Would I have the same feeling of freedom? But I like that, to be very anonymous.

London work life also makes socializing easy. Nicole had no problem doing as provincial newcomers to London have always done, using social contacts inside and out of work to structure their new life in the city.

> In an English company, it's easy to get a social life with English people. This is a big difference. Here you socialize in your work environment. In France, you work during work hours but you keep the same friends you had at school. You don't expect to make friends with workmates.

Nicole's social life improved after she no longer had a French boyfriend and joined in the usual work-based social life that is common in many companies. London, also, is apparently welcoming as an identity. When I ask her if she considers herself a Londoner now, Valerie tells me of an email that has been going round the office: "The 100 things that make you a Londoner." Most of these refer to becoming used to the extortionist price of cinema tickets, sushi or rent, the terrible weather, the lack of clothes clubbers in winter wear, or paying council taxes, etc. I asked her, was there anything on the list that prevented foreigners from being Londoners?

> No, I don't think so. No, well then, I must be a Londoner. It's basically that you don't feel astonished anymore, that we could accept crazy things like that we accept. That's what the email was all about.

Whether "true" Londoners born within the sound of Bow Bells would look at it in these terms is, of course, another question.

The prototypical migrant reasoning illustrated by Nicole and Valerie works both generally—in terms of the extraordinary openness of the London labor market—and specifically in terms of sectors for which London is the true European capital, particularly in finance, IT and media. Others who came later for professional reasons, can also trace their choices in equally rational terms. Laure, a high earning media manager in her early forties, who had been in London since joining CNN during its halcyon days in the early 1990s (well before the big rush of French migrants later), stressed her mixed feelings about her own very rational choices. Commenting on her experiences as a student at Sciences Po, Paris:

> It was awful....I had a very bad time there because I'm a bit of a non-conformist [laughs]. Basically, you get out of your own country as a young professional when you think the opportunities are greater elsewhere, when you think the flexibility is going to be better. I'm sure everybody thinks the same. In my case, the opportunities were very specific at that time: the [cable TV] industry was young and new here [in London], because of the link with America. All the multi-channel TV industry in Europe is born and bred from the States or is very immature, so you just feel this pool of expertise is going to come first to England and then later to the continent which is, in fact, what happened. I hate to think of that—the American influence—[laughs] but that's why I came.

The irony of her chosen Americanized path is not lost on Laure, who married an English man, but yearns for France. Her engaging, corporate articulacy is peppered with socialistic, anti-materialist side remarks and self-questioning. Again, she has a provincial background, very typical of many of the new generation of free movers. These are not the global elites of social theory fame (i.e., Bauman, 1998; Castells, 2000; Sklair, 2001) but, rather, a new middle-class of mobile "spiralists," echoing the famous article by Watson (1964) on the socially and spatially mobile new middle-class from English northern towns in the 1950s and 1960s (see also Fielding, 1995). The bottom line is they would *not* have moved were it not for the new open EU free movement opportunities; and they would *not* have moved if the opportunities were global rather than regional. Freedom of movement in Europe has extended privileges once thought to be exclusively "elite" to a much larger, more provincial, European population. They, thus, combine ambitious social mobility, with international movement born of frustration with the "classic" French system of going to Paris to make it, where, as Bourdieu has shown repeatedly in his work, well-entrenched upper-class cultural capital always succeeds best (Bourdieu, 1979). They are trying to use Europe as an alternative route and trajectory to the classic one through the national capital, a route that builds on the energy of feeling like an "outsider." Another key aspect of their ease of mobility within the European space is that the distances involved have not really disrupted their extended family life in any significant way. Mobility of children is becoming more common and more acceptable for European middle-class parents. With cheap airlines and improving international rail networks, European regional integration is becoming a reality in this sense with London a key hub.

All my respondents recognize certain aspects of Parisian life as better. They can cogently enumerate the comparative benefits of Paris, particularly in terms of "quality of life" (a key term for all my Eurostars). But this has its downsides. As Laure puts it:

> Yeah, it's very good [life in Paris] but it's a bit like '*la pensée unique*' [one way thinking]. Everybody goes in the same direction and thinks politically correct things which I do find a bit oppressive in terms of my own outlook in life.

This viewpoint is echoed by Nour, a successful cable television news journalist, particularly in professional terms. Above all, there is the American suspicion of French colleagues and friends:

> I bump into French journalists here and there and I always get this: Why are you working for an American company!?

Nour, thirty-four-years-old, was born in Algeria, but comes from a more international background, a family of diplomats. London, for her, did represent simply the next nodal point in a global career that went from a childhood in London, to Sciences Po in Paris, to journalism school in New York, to Washington DC, to cable news in London ("It was the best jumping board at the time," she says). Pointedly, she is the only one of these five respondents *not* benefiting from European free movement and points out with frustration the consequences of Britain's non-participation in the Schengen agreement: she cannot work here without a work permit. Her ability to move and work rests on a different kind of "mobility capital" than the four other French respondents, a more recognizably "elite" globalized social background (of the kind wrongly assumed by most scholars to be typical of *all* international professional migrants). Being a high flyer, the company has taken care of her permit problems but she is convinced she has to work that bit harder for it.

> I have to say I think there is always an unfairness in that respect because you do have to prove yourself more....Maybe if you were an English person you'd think it was normal. Why would they hire someone else when I'm just as qualified? For me it's always seemed to me a little bit unfair. I always have the feeling I had to prove myself more to make it worth any employers hiring me because they have to go through this whole work permit thing just to hire me, then they have to decide between me and someone else who has the same qualifications...

This situation translates into a tougher work life which she compares with the kind of conditions she might have enjoyed in France:

> I like the social system (in France), I like the fact people don't have to work the same crazy hours we do because of the law. You'd never be able to get away with it, you know, the nightshift I've had to do here....I would never have done it in France because it's a more humane system. But on the other hand, when we have to work all day with a French cameraman and he's like, "I'm sorry, I have to stop to have my lunch break," and "I've got to have this break and that break," and I'm like, "Come on, let's get on with it!"....So you get used to it whether you like it or not. It's difficult to adapt to another system.

The working hours and stress she complains about are a reminder of the downsides of London compared to continental Europe, something you get in return for a more challenging career environment. It has also taken its toll on Laure and is beginning to be felt by the others such as Valerie.

That [the appeal of London] is perhaps beginning to *déchanter* [lose its allure]. It's such an expensive place, when I arrived it was already a *bordel* [nightmare, lit. 'whorehouse'].....Now I'm looking for work, I don't want to arrive at the point where I ask is this game even worth playing? I might be able to earn a good wage but there's apartment rent to pay and the quality of life, all the same, is not fabulous either. For the moment, I stay because I'm still... [pause] I think I'm going to stay here, I'm very happy with London, for the moment, but we'll see. *Je ne me vois pas ailleurs pour le moment* [I can't see myself anywhere else at the moment].

Valerie is apparently committed to the city. She says this but she has also recently interviewed for jobs in Monaco and Switzerland and is ready to go anywhere with the right boyfriend at the drop of a hat. Being a Londoner perhaps does not run as deep as these respondents at first claim.

Settlement

The experiences of movers begins, quite rapidly, to diverge with the counterfactual life (and career) as it would have been back home, and as they match their expectations with carving out a new life in a new city. The settlement process tends to reveal other aspects of the experience of migration, in particular, the nationally specific limitations of the apparently "global city" they have chosen.

Valerie and Nicole recount in detail the peculiar life of the new Londoners, huddling together in the cheapest hostels in Bayswater and Chelsea, a part of the town long established as a first port of call for expatriates in the city.

Nicole: When I first came, I used to sleep in a hostel in Bayswater which is a brilliant place to meet people. You have people from everywhere around the world. They are just like you, have been here for two weeks, they don't know how long they are going to stay and they're very excited because they've just got a job....Everything you do is new, so it's full of energy. You meet people and spend all your time with them. You are never alone, you eat together and share everything....After six months I couldn't stand it anymore but the first three months were wonderful.

Valerie: It's really a family, everyone knows each other. It's also a network for information, jobs, visiting places. The Spanish always know where to go out in the evening....They are not exactly spoiled by the mode of life here [i.e., London's notorious limitations in terms of closing hours and going out late, compared to Spain]. That's the reason most of the Spanish go home.

Like accommodation anywhere in London, it is not cheap. Valerie was paying 110 pounds a week which included dinners that had to be eaten at the hostel:

I had some savings so it wasn't like the people who have to work at *Prêt-à-Manger* making sandwiches. There were several at the hostel who were doing that. There were

> those that had to get up at 5 a.m. to make muffins, I don't know where….It wasn't like that for me.

Their positive memories perhaps belie how tough it might have been for some of their *camarades*.

What is extraordinary about all this are the compromises in lifestyle they accept in return for a slice of the London action. These accumulate over time relative to a specific peer group back home who, a few years on, now have high-paying jobs, own houses and live established "bourgeois" lives. Laure refers to these as the "golden youth" [*jeunesse dorée*] of continental Europe, the middle-class children from countries with higher average standards of living than Britain, more close-knit conventional family lives, and a sense of over-protection as they grow up. Those who opt to leave, opt out of a settled and more guaranteed social trajectory that would otherwise make them affluent and settled in married life—most likely in their home region—much earlier. Nathalie, like Valerie, is from the south of France, in her sixth year in London, and works in an administrative job for a major retail company.

> Compared to all my friends in France, they don't understand because they now have a three room *bourgeois* in Nice with a chimney….And they see I live in ten square metres [in a London hostel] and share my bathroom with thirty other people, and they are really... *quoi?!*….And, no, I'm not married, I don't have kids, all the thirty-three-year-olds I know are more or less in the family life...

This standard middle-class trajectory back home compares to the many late twenty- or thirty-something French, Spanish, Italian and Greek graduates still living after several years in provisional, shared accommodations before establishing residential independence in the ferociously expensive London rental market.

A sense of wistful no-going-back realism pervades Valerie's reflections on this:

> In France, I don't really have links with people, all my friends who I knew are all married now, all settled [*installées*], whilst here we are all single (even if you have a boyfriend)….So there's none of that sentiment of 'Ok, I'm married now, so I'm not going out anymore'—which is not necessarily a good thing, by the way. But maybe that's why I don't want to settle down because I don't have any examples around me. I don't know! I'll maybe finish by becoming English.

Her feelings are confirmed by Nathalie. She only managed to leave the hostel when she moved in with her Dutch boyfriend, a commercially-based research scientist, who had bought a house near Paddington. Although she misses the fun of the hostel, she also recognizes that by age thirty-three this kind of serially instable lifestyle had parents and friends back home worried.

> I'm both happy and worried it's maybe just because I don't want to make a commitment.

The London French are fully aware of what they are doing, and such interpersonal comparativism pervades their talk, embodying a sharp cross-national Europeanism—shared by all Eurostars—who are acutely aware of qualitative differences between cities and national contexts. In a sense, they are the real comparative experts whose experiences and more insightful, even-handed observations, transcend the usual parade of clichés that pervade public discussion about the characteristics and merits of each European country.

One area on which they have much to say is the relative merit of the British National Health Service, universally assessed as one of the worst medical systems in Europe. Nathalie, Laure and Nour all laugh and recount nightmare stories of their encounters with this system when asked their experiences:

> Nathalie: I'm scared to go....I've been in the hospital with my job in Portugal, it was ten times cleaner than here. I thought it was just because the French were narrow minded [that they think this], that they like only French things, blah blah blah... But the experience I had here in the emergency are...really I don't know...[laughs]!! Frankly, there was a gynecologist at Paddington Hospital, she opened the door with the same glove she examines the patient with....I was ahh...! Let me out! I thought the hygiene was really bad.

> Laure: What do you think I think of it...? [laughs] What everybody thinks of it! Appalling! They said my daughter had asthma when in fact she had problems with her lungs. I took her to France and they put her in a hospital, did an x-ray....In fact, she had double pneumonia! It was not diagnosed properly and it's a general problem of the system. The GP said, "Oh, we don't routinely give x-ray of the chest for a child here." There are lots of stories like this. I don't blame them personally. It's the whole fact that once you are in a system, you start accepting it, you don't question it anymore. Basically, my daughter asked to go to hospital.... And [it]...is the wrong place to go...

> Nour: Don't start me on that one, that is the most awful thing in this country! Much as I appreciate there are a lot of good things that Britain has to offer, the whole medical system....I am totally shocked. The way I've dealt with it is that I go to Paris....What I've done, I often get sick when I'm coming back from a trip and I'll stop in Paris which allows me to see my parents and see my doctor [laughs] so I'll do what I need to do there....[In London] I had to register with a GP and had something serious once....I called for an emergency appointment—that they give you a week later. I go and she says, "There is a philosophy here that as long as you are breathing you are ok." She just said, "It's the air you are breathing in your office, so just drinks lots of fluids." I said, "Can't we do some tests? There's something wrong, I can feel it!" But she was like, "Oh no,

you'll be fine. Just drink a lot of fluids." So I did for three weeks, it just got worse....A friend of mine had to help me on the Eurostar, and I went to Paris and of course the first thing they did was run tests to find out my blood count was totally abnormal in all respects. I do not understand how a civilized, industrialized country would not do that, it's just....The other times when I've needed urgent medical attention I've gone to my doctor, who is Lebanese....When I saw a specialist here, my work doctor referred me. It's a private doctor, you pay 120 pounds for the doctor, 100 for the blood test, then 120 for the x-rays and then the x-rays they do at St. Thomas's Hospital and that's not much better than the hospital I used to go to in Algeria. Filthy!....Ok, I had an insurance, but it's 120 bloody pounds, you know! I just don't understand, there's something messed up with this system, it totally eludes me. I was talking with friends, one who's Brazilian, one from Sri Lanka....This is one thing we are really scared of, if anything happened to us here we'd have to go abroad. The system doesn't allow you to run the tests you have to do and there's no prevention either, it's just zero. If I go see a doctor in France, he will ask me if I'm happy with my weight, skin, psychology, he'll look at the whole picture, even if he's only a GP....Here, as long as you are breathing you are fine. [All these other things] It's just totally irrelevant to them, it's considered luxury. If you can afford it, fine, go to a luxury doctor. But it's not considered an essential part of your well being as it is in many other European countries and that's a shame. It's really something I don't understand.

In the light of this, it is a surely a poor joke British politicians still insist on playing the welfare spongers card, talking about NHS access as an argument for why migrants come to the U.K. (as opposed to elsewhere). This is nonsense: European migrants nearly all maintain doctors and dentists at home. It is true that among these migrants Nicole did get access to unemployment benefits, and other interviewees have confirmed the way they have managed to get housing benefits and access to job centers. However, this ease of access has to be linked to the extraordinary openness of the economy and the willingness to exploit available labor pulled into the country.

Respondents are critical of these aspects, as readily as they give credit to London's easy going attitudes on bureaucracy and its accomplished multiracial, cosmopolitan environment. Laure, in particular, was very positive on this in relation to France:

That is the extraordinary side of London, the acceptance of 'the other'... .I think the English are less neurotic than the French....In general, the English are perhaps less racist...

Contrary to the poor image of British state schools, Laure has found great satisfaction getting involved in a typically multicultural London school.

One of the reasons why we are still here is probably because of the school. I had a complete change of attitude vis-à-vis that, because I think the parents involvement in the school is so much greater in England than it could possibly be in France....It's a school where 50 percent of the children are non-English speaking.

It is interesting that, of the movers here, it is Nour who is the least impressed by what London has to offer culturally. A self-styled "classic" dresser, she is a firm believer in doing all her shopping in Paris, exchange rates permitting. This was particularly good at the time of the interview, with a very strong pound. She would join dozens of other people arriving back in London on the Eurostar, armed with foie gras and wine, that would have cost three times as much at Harrods. She points out these good things in life, that get coded as upper-class "elite" luxuries in Britain, are, in fact, available to a much broader range of the population in France.

> A lot of people here thought I was being very snobbish [shopping in Paris]. But again it's this class thing. People tend to identify you here by how you look and they are "Oh yes *of course* she buys her clothes in Paris"....But it has nothing to do with that. It's because it was much cheaper [laughs].

Cross-border shopping is another big benefit of mobility as well as another tangible fruit of European integration. Other aspects of daily life require settlement, inevitably, over time. But settlement involves the competitive struggle with natives and other residents for access to, and control over, scare "quality of life" resources in the city—the very thing that most motivates domestic middle-classes (Butler and Savage, 1995). This takes its most tangible shape, in London as elsewhere, on the housing market and over questions of childcare and education for children. Laure rails about the extortionist price of childcare and the professional compromises it imposes on families who would have it much easier in Brussels (where childcare is good), or in Amsterdam (where international school options are better). Paris, too, would have had more options.

> You have the crèche, the crèche is never ill. A nanny is. The crèche is always open [laughs]. Financially it's much better, too....When I had a child, I went back to work straight away. A lot of English women who have a child leave work. I come from the feminist culture in France. You don't even think about it.

Nour points out one of the other absurdities with overpriced childcare and double income professionals at full-financial stretch.

> They both have high-paid jobs, working really hard....Quite a few friends get into a pattern where they work hard to pay for someone else to look after their children. Frankly, what is the point of having kids, you know [laughs]. It defeats the purpose I think.

On housing, several of the respondents demonstrate the lack of real local knowledge that sees them renting in well-trodden, higher-price neighborhoods in north and west London, as opposed to doing as British newcomers would do and looking south of the river or in the east end for better value housing. Nicole's ever-temporary existence seems to be always rising in cost. She is having to move down-scale now.

> I moved every year. I wish I didn't have to do that, but I always had a good reason to move. I used *The Guardian*, flat shares, etc. Queensway, Bakerloo, then Shepherds Bush, then here (St.Catherine's Dock). I was working in Shoreditch. It's always an improvement of some sort. I work now in Ladbrook Grove so need to move back west. For the first time, I'm going to go backward, cheaper....London is very, very, very expensive. When you look at salaries they are really high, I would have never earned that in France, but still...you only just live. I didn't know London well enough. What I thought, I'm just going to find out....I didn't have any idea beforehand, I could leave, its still the way I feel about things. I have friends living in the hostel for four years. I have no attachment to neighborhoods.

Her lack of settlement here precludes the kind of more localized ties and networks—a tangible form of social capital—that other residents use to make London livable and affordable.

Nour—who lives with even more professional mobility and more like the image of "global elites" in the city—opted to ignore the prices and move into the most obviously accessible international area of London in Kensington/Chelsea. Although on a relatively average wage, she invested everything she could in a nice flat in this classic expatriate part of town to make relaxation in her hectic mobile life easier.

> I think people also have different priorities when you are a foreigner compared to when you are British. People may have been a bit shocked I would put so much money into that but for me it was absolutely very, very important....Even if it meant I was not going out so much or buying clothes.

On and off planes, working nights and highly global in her orientation (when not back "home" in Paris), she admits to not knowing her way around London much and is still not sure about where to take out-of-town friends when they come to visit.

> I have to say, I'm extremely attached to my neighborhood. Partly it's just laziness, a lot of people are like that in London, you stick to it. A lot of friends at work live next to where I live or in North London....My best friend lives in Camden, I make an exception just for her because I love her [laughs] but otherwise it's just hell to get me out of Earls Court or Kensington.

Integration

It is almost an unquestioned assumption of the global cities theorists, particularly those that home in on the cosmopolitan nature of

the "glocal" in these places (Hannerz 1996), that these former national capitals now embody, in time and space, the wide-open
"scapes" of a truly mobile, global culture. Yet what is striking from
the Eurostars' stories in London, is just how coercive and assimilatory
to specifically *national* norms of behavior life in this city in fact is:
especially in terms of the everyday rhythms, patterns of sociability
and choices and compromises people make between quality of life
and career. Yet it is remarkable, too, how the resident French see this
and accept the ways it has changed them. Valerie, fresh back from
her holiday in continental Europe, reflects:

> You see, there, the life is less stressed, you see people are more calm. Take Milan,
> people move [*bouge*] there, but there is an atmosphere there which you don't find here.
> But in France, I couldn't believe it, to buy something, I just wanted to shout, "*Bouge!
> c'est pas possible!*" I could do three tours of the supermarket while I'm waiting to pay
> at the checkout [laughs] but anyway, when I came back, relaxed etc, I appreciated that
> [their speed of life]. Whether I would like that long-term...[shrugs] You need things to
> move a bit but it's good people were not running, they appreciated things. There isn't
> the same competition, like here. I'm always amused here at 11 p.m. when the bell rings
> [in the pub] people always take three or four pints of beer, as if they don't really
> appreciate what they are doing. In France and Italy, you taste life, you are not just there
> to waste your energies. But I'm just as crazy [*folle*] except that I don't drink. I'm from
> the south of France, it annoyed me a lot when I worked—my job was intense, 8 a.m. to
> 5 p.m.—and you just don't eat, you just work. It's true that for me also today when I
> went to this interview at Canary Wharf, there were all these sandwich shops and all that
> and I say to myself [in English] "Ah, I don't want that." I can't do fast food while I'm
> walking, that stressed me [*angoissée*] because I'd forgotten that. At the moment I have
> the time. If I go back into the system, in finance especially, I will have to eat lunch in
> front of my computer. That's what I call the *non qualité de vie*—where you can't take
> pleasure in eating, when you don't take more than two minutes.

Being a Londoner means living the same way. Valerie jokes she is
not so well integrated because she does not share the British culture
of drinking and of dating (which she describes in French as "*fla-
grant*"). Her best friend is "more integrated because she drinks"—
hardly the most edifying aspect of British culture.

On other aspects, the respondents frequently despair of the destructive quality of life native Londoners put up with and London
also imposes on you.

> The strain of living in England has started to show....There is very little support for
> working mothers with huge problems of childcare and so on...so that was when the train
> started to derail [laughs].

Laure's choice of metaphor is very telling. Perhaps nothing has
symbolized the break down of London life more dramatically than
recent disasters on public transport. Nathalie recalls often taking the

same train involved in the Paddington Station train disaster and how upset she was the following week at the station when she got into an argument with an unhelpful and uncontrite ticket conductor. Nobody else seemed to be complaining, but she was outraged.

> You know the Paddington accident, it was the train I was taking every day. This day, I had a stomach ache, I stayed in my bed. Everybody was calling me to see if I was alive and I was saying, "Its ok, my stomach ache is not that bad!"....I didn't know the accident had happened, there were really people I saw everyday on that train, but never saw them after....At this time [afterwards] they [British Rail] didn't do anything to help people get around at the station. Everyone was lost and so on and I asked a question and they say [shouts] "You cannot read" and I was like "How dare you talk to me like that?"....All the other English are there, queuing, saying nothing...[angrily] "I haven't just killed all these people so you should just shut up. I just asked you a question, it's your job to answer me normally," and everyone was [makes a shocked face]!! It's not possible, they were not saying anything. We had to spend more money, we had to take more trains, they make us lose our time, they have killed people...and still they continue to say, "Oh, it's not our fault" and 'You have to pay and go there"....I was really amazed, they showed no compassion. I was reading in the *Metro* thing [free commuter newspaper]. It says people are really fed up but where do they see that!? I don't see that! I haven't seen anyone saying "It's a shame what happened!"

Nour makes a similar point about the managers of her housing block:

> When I complained, they were utterly shocked. I think it's a British thing—you don't complain. They said, "Oh, you are making a bit of a fuss aren't you?"

Others point to Britain's terrible service culture that ironically belies the British economy's highly "Americanized" self-image. Nour, again:

> One thing that does disturb me in terms of services....Maybe you get spoiled when you are in America. Here nobody cares, you can yell your lungs out, you can point out you are not getting what you are paying for and nobody gives a damn....Then they say "Ok we'll put it back but it will take three weeks." Which country in the bloody world, which industrialized country, takes three bloody weeks to install cable! It's totally ridiculous, they don't care. In my area they are the only ones to provide cable that's just not on. I was furious, I don't have three weeks. When I'm here, I can't wait for three weeks! [Privatized monopolies]... You get the worst of both worlds.

Laure equates bad service with "rip-off Britain" and the collapse of engineering expertise in the cradle of the Industrial Revolution, in one very funny story:

> One aspect of the English, which I don't like...a lot of people take a lot of advantage. That something [i.e., a plumber] can cost ninety pounds, it's disgusting, for nothing...there are shitty schools, lots of people making a quick buck....In France, we have more respect for *métiers* [trades]. You don't just become a plumber just like that. There is a respect [for the trade]. Here there's no respect. At last I understand after thirteen years why it is the trains don't work. It's because there is no respect for engineers. Intelligent people never study to be engineers, they go work in the City. I didn't understand that. I met this

guy [in the City] and asked, "What was your degree?" "I was an engineer," he said, "but no way was I going to work as one!" Then I understood why the Millennium Bridge didn't work [laughs]!! It's a pity. The quick buck. Ok, they're not racist here but how people are exploited, that really shocks me.

For all the talk of Americanization—for all *The Sun* editorials proclaiming "We work like America, think like America, etc."—Great British peculiarities remain just that, British. Rupert Murdoch may well be successful selling the British masses a lowest common denominator image of American society and its similarities to Britain but it is clear too Americans would have exactly the same complaints. On the other hand, it can be argued a parallel Europeanization might be a having an effect in raising London's quality of life and in transcending British class divisions. Jamie Oliver ("The Naked Chef") has indeed brought simple Italian food to the same masses, although (an equally simple) dinner at the River Café still requires a blue chip income. However, quantitatively, economically, the impact of the new European population on London has been considerable. In many ways, these European residents and their lifestyle preferences have become a conduit for the progressive Europeanization of some of London's worst eating and going out habits, with the new vogue for restaurants, street cafés and Euro-chic. A good example is the transformation of Islington, a Europeanized, cosmopolitan neighborhood highly popular with Eurostars who can afford it.

What is noticeable however, in London as elsewhere, is how this involvement almost never translates into political participation. The EU studies literature on European citizenship indeed is way off-beam in its hopes this might be an effective route towards Europeanization and a more democratic Europe. Nicole, when asked about this, shrugged in a way typical of nearly all interviewees—who would be classified among some of the most politically and culturally aware members of the European population, as well as those most likely to care about European citizenship.

I don't have the energy. I didn't ever vote [as a European citizen]. I didn't know anything about it. I didn't receive any information and I didn't look for it. I was expecting information but I was lazy. I read the papers, follow the news and everything but I'm much more interested in French politics and I have voted in France. I think if I had a family here, I would. But I know that I'm not going to stay here for twenty years.

Freedom...or anomie?

Nicole's crisp statement here summarizes the sojourner mentality: a way of life made possible by the European free movement provisions and the new forms of mobility it encourages. For the younger movers, provisionality is the key to this freedom, and it is this that Eurocities—whether London or any other—most usefully enable:

> Deciding to stay for two years was a bit scary. It's stupid, I know, when you've been staying each time, "just another year." This is just two years but it was a big step for me. It's funny. I think it's maybe because I like the idea of knowing it's ok if I change my mind tomorrow. I can just go, give up everything in one month. It's a kind of freedom but now I have to be a bit more responsible.

She adds:

> To me, I feel kind of settled, you can be settled and still traveling. If I could meet someone who likes traveling and we have the opportunity work wise to travel, live five years here, five years there, I think it's fantastic. I didn't lose my friends in France, they are still there for me and I feel very close to friends in London. It's just great, I keep meeting new people....I feel French in England and English in France. I like that line. I love that. Being abroad, being a stranger, being different and I love going back to France and being different, I have a little more.

Valerie, defines her own notion of this trans-European, *de-nationalized* freedom, by comparing life in cosmopolitan London with Paris:

> In Paris, it's perhaps just as good for all that but you don't feel that de-nationalized aspect of life [*côté depaisé*]. I'm a foreigner here, that's what I like. That gives me the right to be different because I'm not from here. When we go out with colleagues, I'm the one who doesn't take beer, who doesn't get drunk, because it's not in my culture. I'm different here but also I'm different now in France because I'm not like everyone now....I like this way of not belonging to anyone, of making myself distinct [*me distinguer*].

But Valerie is slightly older than Nicole and has passed a certain threshold where she, in fact, now feels there is no real going back:

> Yes, that's the only thing that makes me afraid, the more it goes, the less I'll be able to go back to France, even if you take a taste for that, being elsewhere.

A few further years later down the road, married with children, ostensibly settled and successful in London, Laure is even more doubtful of the longer-term commitments she is making:

> I think although I don't like talking about middle-class problems—at the end of the day we are so much more privileged than people who *have* to move—but I would still like to know why it is there are more and more people who make that choice where to go live, to places where they can *project* themselves....What we are all doing is forgetting the most important thing is involvement in *where* we live, not where we *could* live...and I put myself in the same basket because I ate my breakfast today looking at a map of France [laughs].

Her words express the anomie that comes with the European freedoms; an anomie—life without norms—that harks back towards the specific frustrations of life as a foreigner in a foreign city, but also points further to a sense of how unsettling a truly de-nationalized life in the European context might be.

One way this plays out over time is in one's closest social networks, one's "best friends," something always especially important for women. Valerie explains why her three best friends turn out to be French women as well:

> The English are *chez eux* here, why should they bother getting to know people who don't really speak the language, understand everything. As I said, after a while I needed to get to know French people.

Nicole also points to a specifically gendered *and* nationalized scenario *vis-à-vis* male or female friends:

> I notice my male friends are all English or foreign, my female friends are all French. It's easy with English guys, easier than French guys. They are very chatty, willing to get to know you. They can be close friends. I never had the same feeling with an English girl. They were never interested, it was always conversation about clothes, what you did last night, nothing personal. If you have a problem, that's just not close enough for you to go and talk to them. It never happened. I don't know if it's me, I never felt invited to get closer.

Nathalie, with her boyfriend Jeroen, express frustration with this kind of nationalized "social closure" on a different question: why there is no appeal in doing what other English of their age are doing and moving out of the city to the suburbs (which is also why they don't have English friends). Here Jeroen voices their thoughts:

> It happens the English at work are often with families, they go home. They are not living the same life [as us], they tend not to live in London, very few people want to live in London....I grew up a little bit in the suburbs, I find it's not that interesting....Here, you see different people, different clothes, weird or not, Here I look out my window and things happen... I feel the suburbs, they lack something...

The suburban middle-class option has been the routine way native Londoners have, since the early nineteenth century, squared the circle between the impossibly competitive struggle over housing, childcare, affordable education, space and greenery, with urban life in the city they love.

> I should wait until I'm in the situation [having children] but I'm not so sure it's necessary, I think it's a little bit what people want.

The normal route out of the city is just not an option for Eurostars, after all that's not why they came to London or why they continue to be there. But this kind of attitude gets harder to maintain. As Nicole says,

> I miss the fact I can't afford a one-person flat. It's very hard for my parents to understand. Why? Why are you paying 500 pounds rent to share with someone, it's just…One of the reasons why I know I'm not going to spend my life here, you just can't afford it.

I ask her when will it be that she's had enough of the struggle?

> Different situations. If my salary doesn't go up but the cost of living goes up, I just won't enjoy myself anymore. And I will go back and I will be very happy to go back..

The single women here seem to be somewhat out of synch, out of time with the norms around them. They identify buying a house with being a couple and settling down—and think they won't do that until they return. This is precisely the step that the younger Eurostars don't want to take. It leaves them in a kind of limbo land in terms of age and lifestyle, increasingly living a different schedule to both their peer group back home and their age cohort of native British people in London. Nicole identifies how out of time she is, compared to her friends and the astonishment of her family.

> I'm in a minority. My friends…they didn't go to Paris, they stayed in Lille or returned to our first town that is very small. It's a different kind of idea of what you want. Most of them are in a relationship and they find it very hard for me not to be in a relationship and they feel very sorry for me. They think it's a dramatic situation and they have a job and they like to have the family around. Some are married with a child or two; it's just another idea. I guess some of them understand me but some of them think I just don't want to be an adult in a way, that I don't want a relationship, a house, to settle down. It's just peoples' ideas. It's very much something to do with what they were told to do, told what success was, what they were expected to do. Some of them got married at twenty-four, twenty-five and had a child straight away. I know that for me I was absolutely not ready.

Such a situation cannot help but produce a certain degree of weariness and malaise. As Nathalie says:

> The only thing I'm really frightened for me is that because I don't want to think what I'm really doing in terms of jobs, in terms of life...I don't take decisions, because I'm in transit….Sometimes I think you can just forget to make decisions...

In other, generally older, interviewees, I have found older single women and gay men have managed to transcend these conventional lifestyle pressures by opting for distinctly alternative urban lifestyles in the cities studied. Here, however, all of my respondents report more or less conventional wishes in terms of heterosexual romance and partnerships, something that in relationships or outside, London is increasingly failing to deliver.

Valerie: I don't feel completely *installée* [settled] because, after all, I rent my apartment, I can't really feel that until I'm in a couple. I think that is more of a girl's emphasis. A friend of mine, she's in a couple and they've bought a house but my best friend, for example, she thinks she will return to France because she doesn't think she is going to meet someone here. I'm not able to see myself as an individual on my own that way buying, I know it's something in my mentality but I wouldn't do it, the idea wouldn't come to me. You buy something as, and when, you are two people. I can't buy anything by myself, because that's going to be broken up the day that someone comes into my life....I should have bought a house six years ago, now it's too late. The prices are less and less approachable. Once again I have the image of my parents buying a house. I don't want to buy a house by myself....There are many girls that have said that to me, that girls often think about the future in terms of their future partner....But that's a difference here, the English are more independent, while the French do everything in a couple. When you're a couple you're a couple, *ça se rigole pas* (it's no joke) but I can't imagine constructing myself on my own something. I am waiting...for the Messiah, *voilà*!

Valerie's nice piece of self-irony here points to doubts about the longer-term viability of their chosen lifestyle. And, given these things are so much more easily and naturally accessed by natives of the country they live in, one also questions just how truly international, London, this *place*, really is. Laure, speaking of East European au pairs, reflects again on the toughness of the city on other young migrants:

I know many non-English in London and it's pretty easy to see which of those are going to do ok and which are not (*s'en sortir*). Even the Eastern European girls, that's an amazing phenomenon, these girls, you know, nannies and so on. It depends, unfortunately, on the background they had before they came here. The girls that are a bit more polished, better brought-up, they start as secretaries, then they move out. They have this possibility, where they can be mobile. And then there are the others, from simple backgrounds, farms, factories, and it's so tough for them...but they are extraordinary people. I don't want a little French girl '*na na na*' [imitates a French girl]....In human terms you have amazing exchanges with them, but that's only something I have here, not in Paris where everyone would be just like me...

Laure then goes on to diagnose a mismatch between migrant aspirations and the personal development you need to get on with your life, whether at home or abroad.

These girls, it's ok at first, but they are going to arrive at the point when they need to leave and they are not going to be able to do it. They've had no professional development, there is a gap [in their development]. The curve is like that [hand goes up] and they are like that [going down]. At the moment they want to have a family, when they are less fixed on personal achievement, they need to go back to their own country where they are needed...it's a horrible situation.

Laure is talking about a different group of migrants in London, a different set of stories, young East European women with a very different background and social origin than the young French women

I interviewed. For sure, these latter are not so vulnerable. Their middle-class family resources are more solid, their personal and career development in London has been remarkable, and they might still be able to make all that count going back to their home job market or elsewhere. But one might look again at these smart, rootless, unfulfilled young French women in London and wonder to what extent Laure's words are also addressed to herself and her own co-nationals.

The Human Face of Trends in Economic Geography

Talk of mobility is all the rage these days. We have been rightly urged to push sociology and other social sciences beyond the nation state (Urry, 2000) with an integrating Europe a key research terrain (Therborn, 1995). One or two historians have written brilliant, sweeping overviews of mobility—and immobility—in Europe's past (Kaelble, 1990; Moch, 2003). Now, in the contemporary situation, it is only geographers who are likely to be equipped enough—with their distinctive sense of spatial scales, flows, place and time—to begin to capture the fundamental changes afoot on the European continent in empirical terms (see, e.g., Rodríguez-Pose, 2002).

Unfortunately, however, the most well know geographical literature of relevance here—the economic geography literature on global cities and transnational economies—has, on the whole, proceeded apace with scant attention to the *human* dimension of these phenomena. Flows and networks between locations are measured by counting the number of offices corporations have in different cities, measuring foreign direct investment and information exchange, or by quantitatively charting shifts in business activities from production to service industries (Taylor, Walker and Beaverstock, 2000; Sassen, 2000b Brenner, 1999). But rarely is any kind of human face given to these macro-level transactions and data-sets (rare exceptions are the work of Beaverstock, i.e., 2002, 2005; Yeoh and Willis, 2005). Urry's mobile manifesto, meanwhile, offers the right diagnosis as premise but totally the wrong remedy methodologically. It exhorts a cavalier abandonment of all empirical method—the tools of comparativism, carefully constructed case-studies, data collection—in favor of a post-humanist, metaphors strewn theorizing about "global complexity." Sociologists are supposed to now study flows of waste, symbolic networks of meaning, virtual transactions and other abstract ideas rather than ask questions of real people with real lives. Theories of globalization are full of such rhetorical excess. As this suggests, what is most needed is a way of mediating between the necessarily abstract, macro-data driven perspectives on globalization, economies and regional integration, and the equally necessary call for phenomenological insight into the lives and experiences of flesh and blood individuals who are the true face of these global and regional trends.

The other literature on which such research may put a face is, of course, the literature on European (EU) integration. Dominated by top-down policy studies and, hence, mainly legal and institutional analysis; very few have thought about what it might mean to study Europeanization from below. The experiences, attitudes and social trajectories of prototypical free moving European citizens offers a tangible grounding by which we might be able to chart the actual effects of European integration on the ground. They are among the most obvious avatars of the broader institutional process.

All of these processes are located in a global city like London and can be read through the mobile lives and experiences of individuals who best embody these macro-trends. The French women I interviewed in London found new opportunities and different economic practices that satisfied their quest for mobility. Yet much of their ease and adaptation to the city was dependent on not being far from home as well as not needing to make the kinds of routine cultural compromises other immigrants must make in order to integrate. Over time, the experience grew less satisfactory and aspects of the city and the trajectories that natives follow through it were closed to them. The benefits of mobility are often transparent and accessible in the short-run; some of the costs of these life choices only become apparent later.

The growing European presence in London suggests a regional embedding of this particular city, in a way that qualifies some of the excesses of the general literature on globalization and global cities. London is an extraordinary international place but as we have seen it also has its provincial dimensions; for all its global networks and nodal centrality, it remains a highly nationalized, specific place in many ways. The image of effortless, frictionless mobility given to us by theorists of globalization, and portrayed in the stylized *übermenschen* of global yuppie magazines such as *Wallpaper*, gives way here to a very different image: of average middle-class Europeans, aware of the benefits and freedoms mobility has bestowed, but struggling to get by in a global city that cannot satisfy all of their cosmopolitan hopes and aspirations. It turns out—as with "flexibility" in the new post-industrial economy (Sennett, 1998)—it is not such an easy thing to build a complete, fulfilled life out of mobility; there are costs as well as benefits to free movement.

The lives of the Eurostars are extraordinary precisely because it is not easy to opt out of the standard social trajectories offered to middle-class children in European nation-state-societies. Thus, they remain, for all their numbers, the exception in a generally immobile Europe. European residents of London are having an impact on the city and do embody one important facet of its current internationalization. Yet their experiences also remind us global mobility is much easier in theory than in practice, and that even in the most of global of cities, not everyone feels as much at home as everyone else.

Notes

1. See their superb website, which brings together all the state-of-the-art research on global cities: http://www.lboro.ac.uk/gawc
2. An earlier version of this chapter appeared as a working paper on the GaWC website in November 2004, after which the story was quickly picked up by journalists in the English quality press, with similar articles appearing in Observer and The Daily Telegraph about French migrants to the U.K.
3. See our website: http://www.obets.ua.es/pioneur/
4. See the Urban Audit website: http://www.europa.eu.int/comm/regional_policy/urban2/urban/audit/index.html
5. See their website: http://www.francelibre.org/
6. All of my interviewees are presented with pseudonyms, with personal details blurred.

Bibliography

AFL-CIO. 2004. "Outsourcing America." Executive Council Actions. Bal Harbor, Fla., March 11.

Agarwal, Vinod B., and Donald R. Winkler. 1985. "United States Immigration Policy and the Indirect Immigration of Professionals." *Economics of Education Review* 4: 1-16.

Aiken, Linda H., James Buchan, Julie Sochalski, Barbara Nichols and Mary Powell. 2004."Trends in International Nurse Migration." *Health Affairs* 23(3): 69-77.

Alaminos, Antonio, Oscar Santacreu, and Mari Carmen Albert. 2003. *Los procesos de aculturación y socialización de extranjeros en Alicante.* Alicante: Obets.

Alarcón, Rafael. 1999. "Recruitment Processes Among Foreign-Born Engineers and Scientists in Silicon Valley." *American Behavioral Scientist* 42: 1381-1397.

American Immigration Lawyers Association (AILA). 2002. "AILA Co-Sponsors April 30th Teleconference on Immigration Issues Encountered in Addressing the Nursing Shortage." http://www.aila.org

American Medical Association. 2001. *Report of the Council on Medical Service: The Growing Nursing Shortage in the United States*, CMS Report 7-A-01. http://www.ama-assn.org/ama/upload/mm/372/a01report7.doc

Angell, Ian. 2000. *The New Barbarian Manifesto: How to Survive the Information Age.* London: Kogan Page.

Armstrong, Richard. 2003. "H-1B Myth: The Best and Brightest." http://www.hireamericancitizens.org

Ascoli, Ugo. 1979. *Movimenti migratori in Italia.* Bologna: Il Mulino.

Auriol, Laudeline and Jerry Sexton. 2002. "Human Resources in Science and Technology: Measurement Issues and International Mobility." OECD Publications, Paris. http://www.ricyt.edu.ar/interior/normalizacion/V_taller/schaperdoc.pdf

Bade, Klaus J. 2000. *Europa in Bewegung. Migration vom späten 18. Jahrhundert bis zur Gegenwart.* München: Beck.

Baganha, Maria I. 2002. "Portuguese Emigration After World War II." Institute of European Studies Working Paper. University of California, Berkeley. http://ies.berkeley.edu/research/files/CP02/CP02 Close_to_Open_Doors.pdf.

Bagchi, Indrani. 2004."Techies Take Heart, H1-B Dream is Still Alive." *The Times of India*, October 12.

Bakan, Joel. 2004. *The Corporation: The Pathological Pursuit of Profit and Power.* New York: Free Press.

Bakker Matt and Michael Peter Smith. 2003. "*El Rey del Tomate*: Migrant Political Transnationalism and Democraticization in Mexico." *Migraciones Internacionales* 2 (1): 59-83.

Bailly, F., M. El Mouhoub, M and J. Oudinet. 2004. "Les pays de l'Union Européenne face aux nouvelles dynamiques des migrations internationales: Ampleur des migrations et charactéristiques des migrants." *Revue française des affaires sociales*, 58, 2 (avr-juin): 33-60.

Balá•, Vladimír, and Allan M. Williams. 2004. "'Been There, Done That': International Student Migration and Human Capital Transfers from the U.K. to Slovakia." *Population, Space and Place* 10 (May/June): 217-237.

Baldoni, Emiliana. 2003. *The Free Movement of Persons in the EU: A Legal–Historical Overview*. PIONEUR working paper 2003/2. Florence: CIUSPO. http://www.obets.ua.es/pioneur/bajaarchivo_public.php?iden=40

Baldwin, Peter. 1990. *The Politics of Social Solidarity: Class Bases of the European Welfare States*. Cambridge: Cambridge University Press.

Barnet, Richard J. 1995. *Global Dreams: Imperial Corporations and the New World Order*. New York: Simon and Schuster.

Bartlett, Christopher A. and Sumantra Ghoshal. 1989. *Managing Across Borders: The Transnational Solution*. London: Century Business.

Batalova, Jeanne. 2005. "Crossing Borders in the Information Age: The Impact of Highly Skilled Migrants on the Labor Market Outcomes of the U.S. Highly Skilled Workers." Dissertation Thesis, Sociology, University of California Irvine, Irvine, CA.

Bauman, Zygmunt. 1998. *Globalization: The Human Consequences*. Cambridge: Polity Press.

Bean, Frank D., Jennifer Lee, Jeanne Batalova, and Mark Leach. 2004. "Immigration and Fading Color Lines in America." Russell Sage Foundation and Population Reference Bureau, New York, NY and Washington, DC.

Beaverstock, Jonathan. 2001a. "Negotiating Globalization and Global Cities in Extending Our Understanding of New Forms of Brain Drain: 'Transient' Professional Migration Flows in International Banking." *GaWC Research Bulletin* 8. http://www.lboro.ac.uk/gawc/rb/rb8.html

———. 2001b. "The Expatriation Business and the Business of Expatriation." *GaWC Research Bulletin* 42. http://www.lboro.ac.uk/gawc/rb/rb42.html

———. 2001c. "Transnational Elite Communities in Global Cities: Connectivities, Flows and Networks." *GaWC Research Bulletin* 63. http://www.lboro.ac.uk/gawc/rb/rb63.html

———. 2002. "Transnational Elites in Global Cities: British Expatriates in Singapore's Financial District." *Geoforum* 33(4): 525-538.

———. 2005. "Transnational Elites in the City: British Highly-Skilled Inter-Company Transferees in New York City's Financial District." *Journal of Ethnic and Migration Studies* 31: 245-268.

Becker, Sascha O., Andrea Ichino, and Giovanni Peri. 2003. "How Large is the 'Brain Drain' from Italy?" CESifo Working Paper Series No. 839. http://ssrn.com/abstract=378522

Beine, Michel, Frédéric Docquier, and Hillel Rapoport. 2001. "Brain Drain and Economic Growth: Theory and Evidence." *Journal of Development Economics* 64 (February): 275-289.

Benhabib, Seyla. 2002. *Claims of Culture: Equality and Diversity in the Global Era*. Princeton, NJ: Princeeton University Press.

Betts, Julian R. and Magnus Lofstrom. 2000. "The Educational Attainment of Immigrants: Trends and Implications." Pp. 51-116 in *Issues in the Economics of Immigration*, edited by G. Borjas. Chicago, IL: The University of Chicago Press.

Bhagwati, Jagdish, and William Dellalfar. 1973. "The Brain Drain and Income Taxation." *World Development* 1 (February): 94-101.

Bhagwati, Jagdish, and Koichi Hamada. 1974. "The Brain Drain, International Integration of Markets for Professionals and Unemployment: A Theoretical Analysis." *Journal of Development Economics* 1: 19-42.

Biao, Xiang. 2003. "Emigration from China: A Sending Country Perspective." *International Migration* 41 (September): 21-48.

Boeri, Tito and Herbert Brücker. 2001. *Eastern Enlargement and EU–Labour Markets: Perceptions, Challenges and Opportunities*. Discussion Paper No. 256. Bonn: Forschunginstitut zur Zukunft der Arbeit.

Bollag, Burton. 2004. "Enrollment of Foreign Students Drops in U.S." *The Chronicle of Higher Education, International*, November 19. http://chronicle.com/weekly/v51/i13/13a00101.htm

Boo, Katharine. 2004. "The Best Job in Town: The Americanization of Chennai." *The New Yorker* (July 5): 54-69.

Booz, Allen, and Hamilton, Inc. 1988. *Characteristics and Labor Market Impact of Persons Admitted Under the H-1 Program*. Bethesda, MD.

Borjas, George. 1989. "Economic Theory and International Migration." *International Migration Review* (23) 3: 457-485.

———. 1994. "The Economics of Immigration." *Journal of Economic Literature* 32: 1667-1717.

———. 1995. "Assimilation and Changes in Cohort Quality Revisited: What Happened to Immigrant Earnings in the 1980s?" *Journal of Labor Economics* 13:201-245.

———. 2000. *Labor Economics,* 2nd ed. Boston: McGraw-Hill.

———. 2002. "An Evaluation of the Foreign Student Program." Backgrounder, Washington, DC: Center for Immigration Studies. http://www.cis.org/articles/2002/back602.html

———. 2003. "The Labor Demand Curve is Downward Sloping: Reexamining the Impact of Immigration on the Labor Market." *The Quarterly Journal of Economics*:1335-1374.

———. 2004. *Increasing the Supply of Labor Through Immigration: Measuring the Impact on Native-born Workers*. Backgrounder. Washington, DC: Center for Immigration Studies.

Bourdieu, Pierre. 1979. *La distinction*. Paris: Éditions de minuit.

Bousetta, Hassan. 2000. "Political Dynamics in the City. Citizenship, Ethnic Mobilisation and Socio-Political Participation: Four Case Studies." in *Minorities in European Cities: The Dynamics of Social Integration and Social Exclusion at the Neighbourhood Level*, Sophie Body-Gendrot and Marco Martiniello (eds). London: Macmillan.

Bouvier, Leon and David Simcox. 1994. "Foreign Born Professionals in the United States." Center for Immigration Studies, Washington, DC.

Bouvier, Leon and John Martin. 1995. "Foreign-Born Scientists, Engineers and Mathematicians in the United States." Center for Immigration Studies, Washington, DC.

Boyd, Monica. 1989. "Family and Personal Networks in International Migration:Recent Developments and New Agendas." *International Migration Review* 23: 638-70.

Boyer, Robert, and Daniel Drache (eds.) 1996. *States Against Markets*. London : Routledge.

Branigin, William. 1999. "A Push for More Special Work Visas; Tech Employers Say Higher Limit on Foreigners Isn't High Enough." *The Washington Post*, June 25.

Bratsberg, Bernt. 1995. "The Incidence of Non-Return Among Foreign Students in the United States." *Economics of Education Review* 14 (December): 373-384.

Brenner, Neil. 1999. "Globalization as Reterritorialization: the Re-Scaling of Urban Governance in the European Union." *Urban Studies* 36: 431-52.

Brettell, Caroline B and James F. Hollifield (eds.) 2000. *Migration Theory: Talking Across Disciplines*. New York: Routledge.

Briggs, Vernon. 1996. *Mass Immigration and the National Interest*. Armonk, NY: M.E. Sharpe.

Broaded, C. Montgomery. 1993. "China's Response to the Brain Drain." *Comparative Education Review,* 37 (August): 277-303.

Brochmann, Grete. 1999. "The Mechanisms of Control." in *Mechanism of Immigration Control: A Comparative Analysis of European Regulation Policies*. Grete Brochmann and Tomas Hammar (eds.). Oxford: Berg: 1-27.

Brubaker, Rogers. 1995. "Comments on 'Modes of Immigration Politics in Liberal Democratic States.'" *International Migration Review* 29/112: 903-908.

Brush, Barbara L., Julie Sochalski, and Anne M. Berger. 2004. "Imported Care: Recruiting Foreign Nurses to U.S. Health Care Facilities." *Health Affairs* 23(3): 78-87.

Buerhaus, Peter I., Douglas O. Staiger and David I. Auerbach. 2003. "Is the current shortage of hospital nurses ending?" *Health Affairs* 23(6): 191-198.

Burawoy, Michael et al. 2000. *Global Ethnography: Forces, Connections, and Imaginations in a Postmodern World*. Berkeley. University of California Press.

Butler, Tim and Mike Savage (eds.) 1995. *Social Change and the Middle Classes*. London: UCL Press.

Butz, William, Terence Kelly, David Adamson, Gabrielle Bloom, Donna Fossum, and Mihal Gross. 2004. *Will the Scientific and Technology Workforce Meet the Requirements of the Federal Government?* Santa Barbara: Rand Corporation.

Camarota, Steven. 2001. *Immigrants in the United States: 2000*. Washington, DC: Center for Immigration Studies.

Carrington, William J., and Enrica Detragiache. 1998. "How Big is the Brain Drain?" IMF Working Paper.
http://www.imf.org/external/pubs/ft/wp/wp98102.pdf

Carrington, William J., and Enrica Detragiache. 1999. "International Migration and the 'Brain Drain.' " *The Journal of Social, Political, and Economic Studies* 24 (Summer): 163-171.

Castells, Manuel. 2000 (2ⁿᵈ ed.). *The Rise of the Network Society.* Oxford: Blackwell.

Castells, Manuel and Pekka Himanen. 2002. *The Information Society and the Welfare State: The Finnish Model.* Oxford: Oxford University Press.

Castles, Stephen and Mark Miller. 2003 (3ʳᵈ ed). *The Age of Migration.* Basingstoke: Palgrave MacMillan.

Cerny, Philip G. 1994. "Globalization and the Changing Logic of Collective Action." University of York, Department of Politics, Working Paper (5).

Cerny, Philip G. 1999. "Globalization, Governance and Complexity," in *Globalization and Governance,* edited by A. Prakash and J. A. Hart. London and New York: Routledge,188-212.

Chakravartty, Paula. 2001a. "The Emigration of High-Skilled Indian Workers to the United States: Flexible Citizenship and India's Information Economy." in Cornelius et. al. (eds.): 325-350.

———. 2001b. "Flexible Citizens and the Internet: The Global Politics of Local High-Tech Development in India." *Emergences: Journal for the Study of Media and Composite Culture* 11 (1): 69-88.

———. 2005. "Weak Winners of Globalization: Indian H-1B Workers in the American Information Economy." *Asian American Policy Index Nexus* (Summer).

Chanda, Rupa. 2003. *Globalization of Services: India's Opportunities and Constraints.* New Delhi: Oxford University Press.

Chekuri, Chris and Himadeep Muppidi. 2003. "Diasporas Before and After the Nation." *International Journal of Postcolonial Studies* 5 (1): 45-57.

Cheng, Lucie and Philip Yang. 1998. "Global Interaction, Global Inequality, and Migration of the Highly Trained to the United States." *International Migration Review* 32 (3): 626-653.

Clare, Richard and Anne Paternoster. 2003. "Minimum Wages: EU member states and Candidate Countries." *Statistics in Focus–Eurostat* 10: 1–8.

Clasen, Jochen. 2003. *Cross–Border Commuting in the EU: Obstacles and Barriers.* Final Research Report. http://www.dass.stir.ac.uk/CROBOCOB/

Commission on Workforce Quality and Labor Market Efficiency. 1989. *Investing in People: A Strategy to Address America's Workforce Crisis.* Washington, DC: U.S. Department of Labor.

Conradson, David and Alan Lathan. 2005. "Transnational Urbanism: Attending to Everyday Practices and Mobilities." *Journal of Ethnic and Migration Studies* 31, (2): 227-234.

Conradson, David and Alan Latham. 2005. "Friendship Networks and Transnationality in a World City: Antipodean Transmigrants in London." *Journal of Ethnic and Migration Studies* 31, (2) : 287-306.

Cornelius, Wayne A., Philip Martin, and James Hollifield (eds.). 1994. *Controlling Immigration. A Global Perspective.* Stanford, CA: Stanford University Press.

Cornelius, Wayne A., Thomas Espenshade, and Idean Salehyan (eds.). 2001. *The International Migration of the Highly Skilled.* La Jolla: Center for Comparative Immigration Studies, University of California, San Diego.

Cornelius, Wayne A., and Thomas J. Espenshade. 2001. "The International Migration of the Highly Skilled: 'High-Tech *Braceros*' in the Global Labor Market." in Cornelius et al (eds.): 3-19.

Corti, Paola. 2003. *Storia delle migrazioni internazionali.* Roma–Bari: Laterza.

Crouch, Colin. 1999. *Social Change in Western Europe.* New York: Oxford University Press.

CSI, US Coalition of Service Industries. 2000. *Solicitation of Public Comment for Mandated Multilateral Trade Negotiations on Argricultrue and Services in the World Trade Organization and Priorities for Future Market Access Negotiations on Non-Acrigultural Goods.* Washington, DC: CSI.

Das, Man Singh. 1969. "Effects of Foreign Students' Attitudes Toward Returning to the Country of Origin on the National Loss of Professional Skills." Ph.D. dissertation, Oklahoma State University.

Das Gupta, Monisha. 2004 "A View of Post-9/11 Justice from Below." *Peace Review* 16 (2): 141-148.

Desai, Mihir A. et. al. 2001. "The Fiscal Impact of Brain Drain: Indian Emigration to the US." *Weekly Political Economy Discussion Paper.* Cambridge, MA: Harvard University.
http://www.wcfia.harvard.edu/seminars/pegroup/Desai-Kapur.pdf

Desruisseaux, Paul. 1999. "Foreign Students Continue to Flock to the U.S." *The Chronicle of Higher Education, International,* December 10.
http://chronicle.com/weekly/v46/i16/16a00101.htm

Dobson, Janet, Khalid Koser, Gail McLaughlan and John Salt. 2001. *International Migration and the United Kingdom: Recent Patterns and Trends.* London: Home Office.

Dobson, Janet and John Salt. 2002. *Review of Migration Statistics.* PEMINT working paper 7/2002. Universidade de Coimbra.
http://pemint.ces.uc.pt/Working%20Paper–7.pdf.

Dowling, Peter, Schuler, Randall S. and Denice E. Welch. 1994. *International Dimensions of Human Resource Management-* 2nd Edition. Belmont, CA: Wadsworth Pub.

Drèze, Jean and Amartya Sen. 1997. *India: Economic Development and Social Opportunity.* New Delhi: Oxford University Press.

Dumont, Jean-Christophe and Lemaitre George. 2004. "Counting Immigrants and Expatriates: A New Perspective." OECD.
http://www.oecd.org/dataoecd/27/5/33868740.pdf

Dumoulin, Michel (ed). 1989. *Mouvements et politiques migratoires en Europe depuis 1945: le cas italien.* Bruxelles: Ciaco.

Eade, John. (ed).1997. *Living the Global City: Globalization as a Local Process.* London and New York: Routledge.

Ederveen, Sjef and Bardsley, Nick. 2003. "The Influence of Wage and Unemployment Differentials on Labour Mobility in the EU: A Meta–Analysis." Paper presented at the conference "Ageing and Welfare Systems: What Have We Learned? A Comparative EU–US Perspective." Brussels: National Bank of Belgium, 24–25 January. http://www.enepri.org/PapersENEPRIfinalconference/paper5.pdf

Edsall, Thomas. 2001. "Amnesty Proposal is Huge Gamble for Bush: President Could be Rewarded with Hispanic Vote but Risks Angering GOP's Conservative Wing." *The Washington Post,* July 17.

Edström, Anders and Jay R. Galbraith. 1977. "Transfer of Managers as a Coordination and Control Strategy in Multinational Corporations." *Administrative Science Quarterly* 22: 248-263.

Ekberg, Jan and Björn Gustafsson.1995. *Invandrare på Arbetsmarknaden* (Immigrants in the Labor Market). Stockholm: SNS Förlag.

Endelman, Gary. 2003. "Firebell in the Night: The Coming L-1 Crisis and What We Can Do About it." *The Immigration Portal.* http://www.ilw.com/lawyers/articles/2003,0305-endelman.shtm

ESF, European Services Forum. 2000. *Second Position Paper of the European Services Forum on The Temporary Movement of Key Business Personnel.* Brussels: European Services Forum.

ESF, European Services Forum. 2001. *Third Position Paper of the European Services Forum on The Temporary Movement of Key Business Personnel.* Brussels: European Services Forum.

ESN, European Services Network. 1999. *First Position Paper of the European Services Forum on The Temporary Movement of Key Business Personnel.* Brussels: European Services Forum.

Espenshade, Thomas J. 2001. "High-End Immigrants and the Shortage of Skilled Labor" *Population Research and Policy Review* 20, (1-2) : 9-31.

Esping-Andersen, Gösta.1990. *The Three Worlds of Welfare Capitalism.* Cambridge: Polity Press.

Esposito, Joseph. 1999. "Testimony before the House Judiciary Committee, May 5." Directorate for Visa Services, Department of State.

Ethier, Wilfried. 1996. "Theories About Trade Liberalisation and Migration: Substitutes or Complements?" In *International Trade and Migration in the APEC Region.* Edited by Peter Lloyd and Lynne Williams. Melbourne: Oxford University Press, 50-68.

Eurobarometer. 2001. *Young Europeans in 2001.* Summary report. http://europa.eu.int/comm/public_opinion/archives/eb_special_en.htm

European Commission. 1995. "Opinion 1/94 on the Uruguay Round Treaties," *Common Market Law Review,* 1: 219.

———. 1996. *Putting Services to Work.* Communication to the European Council: CSE 6 Final.

——— 2002. *Commission's Action Plan for Skills and Mobility.* COM (2002) 72 Final. http://europa.eu.int/eur–lex/en/com/cnc/2002/com2002_0072en01.pdf

———. 2004. *Fourth Report on Citizenship of the Union.* COM (2004) 695 Final.

Eurostat. 2004. "Acquisition of Citizenship." *Statistics in Focus–Eurostat* 3: 1–7.

Evetts, Julia. 1999. "Regulation of Professions in Global Economies: Dimensions of acquired regulation." Paper presented at the SASE Conference in Madison, Wisconsin, 07.11.1999.

Faist, Thomas. 2000. *The Volume and Dynamics of International Migration and Transnational Social Spaces.* Oxford: Oxford University Press.

Favell, Adrian. 2001 (2nd ed.). *Philosophies of Integration: Immigration and the Idea of Citizenship in France and Britain.* London: Palgrave.

———. 2003. "Games Without Frontiers? Questioning the Transnational Social Power of Migrants in Europe." *Archives Européennes de Sociologie* XLIV (3): 397-427.

———. 2004. "Eurostars and Eurocities: Free Moving Professionals and the Promise of European Integration." *European Studies Newsletter* 33:1-11. http://www.europanet.org/newsletters/200401/favell.html

———. 2006. *Eurostars and Eurocities: Free Moving Urban Professionals in an Integrating Europe.* Oxford: Blackwell.

Favell, Adrian and Hansen, Randall. 2002. "Market Against Politics: Migration, EU Enlargement and the Idea of Europe." *Journal of Ethnic and Migration Studies* 28 (4): 581–602.

Federal Reserve Bank of Dallas. 2004. "Workers Remittances to Mexico" *Business Frontier* 1. http://www.dallasfed.org/research/busfront/bus0401.html#

Feldblum, Miriam. 2000. "Managing Membership: New Trends in Citizenship and Nationality Policy" in From Migrants to Citizens: Membership in a Changing World, T. Alexander and Douglas Klusmeyer (eds.) : 475-499.

Fetzer, Joseph. 2000. *Public Attitudes toward Immigration in the United States, France, and Germany.* Cambridge: Cambridge University Press.

Field, Kelly. 2004. "Fixing the Visa Quagmire." *The Chronicle of Higher Education, International*, October 8. http://chronicle.com/weekly/v51/i07/07a04001.htm

Fielding, Anthony. 1995. "Migration and Middle-Class Formation in England and Wales 1981-91." In Butler and Savage (eds.): 169-187.

Findlay, Allan. 1995. "The Future of Skill Exchanges Within the European Union." in *Europe's Population: Towards the Next Century*, R. Hall and P. White (eds). London, UCL: 130-141.

Finn, Michael G. 2003. "Stay Rates of Foreign Doctorate Recipients from U.S. Universities, 2001." Oak Ridge Institute for Science and Education. http://www.orau.gov/orise/pubs/stayrate03.pdf

Fischer, Peter A. and Thomas Straubhaar. 1996. "Is Migration into EU-Countries Demand Based?" in *Economics and European Union Migration Policy*, Dan Corry (ed.):11-49.

Fligstein, Neil and Frederic Merand. 2001. "Globalization or Europeanization? Evidence on the European Economy Since 1980." Center for Culture, Organizations and Politics. Working Paper wps-2001-02. http://repositories.cdlib.org/iir/ccop/wps-2001-02

Florida, Richard. 2002. *The Rise of the Creative Class: And How It's Transforming Work, Leisure, Community and Everyday Life.* New York, NY: Basic Books.

Forsander, Annika. 2002. "Glocalizing Capital and Labor- Old Structures, New Challenges." in *Immigration and Economy in the Globalization Process: The Case of Finland.* Annika Forsander (ed). Vantaa: Tummavuoren Kirjapaino Oy: 81-118.

Fragomen, Austin A.. 1999. Testimony before the House Judiciary Committee. August 5. The American Council on International Personnel.

Freeman, Gary P. 1995 "Modes of Immigration Politics in Liberal Democratic States." *International Migration Review* 29 (Winter): 881-902.

———. 1999. "The Quest for Skill: A Comparative Analysis." in *Migration and Refugee Policies: An Overview,* Ann Bernstein and Myron Weiner (eds.). London: Pinter, 84-118.

———. 2001. "Client Politics or Populism? Immigration Reform in the United States. " in *Controlling a New Migration World,* Virginie Guiraudon and Christian Joppke (eds.). London: Routledge: 65-96.

———. 2002. "Winners and Losers: Politics and the Costs and Benefits of Migration." in *West European Immigration and Immigrant Policy in the New Century.* Anthony Messina (ed.). Westport, CT: Praeger, 77-96.

Friedmann, John. 1986. "The World City Hypothesis," *Development and Change* 17 (1): 69-84.

Friedmann, John and Goetz Wolff. 1982. "World City Formation: An Agenda for Research and Action." *International Journal of Urban and Regional Research* 6 (2): 309-339.

Friedman, Thomas L. 2000. *The Lexus and the Olive Tree.* New York: Vintage Anchor Publishing.

Fröbel, Folker, Jürgen Heinrichts, and Otto Kreye. 1977. *Die neue internationale Arbeitsteilung : strukturelle Arbeitslosigkeit in den Industrieländern und die Industriealisierung der Entwicklungsländer.* Reinbek: Rowohlt.

Frykman-Povrzanovic, Maja (ed.). 2001. *Beyond Integration: Challenges of Belonging in Diaspora and Exile.* Lund: Nordic Academic Press.

Geddes, Andrew. 2003. *The Politics of Migration and Immigration in Europe.* London and Thousand Oaks, CA: Sage.

Ghosh, Bimal. 1997. *Gains from Global Linkages. Trade in Services and Movement of Persons.* London and New York: Macmillan in association with International Organization for Migration (IOM).

Ghoshal, Sumantra. 1987. "Global Strategy: An Organizing Framework." *Strategic Management Journal* 8: 425-440.

Ghoshal, Sumantra and Christopher A. Bartlett. 1990. "The Multinational Corporation as an Interorganizational Network." *Academy of Management Review* 15: 603-625.

Giddens, Anthony. 1990. *The Consequences of Modernity.* Cambridge: Polity Press.

Gimpel, James and James Edwards, Jr. 1999. *The Congressional Politics of Immigration Reform.* Boston: Allyn & Bacon.

Glaessel-Brown, Eleanor E. 1998. "Use of Immigration Policy to Manage Nursing Shortages." *Image: Journal of Nursing Scholarship* 30(4): 323-27.

Glaser, Thomas. 2001. "Immigration: What Effect on the Progress of Enlargement?" *The Courier ACP–EU* 187: 33.

Glaser, William A. 1978. With the assistance of G. Christopher Habers). *The Brain Drain: Emigration and Return.* New York: Pergamon.

Glick-Schiller, Nina. 2005. "Transborder Citizenship: An Outcome of Legal Pluralism within Transnational Social Fields." in *Mobile People, Mobile Law: Expanding Legal relations in a Contracting World*, Franz Bender Beckman and Keebit Bender Beckman (eds.). London: Ashgate.

Glick-Schiller, Nina, Linda Basch and Cristina Blanc Szanton (eds.). 1999. *Towards a Transnational Perspective on Migration: Race, Class, Ethnicity, andNationalism Reconsidered.* New York: New York Academy of Science.

Golini, Antonio and Flavia Amato. 2001. "Uno sguardo a un secolo e mezzo di emigrazione italiana," in *Storia dell'emigrazione italiana*, Piero Bevilacqua, Andreina De Clementi and Emilio Franzina (eds.). Roma: Donzelli.

Gouldner, Alvin W. 1957. "Cosmopolitans and Locals: Toward an Analysis of Latent Social Roles – I." *Administrative Science Quarterly* 2: 281–306.

———. 1958. "Cosmopolitans and Locals: Toward an Analysis of Latent Social Roles – II." *Administrative Science Quarterly* 2: 444–480.

Greenwood, Michael J. and Fred A. Ziel. 1997. "The Impact of the Immigration Act of 1990 on U.S. Immigration." Washington, DC.
http:/ www.utexas.edu/lbj/uscir/respap-t.html

Grewal, Inderpal. 1999. "Traveling Barbie: Indian Transnationality and New Consumer Subjects." *Positions* 7 (3): 799-826.

Grubel, Herbert B., and Anthony D. Scott. 1966. "The International Flow of Human Capital." *The American Economic Review* 56 (March): 268-274.

Guarnizo, Luiz E. and Michael Peter Smith (eds). 1998. "The Locations of Transnationalism," in *Transnationalism From Below*, Michael Peter Smith and Luiz E. Guarnizo (eds.). New Brunswick: Transaction Publishers, 3-34.

Guild, Elspeth. 2001. *Immigration Law in the European Community.* The Hague: Kluwer.

Guimarães, Reinaldo. 2002. "A Migracão de Pesquisadores do Brasil." *Ciência Hoje* 32 (October): 40-43.

Guiraudon, Virginie. 1998. "Citizenship Rights for Non-Citizens: France, Germany and the Netherlands" in *Challenge to the Nation State*, Christian Joppke (ed). Oxford: Oxford University Press: 272-318.

———. 2000. "European Integration and Migration Policy: Vertical Policymaking as Venue Shopping." *Journal of Common Market Studies*, 38: 251-271.

Guiraudon, Virginie and Gallya Lahav. 2000. "A Reappraisal of the State-Sovereignty Debate: The Case of Migration Control." *Comparative Political Studies* 33(2): 163-195.

Guiraudon, Virginie and Christian Joppke (eds.). 2001. *Controlling a New Migration World.* London: Routledge.

Gupta, Akhil and James Ferguson (eds.). 1997. *Culture, Power, Place: Exploration in Critical Anthropology.* Durham and London: Duke University Press.

Gupta, Anil K. and Vijah Govindarajan. 2000. "Knowledge Flows Within Multinational Corporations." *Strategic Management Journal* 21: 473-496.

Gurak, Douglas T. and Fe Caces. 1993. "Migration Networks and the Shaping of Migration Systems." in *International Migration Systems: A Global Approach*, Mary M Kritz, Lin Leam Lim and Hania Zlotnik (eds.). Oxford: Clarendon Press: 150-176.

Gurcak, Jessica C., Thomas Espenshade, Aaron Sparrow, and Martha Paskoff. 2001. "Immigration of Scientists and Engineers to the United States: Issues and Evidence." in Cornelius et. al. (eds.): 55-84.

Hannerz, Ulf. 1996. *Transnational Connections: Culture, People, Places*. London: Routledge.

Hardill, Irene and S. MacDonald. 2000. "Skilled International Migration: The Experience of Nurses in the U.K." *Regional Studies*. 34, 7: 681-92.

Haque, Nadeem U., and Se-Jik Kim. 1995. "'Human Capital Flight': Impact of Migration on Income and Growth." *IMF Staff Papers* 42 (September): 577-607.

Harvey, David. 1989. *The Condition of Postmodernity*. Cambridge, MA: Blackwell.

Harvey, David. 2001. *Spaces of Capital: Towards a Critical Geography*. London: Routledge.

Hatono, Daryl. 1998. "Testimony before the House Judiciary Committee, Subcommittee on Immigration and Claims, April 21." Semiconductor Industry Association.

Havel, Vaclav. 1998. "Europe as Task," in *The European Challenge*, ed. Hans Magnus Enzensberger (ed.)'s–Gravenhage: Vuga.

Heilemann, John. 1996. "Do You Know the Way to Ban Jose?" *Wired.* http://www.wired.com/wired/archive/4.08/netizen_pr.html

Held, David, Anthony McGrew, David Goldblatt, and Jonathan Perraton. 2000. *Global Transformations. Politics, Economics and Culture*. Cambridge: Polity Press.

Helsinki City Urban Facts Office. 2004. "Population By Citizenship 2000-2004" in *Statistical Yearbook of the City of Helsinki 2004*. http://www.aluesarjat.fi

Héritier, Adrienne. 2002. *Common Goods. Reinventing European and International Governance*. Lanham: Rowman and Littlefield.

Hernández-Léon, Rubén. 2004. "Restructuring at the Source: High-Skilled Industrial Migration from Mexico to the US." *Work and Occupations* 31: 424-452.

Hira, Ron. 2003a. "Global Outsourcing of Engineering Jobs: Recent Trends and Possible Implications." *Testimony to the Committee on Small Business, United States House of Representatives*. Washington, DC: The Institute of Electrical and Electronics Engineers. http://www.whomovedmyjob.org/files%5CRonHiraOutsourcing20030618pdf

———. 2003b. "Utilizing Immigration Regulations as a competitive Advantage: An Additional Explanation for India's Success in Exporting Information Technology Services." New York: Center for Science, Policy and Outcomes. http://www.cspo.org/products/papers/Bangalore.pdf

———. 2005. *Outsourcing America: What's Behind Our National Crisis and How We Can Reclaim American Jobs.* Washington, DC: American Management Association.

Hirst, Paul, and Grahame Thompson. 1996. *Globalization in Question. The International Economy and the Possibilities of Governance.* Cambridge: Cambridge University Press

Hoerder, Dick. 1996. "From Migrants to Ethnics: Acculturation in a Societal Framework," in *European Migrants: Global and Local Perspectives,* Dick Hoerder and Leslie Page Moch (eds.). Boston: Northeastern University Press.

Hollifield, James F. 1992a. *Immigrants, Markets, and States: The Political Economy of Postwar Europe.* Cambridge: Harvard University Press.

———. 1992b. "Migration and International Relations: Cooperation and Control in the European Community." *International Migration Review* 26 (2).

Holzmann, Robert and Münz, Rainer. 2004. *Challenges and Opportunities of International Migration for the EU, its Member States, Neighboring Countries and Regions: A Policy Note.* Stockholm: Institute for Future Studies.

Huang, Wei-Chiao. 1988. "An Empirical Analysis of Foreign Student Brain Drain to the United States." *Economics of Education Review* 7: 231-243.

Hudson Institute. 1987. *Workforce 2000: Work and Workers for the 21st Century.* Indianapolis: Hudson Institute, Inc.

ImmSpec.com. 2001. "Senate Subcommittee Hears Testimony on Shortage of Healthcare Professionals, Examines Immigration Options." http://www.immspec.com/RN/subcomm-shortage.htm

Information Technology Association of America (ITAA). 2002. *Bouncing Back: Jobs, Skills and the Continuing Demand for IT Workers.* Arlington, VA.

Institute of International Education. 2004. *Open Doors: Report on International Educational Exchange.* New York: Institute of International Education.

Iredale, Robyn. 2001. "The Migration of Professionals: Theories and Typologies" *International Migration* 39 (5): 7-26.

ISTAT. Various years. *Compendio statistico italiano.* Rome: Istat.

Iyer, Pico. 2000. *The Global Soul: Jet Lag, Shopping Malls and the Search for Home.* New York: Vintage Books.

Jackson, S. 2003. *Envisioning 21st Century Science and Engineering Workforce for the United States: Tasks for Universities, Industry, and Government.* Washington, DC: The National Academies.

James, Scott C. 2000. *Presidents, Parties and the State: a Party System Perspective on Democratic Regulatory Choice 1884-1936.* Cambridge; New York: Cambridge University Press.

Jacobson, David. 1996. *Rights Across Borders: Immigration and the Decline of Citizenship.* Baltimore: Johns Hopkins University Press.

Joronen, Tuula, Pajarinen, Mika and Pekka Ylä-Anttila. 2002. "From Hanseatic Trade to Hamburger Chains- A Historical Survey." in *Immigration and Economy in the Globalization Process: The Case of Finland.* Annika Forsander (ed) Vantaa: Tummavuoren Kirjapaino Oy, 48-65.

Jasso, Guillermina, Douglas S. Massey, Mark R. Rosenzweig, and James P. Smith. 2000. "The New Immigrant Survey Pilot (NIS-P): Overview and New Findings about U.S. Legal Immigrants at Admission." *Demography* 37:127-138.

Johnson, C. 2001. "Panel Declines to Address Visa Issue; Foreign Workers Said To Lower Tech Pay." *Washington Post,* October 25.

Johnson, Jean M., and Mark C. Regets. 1998. "International Mobility of Scientists and Engineers to the United States-Brain Drain or Brain Circulation?" Arlington, VA: National Science Foundation. http://www.nsf.gov/sbe/srs/issuebrf/sib98316.htm

Joppke, Christian. 1998. "Immigration Challenges the Nation State." in *Challenge to the Nation State.* in Christian Joppke (ed). Oxford: Oxford University Press: 5-46.

———. 1998. "Why Liberal States Accept Unwanted Immigration." *World Politics* 50: 266-293.

Kaelble, Hartmut. 1990. *A Social History of Western Europe 1880-1980.* Dublin: Gill and Macmillan.

Kapur, Davesh. 2001. "Diasporas and Technology Transfer." *Journal of Human Development* 2 (2): 265-286.

———. 2003. "India's Diaspora as a Strategic Asset." *Economic and Political Weekly* (February 1). http://www.epw.org.in showArticles.php?root=2003&leaf=02&filename=5445&filetype=html

Khadria, Binod. 2001. "Shifting Paradigms of Globalization: The 21st Century Transition Towards Generics in Skilled Migration from India." *International Migration* 39(5): 45-71.

———. 2002. "Skilled Labour Migration from Developing Countries: Study on India." *International Migration Papers 49.* Geneva: ILO. http://www.ilo.org/public/english/protection/migrant/publ/imp-list.htm.

King, Russell. 1993. "European International Migration 1945–90: A Statistical and Geographical Overview." in *Mass Migrations in Europe: The Legacy and the Future.* Russell King (ed). London: Belhaven.

———. 2002. "Towards a New Map of European Migration." *International Journal of Population Geography* 8 (March/April): 89-106.

King, Russell and Enric Ruiz-Gelices. 2003. "International student migration and the European 'year abroad': effects on European identity and subsequent migration behaviour." *International Journal of Population Geography* 9: 229-252.

King, Russell, Tony Warnes and Allan M. Williams, Allan M. 2000. *Sunset Lives: British Retirement Migration to the Mediterranean.* Berg: Oxford.

Klein, Naomi. 2002. *No Logo: No Space, No Choice, No Jobs.* New York: Picador.

Kloosterman, Robert, Joanne van der Leun and Jan Rath. 1998. "Across the border: immigrants' economic opportunities, social capital and informal business activities." *Journal of Ethnic and Migration Studies* 24, (2): 249-268.

Knill, Christoph, and Dirk Lehmkuhl. 2002. "Private Actors and the State: Internationalization and Changing Patterns of Governance." *Governance: An International Journal of Policy, Adminstration and Institutions* 15 (1):41-63.

Koehler, Matthias. 1999. *Das Allgemeine Übereinkommen über den Handel mit Dienstleistungen (GATS): Rahmenregelung zur Liberalisierung des internationalen Dienstleistungsverkehrs unter besonderer Berücksichtigung des grenzüberschreitenden Personenverkehrs von Dienstleistungsanbietern.* Berlin: Duncker & Humblot.

Kofman, Eleonore. 2000. "The Invisibility of Skilled Female Migrants and Gender Relations in Studies of Skilled Migration in Europe." *International Journal of Population Geography* 6: 45-59.

Konrad, Rachel. 2001. "Foreign Workers Face New Opposition in Tech Slump." *CNETNEWS.COM,* August 13.

Koopmans, Ruud and Paul Statham (eds.) 2000. *Challenging Immigration and Ethnic Relations Politics: Comparative European Perspectives.* Oxford: Oxford University Press.

Koshy, Susan. 1998. "Category Crisis: South Asian Americans and Questions of Race and Ethnicity" *Diaspora* 7 (3): 285-319.

Kostakopolou, Theodora. 2001. *Citizenship, Identity, and Immigration in the European Union.* Manchester: Manchester University Press.

Kazmierczak, Mark. 2005. *Losing the Competitive Edge: The Challenge for Science and Technology in the United States.* Washington, DC: American Electronics Association.

Krikorian, Mark. 2004. "Strange Bedfellows: Left and Right on Immigration." *National Review Online.* March 31. http://www.nationalreview.com

Kritz, Mary M., and Fe Caces. 1992. Science and Technology Transfers and Migration Flows. In *International Migration Systems: A Global Approach,* Mary M. Kritz, Lin Lean Lim, and Hania Zlotnik, (eds.). Oxford: Clarendon Press, 221-242.

Krugman, Paul R. 1991. *Geography and Trade.* Leuven, Belgium: Leuven University Press; Cambridge, MA: MIT Press.

Kuh, Charlotte V. 2000. "Information Technology Workers in the Knowledge Based Economy" in *Building a Workforce for the Information Economy.* Washington, DC: National Academy Press.

Kurzban, Ira J. 2000. *Immigration Law* Sourcebook, 7th ed. Washington, DC: American Immigration Law Foundation.

Kyle, David. 2000. *Transnational Peasants: Migration, Networks and Ethnicity in Andean Ecuador.* Baltimore, MD: Johns Hopkins University Press.

Lamont, Michèle. 2002. "Working Men's Imagined Communities: The Boundaries of Race, Immigration, and Poverty in France and the United States" in *The Postnational Self: Belonging and Identity.* Ulf Hedetoft and Mette Hjort (eds.). Minneapolis: University of Minnesota Press: 178-197.

Lariviere, Richard. 1998. "Testimony before the House Judiciary Committee, Subcommittee on Immigration and Claims." April 21.

Lavenex, Sandra. 2004. "Towards an International Framework for Labor Mobility? The Case of the GATS." *IMIS-Beiträge* 25 (2004): 23-46. http://www.imis.uni-osnabrueck.de/pdffiles/imis25.pdf.

Lee, Yong-Shik. 1999. "Emergency Safeguard Measures under Article X in GATS. Applicability of the Concepts in the WTO Agreement on Safeguards." *Journal of World Trade* 33 (4):47-59.

Levitt, Peggy. 2001. *The Transnational Villagers*. Berkeley, CA: University of California Press.

Li, F. L. N., A. M. Findlay, A. J. Jowett, and R. Skeldon. 1996. "Migrating to Learn, Learning to Migrate: A Study of the Experiences and Intentions of International Student Migrants." *International Journal of Population Geography* 2 (March): 51-67.

Lieberson, Stanley. 1969. "Measuring Population Diversity." *American Sociological Review* 34: 850–862.

Livi Bacci, Massimo. 1972. "The Countries of Emigration," in *The Demographic and Social Pattern of Emigration from the Southern European Countries*. Massimo Livi Bacci (ed). Firenze: Dipartimento Statistico Matematico dell'Università di Firenze.

Lofstrom, Magnus. 2001. "Self-Employment and Earnings among High-Skilled Immigrants in the United States." in Cornelius et al (eds.): 163-197.

Lowell, B. Lindsay. 1996. "Skilled and Family-based Immigration: Principles and Labor Markets." in *Immigrants and Immigration Policy: Individual skills, Family Ties, and Group Identities*, H. O. Duleep and P. V. Wunnava (eds.). Greenwhich, CT: AIS Press, 353-372.

———. 2001a. "The Foreign Temporary (H-1B) Workforce and Shortages in Information Technology." In Cornelius et. al. (eds.): 131-162.

———. 2001b. "State of Knowledge on the Flow of Foreign Science and Technology Workers to the United States." Washington, DC.

———. 2001c. "Skilled Temporary and Permanent Immigrants to the United States." *Population Research and Policy Review* 20 (1-2): 33-58.

———. 2004a. "Immigrant Labor Market Assimilation in the United States: A Critique of Census Data and Longitudinal Outcomes." in *U.S.-EU Seminar on Integrating Immigrants into the Workforce*. Georgetown University.

———. 2004b. "Policies and Regulations for Managing Skilled International Migration for Work." United Nations, Mortality and Migration Section of the Population Division/DESA, New York, NY.

Lowell, B. Lindsay, and Allan Findlay. 2001. "Migration of Highly Skilled Persons from Developing Countries: Impact and Policy Responses." International Migration Papers 44, Geneva: International Labour Office. http://www.ilo.org/public/english/protection/migrant/download/imp/imp44.pdf

Lowell, B. Lindsay, Allan Findlay, and Emma Stewart. 2004. "Brain Strain: Optimising Highly Skilled Emigration from Developing Countries." Asylum and Migration Working Paper 3, London: Institute for Public Policy Research.http://www.ippr.org.uk/research/files/team19/project183/WP3FINAL6.pdf

Lowi, Theodore J. 1964a. "American Business, Public Policy, Case-Studies, and Political Theory." *World Politics 16* (July): 677-715.

———. 1964b. *At the Pleasure of the Mayor: Patronage and Power in New York City, 1898-1958.* New York: The Free Press of Glencoe.

Lynch, James P. and Rita Simon. 2003. *Immigration the World Over: Statutes, Policies, and Practices.* Lanham, MD: Rowman and Littlefield.

Mair, Andrew. 1997. "Strategic Localization: The Myth of the Postnational Enterprise." in *Spaces of Globalization.* Kevin Cox (ed). New York: Guildford Publications, 64-88.

Martin, Philip and Elizabeth Midgley. 1994. "Immigration to the United States: Journey to an Uncertain Destination." *Population Bulletin* 19(2).

Maas, Willem. 2004. "European Rights and Migration within the Union." Paper presented at the 14th International Conference of Europeanists'. Council for European Studies. 11–13 March, Chicago.

Massey, Doreen. 1988. "Uneven Redevelopment: Social Change and Spatial Divisionsof Labor." in *Uneven Redevelopment: Cities and Regions in Transition.* Doreen Massey and John Allen (eds.) London: Hodder&Stoughton.

Massey, Douglas S. 1999. "International Migration at the Dawn of the Twenty-First Century: The Role of the State." *Population and Development Review* 25 (2):303-322.

Massey, Douglas S., Rafael Alarcon, Jorge Durand and Humberto Gonzalez. 1987. *Return to Aztlan: The Social Process of International Migration from Western Mexico.* Berkeley: University of California Press.

Massey, Douglas S., Joaquin Arango, Graeme Hugo, Ail Kouaouci, Adela Pellegrino, and J.E. Taylor. 1993. "Theories of International Migration: A Reviewand Appraisal." *Population and Development Review* 19: 431-466.

Matloff, Norman. 2002. "Debunking the Myth of a Desperate Software Labor Shortage" Testimony to the US House Judiciary Committee Subcommittee on Immigration.
http://heather.cs.ucdavis.edu/itaa.html

———. 2003. "On the Need for Reform of the H-1B Non-Immigrant Work Visa in Computer Related Occupations." *University of Michigan Journal of Law Reform* 36: 815-914.

———. 2004. "Needed Reform for the H-1B and L-1 Work Visas (And Relation to Off-shoring)."
http://heather.cs.ucdavis.edu/Summary.pdf

Maxwell, Joseph A. 1996. *Qualitative Research Design: An Interactive Approach.* Thousand Oaks, CA: Sage Publications.

Mayor of London. 2002. *The Draft London Plan: Draft Spatial Development Strategy for Greater London.* London: Greater London Authority.

McCarthy, E. 2003. "Paring A Foreign Guest List" *The Washington Post,* September 18.

McLaughlan, Gail and John Salt. 2002. "Migration Policies Towards Highly Skilled Foreign Workers: Report to the Home Office." Migration Research Unit, Geography department, University College London, London.

McMichael, Philip. 1996. *Development and Social Change: A Global Perspective.* Thousand Oaks, CA: Pine Forge Press.

McMurtie, Beth. 2001. "Foreign enrollments grow in the U.S., but so does competition from other nations." *The Chronicle of Higher Education, International,* November 16.
http://chronicle.com/weekly/v48/i12/12a04501.htm

Merton, Robert K. 1957. *Social Theory and Social Structure.* Glencoe: Free Press.

Messina, Anthony M. 1990. "Political Impediments to the Resumption of Labour Migration to Western Europe." *West European Politics* 3: 31-46.

Meyer, Jean-Baptiste. 2001. "Network Approach Versus Brain Drain: Lessons from the Diaspora." *International Migration* 39: 91-110.

Meyers, Eytan. 2004. *International Immigration Policy: A Theoretical and Comparative Analysis.* London: Palgrave.

Migration News. Various.
http://www.migration.ucdavis.edu

Migrationsverket. Various.
http://www.migrationsverket.se

Mir, Ali et. al. 2000. "The Codes of Migration: Contours of the Global Software Labor Market" *Cultural Dynamics* 12 (1): 5-33.

Mitter, Swasti and Sheila Rowbotham (eds.) 1995. *Women Encounter Technology: Changing Patterns of Employment in the Third World.* London: Routledge.

Moch, Leslie Page. 1992. *Moving Europeans: Migration in Western Europe since 1650.* Bloomington: Indiana University Press.

———— 1996. "Introduction," in *European Migrants: Global and Local Perspectives,* Dick Hoerder and Leslie P. Moch (eds.). Boston: Northeastern University Press.

————. 2003 (2nd ed.). *Moving Europeans: Migration in Western Europe Since 1650.* Bloomington: Indiana University Press.

Molle, Willem and Van Mourik, Aad. 1988. "International Movements of Labour Under Conditions of Economic Integration: The Case of Western Europe." *Journal of Common Market Studies* 26: 319–342.

Money, Jeannette. 1997. "No Vacancy: The Political Geography of Immigration Control in Advanced Industrial Countries." *International Organization* 51 (4): 685-720.

Money, Jeannette. 1999. *Fences and Neighbors. The Political Geography of Immigration Control.* Ithaca, NY: Cornell University Press.

Mouhoud, El Mouhoub and Oudinet, Joël. 2004. "Les déterminants des migrations dans l'Union européenne: une prime aux effets de réseaux." *Revue française des affaires sociales* 58: 87–108.

Mountford, Andrew. 1997. "Can a Brain Drain Be Good for Growth in the Source Economy?" *Journal of Development Economics* 53 (August): 287-303.

Mukherjee, Neela. 1999. "GATS and the Millennium Round of Multilateral Negotiations. Selected Issues from the Perspective of the Developing Countries." *Journal of World Trade* 33 (4):87-102.

Mundell, Robert A. 1961. "A Theory of Optimum Currency Areas." *American Economic Review* 51: 509–517.

National Commission on Excellence in Education. 1983. *A Nation at Risk: The Imperative for Educational Reform*. A Report to the Nation and the Secretary of Education. Washington, DC.

National Center on Education and the Economy. 1990. *America's Choice: High Skills or Low Wages. Report of the Commission on the Skills of the American Workforce*. Washington, DC.

National Public Radio. 2004. *Immigration in America*. http://www.npr.org/news/specials/polls/2004/immigration

National Research Council. 2000. *Building a Workforce for the Information Economy*. Committee on Workforce Needs in Information Technology. Washington, DC: National Academies Press.

National Science Foundation. 1987. *Future Scarcity of Scientists and Engineers: Problems and Solutions*. Washington, DC.

Nayyar, Deepak.1994. *Migration, Remittances and Capital Flows: The Indian Experience*. New York: Oxford University Press.

———. 2002. "Cross-Border Movements of People." in *Governing Globalization: Issues and Institutions*. Deepak Nayyar (ed). New York: Oxford University Press: 144-176.

Nielson, Jutta. 2002. "Current Regimes for Temporary Movement of Service Providers. Labor Mobility in Regional Trade Agreements." Paper presented a the Joint WTO-World Bank Symposium on the Movement of Natural Persons (Mode 4) Under the GATS. 11-12 April 2002.

Nugent, Walter. 1996. "Demographic Aspects of European Migration Worldwide." in *European Migrants: Global and Local Perspectives*. Dick Hoerder and Leslie P. Moch (eds.). Boston: Northeastern University Press.

OECD. 1995. "The Measurement of Scientific and Technological Activities Manual on the Measurement of Human Resources Devoted to S&T: 'Canberra Manual.'" Paris. http://www.oecd.org/dataoecd/34/0/2096025.pdf

———. 2002. *International Mobility of the Highly Skilled*. Paris: OECD.

OECD, Trade Directorate. 2002. Working Party of the Trade Committee: Service Providers on the Move: A Closer Look at Labor Mobility and the GATS. *TD/TC/WP(2001)26/final*.

OECD Department for Employment, Labor and Social Affairs. 2001. "Skilled Workers, Asylum Seekers Boost Migration Flows, Says OECD Report." http://www.oecd.org/document/290%2C2340%2Cen_2649_33729_2727069_1_1_1_1%2C00.html

Ohmae, Kenichi. 1990. *The Borderless World: Power and Strategy inthe Interlinked Economy*. London: Harper Collins.

Ohmae, Kenichi. 1995. *The End of the Nation State: The Rise of Regional Economics. How New Engines of Prosperity are Reshaping Global Markets*. London: HarperCollins.

O'Keeffe, David. 1998. "Freedom of Movement for Workers in Community Law." in *Thirty Years of Free Movement of Workers in Europe*. Jean-Yves Carlier and Michel Verwilghen (eds.). Brussels: European Commission.

Oleszck, Walter. 2004. *Congressional Procedures and the Policy Process*. Washington, DC: Congressional Quarterly Press.

Olzak, Susan. 1992. *The Dynamics of Ethnic Competition*. Stanford, CA: Stanford University Press.

O'Neil, Kevin. 2003. "Brain Drain and Gain: The Case of Taiwan." Migration Information Source.

Ong, Aihwa. 1999. *Flexible Citizenship: The Cultural Logics of Transnationality*. Durham: Duke University Press.

Ong-Hing, Bill. 1998. "Asian Immigrants: Social Forces Unleashed After 1965." in *The Immigration Reader: America in a Multidisciplinary Perspective*, ed. David Jacobson (ed) Boston: Blackwell: 144-183.

Papademetriou, Demetrious G. and Stephen Yale-Loehr. 1996. *Balancing Interests: Rethinking U.S. Selection of Skilled Immigrants*. Washington, DC: Carnegie Endowment for International Peace.

Pastore, Ferruccio. 2004. *Dobbiamo temere le migrazioni?* Roma–Bari: Laterza.

Patibandla, Murali. and Bent Petersen. 2002. "Role of Transnational Corporations in the Evolution of a High-Tech Industry: The Case of India's Software Industry." *World Development* 30 (9): 1561-1577.

Pelizon, Cristina. 2002. "Is the Italian Brain Drain Becoming a Flood?" *Science Magazine,* May 10.
http://nextwave.sciencemag.org/cgi/content/full/2002/05/08/4

Pehrsson, Anders.1996. *International Strategies in Telecommunications*. London: Routledge.

Peri, Giovanni. 2005. "Skills and Talent of Immigrants: A Comparison Between the European Union and the United States." Institute of European Studies Working Paper 050304. University of California, Berkeley.
http://www.repositories.cdlib.org/ies/050304

Perlmutter, Ted. 1996. "Bringing Parties Back In: Comments on 'Modes of Immigration Politics in Liberal Democratic States.'" *International Migration Review* 30: 375-388.

Piore, Michael J. 1979. *Birds of Passage: Migrant Labor in Industrial Societies*. Cambridge: Cambridge University Press.

Piracha, Matloob E. and Roger Vickerman. 2003. *Immigration, Labour Mobility and EU Enlargement*. Department of Economics, University of Kent.
http://papers.ssrn.com/sol3/cf_dev/AbsByAuth.cfm?per_id=246519.

Porter, Michael E. 1986. "Competition in Global Industries: A Conceptual Framework." in *Competition in Global Industries*. Michael E. Porter (ed) Boston, MA: Harvard Business School Press, 15-60.

Portes, Alejandro. 1996a. "Global Villagers: The Rise of Transnational Communities." *The American Prospect* 2: 74-77.

———. 1996b. "Transnational communities: their emergence and their significance in the contemporary world-system." in *Latin America in the World Economy*, Korzeniewicz, R.P. and Smith, W.C. (eds). Westport, CN: Greenwood Press.

Portes, Alejandro and Ruben G. Rumbaut. 2001. *Legacies: The Story of the Immigrant Second Generation*. Berkeley: University of California Press.

Poulain, Michel. 1996. "Migration Flows Between the Countries of the European Union: Current Trends." in *Population Migration in the European Union*. Philip Rees, John Stillwell, Andrew Convey and Marek Kupiszewski (eds.). Chichester: Wiley.

———. 1999. *Confrontation des statistiques de migration intra–européennes: vers une matrice complete?* Eurostat Working Paper 5/1999 – Theme 3. Luxembourg: Eurostat.

Prakash, Aseem, and Jeffrey A. Hart, eds. 1999. *Globalization and Governance.* London and New York: Routledge.

Prashad, Vijay. 2000. *The Karma of Brown Folk.* Minneapolis: The University of Minnesota Press.

Pries, Ludger (ed). 2001. *New Transnational Social Spaces: International Migration and Transnational Companies in the Early Twenty-First Century,* London and New York: Routledge.

Pugliese, Enrico. 2002. *L'Italia tra migrazioni internazionali e migrazioni interne.* Bologna: Il Mulino.

Rae, Nicol. 1998. *Conservative Reformers: The Republican Freshmen and the Lessons of the 104ᵗʰ Congress.* Armonk, NY: M.E. Sharpe.

Ratha, Dilip. 2003. "Workers' Remittances: An Important and Stable Source of External Development Finance." *Global Development Finance.* Washington, DC: World Bank.
http://www.worldbank.org/prospects/gdf2003/gdf_ch07_web.pdf

Recchi, Ettore and Tina M. Nebe. 2003. "Migration and Political Identity in the European Union: Research Issues and Theoretical Premises." PIONEUR Working Paper 2003/1. Florence: Ciuspo.
http: www.obets.ua.es/pioneur/bajaarchivo_public.php?iden=39

Recchi, Ettore, Damian Tambini, Emiliana Baldoni, David Williams, Kristen Surak and Adrian Favell. 2003. "Intra–EU Migration: A Socio–demographic Overview." PIONEUR Working Paper 2003/3. Florence: Ciuspo.
http://www.obets.ua.es/pioneur/bajaarchivo_public.php?iden=42

Reitz, Jeffrey. 1998. *Warmth of the Welcome: The Social Causes of Economic Success for Immigrants in Different Nations and Cities.* Boulder, CO: Westview Press.

Riccio, Bruno. 2001. "From 'Ethnic' Group to 'Transnational Community'? Senegalese Migrants' Ambivalent Experiences and Multiple Trajectories." *Journal of Ethnic and Migration Studies* 27 (4): 583-99.

Rodenas Calatayud, Carmen. 1994. *Emigracion y economia en España.* Madrid: Civitas.

Rodríguez-Pose, Andres. 2002. *The European Union: Economy, Society and Polity.* London: Oxford University Press.

Rogers, Rosemarie. 1985. "Post–World War II European Labor Migration: An Introduction to the Issues." in *Guest Come to Stay.* Rosemarie Rogers (ed). Boulder: Westview.

Romero, Federico. 1991. *Emigrazione ed integrazione europea 1945–1973.* Rome: Edizioni Lavoro.

———. 2001. "L'emigrazione operaia in Europa (1948–1973)." in *Storia dell'emigrazione italiana.* Piero Bevilacqua, Andreina De Clementi and Emilio Franzina (eds.). Rome: Donzelli.

Rosenau, James. 1997. *Along the Domestic-Foreign Frontier.* Cambridge: Cambridge University Press.

Rosenblum, Marc. 2001. "High-Skilled Immigration and the US National Interest." in Cornelius et al (eds.): 373-400.

—————. 2003. "The Political Determinants of Migration Control: A Quantitative Analysis." *Migraciones Internacionales* 2(1): 161-170.

Rudolph, Christopher. 2003. "Security and the Political Economy of International Migration." *American Political Science Review* 97(4): 603-620.

Ruggie, John G. 1993. "Territoriality and Beyond: Problematizing Modernity in International Relations." *International Organization* 47 (1):139-174.

Rumbaut, Ruben. 2004. "Ages, Life Stages, and Generational Cohorts: Decomposing the Immigrant First and Second Generations in the United States." *International Migration Review* 38:1160-1206.

Salih, Ruba. 2003. *Gender in Transnationalism: Home, Longing and Belonging Among Moroccan Migrant Women.* London: Routledge.

Salt, John. 1976. "International Labour Migration: the Geographical Pattern of Demand." in *Migration in Post–War Europe.* John Salt and Hugh Clout (eds.). Oxford: Oxford University Press.

—————. 1992. "Migration processes among the highly skilled in Europe." *International Migration Review* 26(2): 484-505.

—————. 1997. "International Movements of the Highly Skilled." Occasional Papers No. 3, Directorate for Education, Employment, Labour and Social Affairs, International Migration Unit. Paris: OECD. http://www.oecd.org/dataoecd/24/32/2383909.pdf

Salt, John and Gail McLaughlan. 2002. *Global Competition for Skills: An Evaluation of Policies.* DIMIA conference on 'Migration: Benefiting Australia' Sydney, Australia.

Sapir, André. 1999. "The General Agreement on Trade in Services. From 1994 to the Year 2000." *Journal of World Trade* 33 (1):51-66.

Sapir, André, Aghion, P., Bertola, G., Hellwig, M., Pisani–Ferry, J., Rosati, D., Viñals, J., and Fallace, H. 2004. *An Agenda for a Growing Europe. The Sapir Report.* Oxford: Oxford University Press.

Sassen, Saskia. 1988. *The Mobility of Labor and Capital.* Cambridge and New York: Cambridge University Press.

—————. 1996. *Losing Control? Sovereignty in an Age of Globalization.* New York: Columbia University Press.

—————. 1998. *Globalization and Its Discontents. Essays on the New Mobility of People and Money.* New York: The New Press.

—————. 1999. "Beyond Sovereignty: De-Facto Transnationalism in Immigration Policy." *European Journal of Migration and Law* 1 (2):177-198.

—————. 2000. "Regulating Immigration in a Global Age." *Annals of the American Academy* 570:65-77.

—————. 2000b. *Cities in a World Economy.* Thousand Oaks: Pine Forge Press.

—————. 2001 (2nd ed.). *The Global City.* Princeton, NJ: Princeton University Press.

Savage, Mike, Warde, Alan and Kevin Ward. 2003 (2nd ed.). *Urban Sociology, Capitalism and Modernity.* Houndmills, Basingstoke and New York: Palgrave MacMillan.

Saxenian, AnnaLee. 1999. *Silicon Valley's New Immigrant Entrepreneurs.* Berkeley: Public Policy Institute of California.

————. 2001. "Networks of Immigrant Entrepreneurs." in *The Silicon Valley Edge*, Chong-Moon Lee et al (eds.). Stanford, CA: Stanford University Press: 248-275.

Saxenian, AnnaLee, Motoyama, Yasuyuki and Xiaohong Quan. 2002. *Local and Global Networks of Immigrant Professionals in Silicon Valley*. San Francisco, CA: Public Policy Institute of California.

Sayad, Abdelmalek. 2004. *The Suffering of the Immigrant*. Malden, MA: Polity Press.

Schachter, Jason. 2001. *Geographical Mobility*. Current Population Report. Washington, DC: US Census Bureau.

Schattschneider, E. E. 1960. *The Semi-Sovereign People*. New York: Holt, Rinehart, and Winston.

Schuck, Peter. 1998. *Citizens, Strangers, and In-Betweens: Essays on Immigration and Citizenship*. Boulder, CO: Westview.

Scott, Alan. 1997. (ed). *The Limits of Globalization*. London and New York: Routledge.

Selmer, Jan (ed.). 1995. *Expatriate Management: New Ideas for International Business*. Westport, CT: Quorum.

Sennett, Richard. 1998. *The Corrosion of Character: The Personal Consequences of Work in the New Capitalism*. New York: W. W. Norton.

Shah, Priya. 2004. "Second Generation Indian Americans and the Trope of the Arranged Marriage." UC Transnational and Translocal Research Group: http://repositories.cdlib.org/cmcs/mrg/gsc/Shah/

Shaw, Daron R. 1999. "The Methods behind the Madness: Presidential Electoral College Strategies, 1988-1996." *Journal of Politics* 61(4): 893-913.

Simon, Julian L. 1989. *The Economic Consequences of Immigration*. Oxford: Basil Blackwell.

Sklair, Leslie. 1995 (2nd ed). *Sociology of the Global System*. Baltimore, MD: Johns Hopkins University Press.

Sklair, Leslie. 2001. *The Transnational Capitalist Class*. Oxford: Blackwell.

Smith. David. 1998. "Testimony before the House Judiciary Committee, Subcommittee on Immigration and Claims, April 21." American Federation of Labor/Congress of Industrial Organizations.

Smith, James P. and Barry Edmonston, eds. 1997. *The New Americans: Economic, Demographic, and Fiscal Effects of Immigration*. Washington, DC: National Academy Press for the National Research Council.

Smith, Michael Peter. 1999. "The New High-Tech Braceros? Who is the Employer? What is the Problem?" in *Foreign Temporary Workers in America*, B. Lindsay Lowell, (ed.). Westport, CT. and London: Quorum Books, 1999: 119-147.

————. 2001. *Transnational Urbanism: Locating Globalization*. Oxford: Blackwell.

————. 2005. "Transnational Urbanism Revisited." *Journal of Ethnic and Migration Studies* 31: 235-244.

Smith, Robert C. 2005. *Mexican New York: Transnational Lives of New Immigrants*. Berkeley, CA: University of California Press.

Solimano, Andres and Molly Pollack. 2004. "International Mobility of the Highly Skilled: The Case between Europe and Latin America." Special office in Europe of Inter-American Development Bank.

SOPEMI. Various years. *Trends in International Migration*. Paris: OECD.

Sorensen, Elaine, Frank D. Bean, Leighton Ku, and Wendy Zimmermann. 1992. *Immigrant Categories and the U.S. Job Market: Do They Make a Difference?* Washington, DC: The Urban Institute Press.

Soysal, Yasemin N. 1994. *Limits of Citizenship: Migrants and Postnational Membership in Europe*. Chicago: Chicago University Press.

Stark, Oded. 2004. "Rethinking the Brain Drain." *World Development* 32, 1 (Jan): 15-22.

Stark, Oded, Christian Helmenstein, and Alexia Prskawetz. 1997. "A Brain Gain with a Brain Drain." *Economics Letters* 55 (August): 227-234.

Statistika Centralbyrån. 1997. *Välfärd och Ojämlikhet i 20-Årsperspektiv 1975-1995*. (Living Conditions and Inequality in Sweden: A 20-Year Perspective 1975-1995) Örebro, Stockholm: Statistika Centralbyrån.

Storper, Michael. 1997. *The Regional World*. New York: Guildford Press.

Strange, Susan. 1996. *The Retreat of the State. The Diffusion of Power in the World Economy*. Cambridge: Cambridge University Press.

Tarrius, Alain. 1992. *Les fourmis d'Europe. Migrants riches, migrants pauvres et nouvelles villes internationales*. Paris: L'Harmattan.

———. 2000. *Les nouveaux cosmopolitismes. Mobilités, identités, territoires*. La Tour d'Aigues: L'Aube.

Taylor, Peter J. 2004. "Material Spatiality of Cities and States." *ProtoSociology* 20: 30-45.

Taylor, Peter J. and Hoyler, M. 2000. "The spatial order of European cities under conditions of contemporary globalisation." *Tijdschrift voor Economische en Sociale Geografie* 91: 176-89.

Taylor, Peter J., David Walker and Jonathan Beaverstock. 2000. "Introducing GaWC: researching world city network formation." in *Telematics and Global Cities*, S. Sassen (ed.). Blackwell: Oxford.

Teitelbaum, Michael. 2003. "Do We Need More Scientists?" *Public Interest* 153 (Fall): 40-53.

Therborn, Göran. 1995. *European Modernity and Beyond: The Trajectory of European Societies, 1945-2000*. Thousand Oaks, CA: Sage.

Thorogood, David and Karin Winqvist. 2003. "Women and Men Migrating to and from the European Union." *Statistics in Focus–Eurostat* 2: 1–8.

Thrift, Nigel. 1994. "On the social and cultural determinants of international financial centres: the case of the city of London." in *Money, Power and Space*, S. Corbridge, R.Martin, and N.Thrift (eds.). Blackwell: Oxford, 327-354.

Tichenor, Daniel. 2002. *Dividing Lines: The Politics of Immigration Control in America*. Princeton, NJ: Princeton University Press.

Tilly, Charles. 1990. "Transplanted Networks." in *Immigration Reconsidered: History, Sociology, and Politics*. Virginia Yans-McLaughlin (ed). New York: Oxford University.

Torpey, John. 2000. *The Invention of the Passport: Surveillance, Citizenship, and the State.* Cambridge, Cambridge University Press.

Tri-Council. 2001 "Strategies to Reverse the New Nursing Shortage." http://www.nursingworld.org/presrel/2001/sta0205.htm

UNESCO. 2004. *Global Education Digest 2004: Comparing Education Statistics around the World.* Montreal: UNESCO Institute for Statistics. http://www.uis.unesco.org/ev_en.php?ID=5727_201&ID2=DO_TOPIC

UNIFEM. 2000. *Gender and Telecommunications: An Agenda for Policy.* New York: UNIFEM.

United Nations, Department of Economic and Social Affairs - Population Division. 2001. *Replacement Migration: Is It a Solution to Declining and Ageing Populations?* New York: United Nations.

United Nations. 2003. *The International Migration Report 2002.* New York: United Nations Publications.

United States Bureau of Labor Statistics. 2005a. "Local Area Unemployment Statistics." http://www.bls.gov/lau/home.htm

———. 2005b. "Occupations with the largest job growth, 2000-10." http://www.bls.gov/news.release/ecopro.t07.htm

United States Census. 2000. "Profile of the Foreign-Born Population in the United States, 2000." Washington, DC. http://www.census.gov/population/www/socdemo/foreign/ppl-145.html

———. 2003. "U.S. Census 2000, 5-Percent Public Use Microdata Sample (PUMS) Files."http://www.census.gov/Press-Release/www/2003/PUMS5.html

United States Citizenship and Immigration Services. 2004a. *USCIS To Implement H-1B Visa Reform Act of 2004.* Press Release (December 9).

———. 2004b. *USCIS to Implement L-1 Visa Reform Act of 2004.* Press release, December 9.

United States Commission on Immigration Reform. 1994. *US Immigration Policy: Restoring Credibility.* Washington, DC. USGPO.

———. 1995. *Legal Immigration: Setting Priorities.* Washington, DC: USGPO.

———. 1997. *Becoming an American: Immigration and Immigrant Policy.* Washington, DC: USGPO.

United States Congress. 1992. *Projecting Science and Engineering Personnel Requirements of the 1990s: How Good are the Numbers?* House Committee on Science, Space and Technology, Subcommittee on Oversight and Investigations. Washington, DC.

United States Department of Commerce. 1998. *America's New Deficit: The Shortage of Information Technology Workers.* Washington, DC.

United States Department of Health and Human Services. 1996. *The Registered Nurse Population. Findings from The National Sample Survey of Registered Nurses.* Washington, DC: Division of Nursing.

———. 2003. *Projected Supply, Demand and Shortages of Registered Nurses 2000-2002.* Washington, DC: Government Printing Office.

———. 2005. *Health Professional Shortage Areas: Ad-Hoc Database Query Selection.* http://belize.hrsa.gov/newhpsa/newhpsa.cfm

United States Department of Homeland Security. 2003a. *Characteristics of Specialty Occupation Workers (H-1B): Fiscal Year 2002.* September. Office of Immigration Statistics. Washington, DC.

―――. 2003b. *Fact Sheet.* October 22. U.S. Citizenship and Immigration Services. Washington, DC.

―――. 2004. *Press Release.* February 17. U.S. Citizenship and Immigration Services. Washington, DC.

United States Department of Labor 2005, Bureau of Labor Statistics, *Occupational Outlook Handbook: Registered Nurses.* http://www.bls.gov/oco/ocos083.htm

United States Immigration and Naturalization Service. 1996. *Immigration Information –Statistics: State of Residence Fiscal Year 1996.* http://uscis.gov/graphics/shared/aboutus/statistics/310.htm

―――. 1999. *North American Free Trade Agreement: NAFTA Handbook,* http://uscis.gov/graphics/shared/lawenfor/bmgmt/inspect/naftahan.pdf

―――. 1999-2000. *Leading Employers of Specialty Occupation Workers (H-1B): October 1999 to February 2000* http://uscis.gov/graphics/shared/services/employerinfo/h1top100.pdf

―――. 2000. *Characteristics of Specialty Occupation Workers May 1998 – July 1999.* Washington, DC: Government Printing Office.

―――. 2001a. *Leading Employers of Specialty Occupation Workers (H-1B): October 1999-February 2000.* Washington, DC: Government Printing Office.

―――. 2001b. *Report on Characteristics of Specialty Occupation Workers (H-1B): Fiscal Year 2001.* http://uscis.gov/graphics/shared/services/employerinfo/FY2001Charact.pdf

―――. 2001c. *Fiscal Year 2001 Statistical Yearbook: Table 37 Nonimmigrants Admitted by class of Admission Selected Fiscal Years 1981-2001.* http://uscis.gov/graphics/shared/aboutus/statistics/TEMP01yrbk/TEMPExcel/Table37.xls

United States Public Health Service. 1997. "50 Years at the Division of Nursing." Washington, DC: United States Public Health Service.

Urry, John. 2000. *Sociology Beyond Societies: Mobilities for the Twenty-First Century.* London: Routledge.

Usdansky, Margaret, and Thomas Espenshade. 2001. "The Evolution of U.S. Policy toward Employment-Based Immigrants and Temporary Workers: The H-1B Debate in Historical Perspective." in Cornelius et al (eds.): 23-54.

Utrednings-och-Statistik Kontoret. 2005. "Utrikes-födda samt Utländska Medborgare Efter Medborgarskap" ("Foreign Born Persons and Aliens By Citizenship") in *Statistisk Årsbook 2005.* http://www.stockholm.se/files/88300-88399/file_88327.pdf

Valentine, Lisa. 2004. "Siemens: Planets Aligning for Mobile-Phone Growth." March 18. http://wireless.newsfactor.com/story.xhtml?story_id=23431

Vaughan, Jessica. 2003. *Shortcuts to Immigration: The Temporary Visa Program is Broken.* Backgrounder. Washington, DC: Center for Immigration Studies.

Venugopalan, Arun. 2005. "US RJs Threaten Indian BPO Worker" Rediff.com (Jan 11). http://us.rediff.com/news/2005/jan/11bpo.htm

Visweswaran, Kamala. 1997. "Diaspora by Design: Flexible Citizenship and South Asians in US Racial Formations." *Diaspora* 6 (1) (1997): 5-29.

Waever, Ole. 1993. "Societal Security: The Concept." *Identity, Migration, and the New Security Agenda in Europe*. Ole Waever, Barry Buzan, Morten Kelstrup, and Pierre Lemaitre, (eds.). London: Pinter.

Wagner, Anne–Catherine. 1999. *Les nouvelles elites de la mondialisation*. Paris: PUF.

Waldinger, Roger and David Fitzgerald. 2004. "Transnationalism in Question." *American Journal of Sociology* 109 (5): 1177-95.

Wallace, Claire. 2002. "Opening and Closing Borders: Migration and Mobility in East–Central Europe." *Journal of Ethnic and Migration Studies* 28: 603–625.

Wasem, Ruth Ellen. 2001. *Immigration: Legislative Issues of Nonimmigrant Professional Specialty (H-1B) Workers*.Washington, DC: Congressional Research Service Report for Congress.

Watson, W. 1964 "Social Mobility and Social Class in Industrial Communities." in *Closed Systems and Open Minds: The Limits of Naivety in Social Anthropology*, M.Gluckman (ed.). Edinburgh: Oliver and Boyd, 129-157.

Watts, Julie. 2002. *An Unconventional Brotherhood: Union Support for Liberalized Immigration in Europe*. San Diego: Center for Comparative Immigration Studies.

Weinstein, Eric. "How and Why Government, Universities, and Industry Create Domestic Labor Shortages of Scientists and High-Tech Workers." Cambridge: National Bureau of Economic Research. Date accessed: 11/04. http://www.nber.org/~sewp/weinsteinhowandwhygovernment.pdf

Weinstein, Bernard L. and Terry L. Clower. 2000. "Technology, Workforce and the DFW Business Climate: A Review and Critique of Recent Assessments." Prepared for the North Texas Commission, Center for Economic Development and Research, Denton, TX: University of North Texas. http://www.unt.edu/cedr/NTCreport/pdf

Wernerfelt, Birger. 1984. "A Resource-based View of the Firm." *Strategic Management Journal* 5: 171-180.

White, Paul. 1993. "The Social Geography of Immigrants in European Cities: The Geography of Arrival." *The New Geography of European Migrations,* in Russell King, ed., . London: Belhaven.

Williams, Allan M. and Vladimir Balá•. 2002. "Trans–border Population Mobility at a European Crossroads: Slovakia in the Shadow of EU Accession." *Journal of Ethnic and Migration Studies* 28: 647–664.

Willis, Frank R. 1971. *Italy Chooses Europe*. Oxford: Oxford University Press.

Wilson, James Q. 1973. *Political Organizations*. New York: Basic Books.

——— (ed.) 1980. *The Politics of Regulation*. New York: Basic Books.

World Trade Organization (WTO).1995. Note by the Secretariat of the Working Party on GATS Rules, Document S/WPGR/W/1 of 6.7.1995.

———. 1998. *Council for Trade in Services, Presence of Natural Persons (Mode 4), Background Note by the Secretariat, S/C/W/75 of 8.12.1998.*

————. 2000. Communication from India: Proposed Liberalization of Movement of Professionals under the General Agreement on Trade in Services (GATS). *S/CSS/W/12* 24.11.2000.

Yale-Loehr, Stephen. 2003. "Examining the Importance of the H-1B Visa to the American Economy." Statement of Stephen Yale-Loehr to Senate Committee on the Judiciary on H-1B Visas. Ithaca, NY: True, Walsh & Miller, LLP Attorneys at Law.
http://www.twmlaw.com

Yeoh, Brenda S. A. and Katie Willis. 2005. "Singaporean and British transmigrants in China and the cultural politics of contact zones." *Journal of Ethnic and Migration Studies*. 31 (2): 269-285.

Young, Allison. 1999. "Labor Mobility and the GATS: Where Next?" Paper presented at the World Services Congress "Services: Generating Global Growth and Opportunity." Washington, DC.

Zakaria, Fareed. 2004. "Rejecting the Next Bill Gates." *The Washington Post,* Nov 23.
http://www.washingtonpost.com/ac2/wp-dyn/A6008

Zhao, John et al. 2000. "Brain Drain and Brain Gain: The Migration of Knowledge Workers from and to Canada." *Education Quarterly Review* 6 (3): 8-35.

Zhou. Y. and Tseng, Y-F. 2001. "Regrounding The 'Ungrounded Empires': Localization As The Geographic Catalyst For Transnationalism." *Global Networks* 1 (2): 131-153.

Zogby, James. 2000. "Abraham Under Attack." *Washington Watch.* April 24.
http://www.aaiusa.org/wwatch/042400.htm

Zolberg, Ari. 1999. "Matters of State: Theorizing Immigration Policy." in *Handbook of International Migration*. Charles Hirschman, Josh Dewind, Philip Kasinitz (eds.). New York: Russell Sage Foundation.

Zürn, Michael. 1998. *Regieren jenseits des Nationalstaates. Globalisierung und Denationalisierung als Chance.* Frankfurt a.M.: Suhrkamp.

Zweig, David. 1997. "To Return or Not to Return? Politics vs. Economics in China's Brain Drain." *Studies in Comparative International Development* 32 (Spring): 92-125.

Index

Abraham, Senator Spencer, 107, 120
Africa, brain drain effecting, 186
American Association of Colleges of Nursing, 152
American Business for Legal Immigration, 122
American Business Roundtable, 122
American Competitiveness in the Twenty-first Century Act, 144
American Competitiveness and Workforce Improvement Act (ACWIA), 107, 144
American Council on Education, 122
American Council on International Personnel, 122
American Immigration Lawyers Association, 123
American Nursing Association, 152
American Organization of Nurse Executives, 152
"Americanization," 266-267
Amnesty programs, 123-124
Angell, Ian, 19
Armstrong, Richard, 177
Asia Pacific Economic Co-operation Forum, 41
Asia-Pacific movement
  regional migration, 23-24
  US relations and, 24
Association of American Universities, College Personnel Association, 122
Association of International Educators, 1227
Association of South East Asian Nations, 20
Australia
  international students increasing, 183
  skilled-based migration, 11
  skilled worker recruiting, 81
Australia-New Zealand Closer Economic Relations, 40

Austria, labor migration rates, 65-66

Baiocchi, Gianpaolo, 180
Bangladesh, government sponsored emigration, 36
Baru, Sundari, 163
Batalova, Jeanne, 7-8, 12, 18, 20, 81, 99
Bauman, Zygmunt, 14
Bean, Frank D., 96
Beaverstock, Jon, 254
Belgium, international students increases, 183
"Bodyshops," 164
Boo, Katherine, 159
Booz, Allen, and Hamilton, Inc., 117
Bozkurt, Ödül, 13, 18, 22, 211
Brain drain
  assumptions challenging of, 11
  concerns over, 166
  cost of, 167
  countries effecting, 11, 186
  countries sponsoring emigration, 36
  global movement easing, 12
  research methodology, 190-193
  skilled migration as, 11
  vs. brain gaining, 12-13
  zero sum logic, 12-13
  See also International graduate students
Brain migrations
  adverse effects of, 186-187
  boundary conceptions of, 206-207
  brain circulation and, 207-208
  forms of, 208
  graduate education decisions, 205-206
  literature changes on, 186
  policy implications for, 208-209
  student responsibilities, 207
  types of, 185-186
  vs. brain gain, 186

303

Lightning Source UK Ltd.
Milton Keynes UK
UKOW04f1114041013

218475UK00002B/88/P